HOLLYWOOD HEARTBREAK

The Tragic and Mysterious Deaths of Hollywood's Most Remarkable Legends

LAURIE JACOBSON

A FIRESIDE BOOK

Published by Simon & Schuster, Inc.
New York

Copyright © 1984 by Laurie Jacobson

A Fireside Book
Published by Simon & Schuster, Inc.
Simon & Schuster Building
Rockefeller Center
1230 Avenue of the Americas
New York, New York 10020

FIRESIDE and colophon are registered trademarks of Simon & Schuster, Inc.

Designed by Paul Chevannes

Manufactured in the United States of America

10 9 8 7 6 5 4 3 2

Library of Congress Cataloging in Publication Data
Jacobson, Laurie.
　Hollywood heartbreak.

　"A Fireside book."
　Bibliography: p.
　1. Moving-picture actors and actresses—United
States—Biography.　2. Entertainers—United States—
Biography.　3. Violent deaths.　I. Title.
PN1998.A2J33　1984　　　791.43'028'0922 [B]　　　84-14113
ISBN 0-671-49998-X

Grateful thanks is extended for permission to quote lyrics from Janis Joplin's "One Good Man,"
ASCAP 1969, Strong Arm Music.

PHOTOGRAPHIC CREDITS

Academy of Motion Picture Arts and Sciences, p. 228; Academy of Motion Picture Arts and
Sciences/Eva Kasday, p. 223; Author's Collection, pp. 21, 23, 33, 34, 60, 80, 83, 94, 103, 111, 128,
149, 154, 159, 164, 169, 195, 198, 208, 211, 244; Collector's Bookstore, p. 201; Columbia Pictures,
p. 151; Columbia Records, p. 239; Delmar Watson Photography, pp. 53, 97; Michel Duplaix for
RCA Victor, p. 192; George Eastman House, p. 122; E. Hazeboucq, p. 117; Hedda Hopper Collection, p. 56; Hurrell for MGM, p. 105; Jon Jacobs Collection, p. 184; Richard Lamparski, p. 77; Marc
Wanamaker Bison Archives, pp. 2, 18, 19, 28, 30, 38, 40, 45, 49, 50, 62, 68, 70, 71, 76, 85, 89, 90,
91, 102, 106, 108, 113, 119, 121, 123, 130, 162, 170, 173, 249; Sally Marr, p. 186; MGM, pp. 134,
135, 209, 225; MGM-TV, p. 158; Motown Records, p. 241; Nick Bougas Collection, p. 138; Paramount Pictures, p. 95; RCA Victor, p. 190; RKO Radio Pictures, Inc., p. 140; Pam Sartori, p. 99;
Bruce Torrence, p. 65; UCLA Special Collections, pp. 143, 145; Universal Studios, pp. 203, 231,
233; UPI, pp. 57, 175, 177, 180, 218; Wide World, p. 216; Louis Wolf, p. 167.

ACKNOWLEDGMENTS

I would like to thank Mark S. Jacobson, my brother. I am deeply grateful for his enormous help and contribution.

I would also like to thank Ernest Kearney, Colin Gardner, Don Hepner, Harry B. Friedman, Forrest J. Ackerman, Tim Eaton, Bill Lomax, Rose Smouse, Ron Silverman, Philip Clarke, Skood, Chuck Pennock, Nick Bougas, Dennis Martino, Jim Ferris, Collector's Bookstore, Larry Edmunds Bookstore, Lori Patterson, Bunny and Jerry Steinbaum, Birthe Hansen, and my parents, Sid and Carol, for their patience, kindness, stories, and criticism.

Special thanks to Sally Marr and Wah Wah Watson.

Very special thanks to Marc Wanamaker/Bison Archives for his infinite patience and invaluable assistance.

Very special thanks also to Allen L. Greene, my agent, for many things, but especially for having a sense of humor.

*This book is lovingly dedicated to
the cherished memories of
Charles Jacobson, Michael Lehman,
and
Harvey Lembeck.*

CONTENTS

III THE SIXTIES, SEVENTIES, AND EIGHTIES

PREFACE

Since the first camera rolled under the California sunshine, no one has moved casually to "Hollywood"—a dream factory, not just a town. One comes here hoping or scheming to win the pot of gold, willing to risk love, limb, and even life to realize that dream. A few succeed where thousands fail. Some win it all and still lose; it's an old story. In this city of extremes, a star can live at the top only to spiral down to the depths of defeat and humiliation in the course of a few years. The pressures at the top can be the same as the pain at the bottom. It all comes down to survival.

Innocents to this town can easily be swept out to sea and eaten by the sharks. Others are tragically dragged down by the undertow. One broken heart leaped to her death from the giant Hollywood sign, in despair over her immobile career. Another died because his career moved too fast. Every Hollywood generation has its legends, scandals, and tragedies. There was always booze here. There were always drugs. There were always big cars and wild parties. In the early days, the world pronounced Hollywood morally improper. The town became, and has remained, the world's largest fishbowl, where a stumble at the top can start an avalanche. The lights are always on, the volume turned up full.

A heartbreak in Hollywood makes the whole world mourn, because these are the people who've made us laugh, and cry, and sing. We've stood in the rain to see them, imitated the way they look and dress, and named our children after them. Their problems have been our concern. Our cheers and support have made some survive, while others have slipped away as we watched helplessly. They have touched us.

Many have died tragically and mysteriously in Hollywood. This is the story of thirty-one luminous, legendary citizens whose lives helped build the dream factory and whose deaths helped create its mystique. Their orbits span seventy years of growth and social change—not quite a lifetime—but history moves at lightning speed in Hollywood.

Hollywood is wonderful. Anyone who doesn't like it is either crazy or sober.

—Raymond Chandler

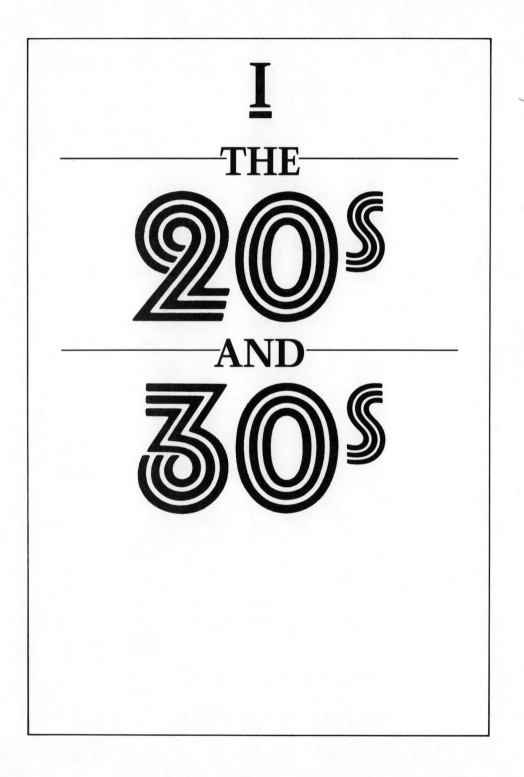

I

THE

20ˢ

AND

30ˢ

RAMON NOVARRO
Anxious to Please

Halloween morning, 1968. Los Angeles police braced themselves for the bizarre trouble all too typical of the late 1960s. Shortly before 9 a.m., they responded to an apparent homicide at the home of silent screen star Ramon Novarro. Braced or not, the officers were stunned.

Novarro's secretary, Edward Weber, led police through the living room, a scene of violent struggle. A magnificent bronze bust of Novarro as he appeared in the 1925 epic *Ben Hur* stood a silent witness to the previous night's devastating rampage. Weber opened the door to the darkened bedroom and turned away.

The room was drenched in blood, from floor to ceiling. Novarro's shattered glasses lay in a red pool on the floor. On the mirror was scribbled a cryptic message, "Us girls are better than fagits." The police carefully edged closer to the motionless figure on the bed.

Ramon Novarro's once strong, handsome features had been savagely beaten to a bloody pulp. His nude body was bound at the wrists and ankles by an electric cord and what was possibly the letter "Z" or "N" was carved into his neck. Police were further baffled by the shaft of a black cane deliberately laid across his legs, its broken ivory tip symbolically placed between his thighs. When they moved the body, a pen fell from Novarro's lifeless hand. On the blood-soaked sheet underneath, the name "Larry" had been scrawled in foot-high letters.

After thirty years, Ramon Novarro was front page news again. Reporters and photographers quickly converged on the North Hollywood home. Police did not have much to tell them. They had found the name "Larry" also written on a telephone pad, and were checking it out. As they spoke, one reporter

As Ben Hur in 1925.

made a crucial discovery. He led police to a pile of bloody clothing in a neighbor's yard. It was the first substantial clue in what was to become an obvious trail. This, plus an intimate investigation into Novarro's well-kept personal life, would enable police to arrest the murderers within a week.

1913. Fourteen-year-old Ramon Samaniegos and his brother stood lonely and bewildered on a dusty dirt road, staring at the citrus groves. *This* was the magical Los Angeles? The town where two hungry boys with less than $10 between them could make bushels of money to send back to mama and papa and their eight brothers and sisters in Durango, Mexico? It looked like the most desolate spot on earth, yet it was sprouting diamonds. Soon the citrus trees would disappear, and the mud beneath their tired feet would be paved and dubbed Hollywood and Vine. Just down the road, Cecil B. DeMille was shooting *The Squaw Man,* Hollywood's first feature length film, in a barn he shared with a horse.

Jobs were plentiful, and young Ramon worked as a grocery clerk, theater usher, piano teacher, cafe singer, and busboy at the elegant Alexandria Hotel, downtown. By 1917, the hotel's bar had become the gathering place for the growing ranks of aspiring movie actors. Another provocative-looking young Latin, a bit player named Rodolfo Guglielmi, tried to attract attention there as a dancer. Eventually he became known to the world as Rudolph Valentino, and he and Ramon became the best of friends.

The marble lobby of the Alexandria Hotel (circa 1917). Elegant meeting place of the stars where Novarro was a busboy and his friend, Rudolph Valentino, was a dancer.

The acting bug bit Samaniegos, too. Out of his impressive performance in a local play came a five-year contract under the very eminent director Rex Ingram, who cast him as an extra and bit player. Ramon waited patiently for his big break. He got it thanks to his pal Valentino's overnight celestial coronation, which came in 1921, with Ingram's *Four Horsemen of the Apocalypse*. The movie made Rudy's name an aria on the lips of women everywhere, but Metro Studios refused to give its red-hot Latin lover a $50-a-week raise. Valentino immediately jumped ship for Paramount. Fortunately, Ingram had a new Latin he-siren hanging around the lot—all he needed was a new, more seductive name. Samaniegos became Novarro, and Ingram cast him brilliantly as Rupert in *Prisoner of Zenda*. He was an immediate hit, and with their combined efforts in 1923's *Scaramouche*, Ramon became a major star. In celebration, Valentino gave his friend a black lead, Art Deco phallic symbol inscribed with his silver signature.

Novarro and Ingram sailed to North Africa for their last collaboration, *The Arab*. "Ramon Novarro is 110° in the shade!" the international press declared with the movie's release. His salary rocketed to a whopping untaxed $10,000 a week. In public he had to have police bodyguards.

When Metro merged with the Samuel Goldwyn production company to become MGM, "Boy Wonder" production chief, Irving Thalberg, took charge of Novarro's career. Women could thank Thalberg for the sight of Novarro's brawny bare chest when he played the title role in *Ben Hur*. It was said that female theater patrons fainted during his nearly nude scenes. Yet some critics called him a second-string Valentino. Some implied that both of the Latin-lover types were part of the "pink powder puff" set; that real men were never so pretty. Nonsense, countered the studio. Though Novarro, to be sure, did not have a record of glamorous ladies traipsing through his boudoir, the publicists explained that unlike hedonist Valentino, Ramon was a man of deep religious and philosophical beliefs. One publicity photo showed him half-naked above a caption that said, "Rather conclusive proof that Ramon Novarro has no intention of entering a monastery." Women thought he was a "religious experience" all right. They wrote to him simply in care of "Mr. Ben Hur; Hollywood, California." When Rudy died suddenly in 1926, Ramon inherited the throne of the world's most popular Latin lover.

No one was more pleased than the maestro of perfection, Irving Thalberg. To enhance the career of his new wife, Norma Shearer, he cast her opposite Novarro in the lavish production of *The Student Prince*, directed by the gifted Ernst Lubitsch. Thalberg's judgement was correct, as usual. Audiences loved the pair.

Novarro's legion of ladies wanted to see "more" of him, and he gave them just that in *The Pagan*. He wore the smallest sarong the censors would allow. To compete with the new "talkies," the silent film packed a double wallop— a recording of Ramon singing "Pagan Love Song." He had a beautiful voice.

"From cabbages to castles" is how MGM described his rise to the top. Hollywood and Ramon grew rich together. In the former dusty hamlet where he'd once stood with an empty stomach, now all heads turned to see him racing down Hollywood Boulevard in his 1928 Lincoln roadster. He was above the orgiastic revelry that got a number of other stars in trouble, and too much the brooding, religious artist for the usual Hollywood gossip to taint him.

He was one of the fortunate stars who made a successful transition to talkies, too. But for some reason, his popularity began to wane when the Depression struck. Thalberg's gimmicks didn't help much. He tried Ramon in an unheard-of variety of roles: college hero, Oriental, American Indian, Ruritarian prince. At last the star maker seemed to be back on the right track when he cast his dark, pensive boy opposite Greta Garbo in *Mata Hari*, made in 1931.

As a college football hero in Sam Wood's The Huddle *(1932).*

The love scene that melted Mata's frigid heart was pure magic. Garbo and Novarro—who wrote the scene themselves—embraced in total darkness except for the glow of two cigarettes. The film not only sent women panting after Ramon all over again, but also sparked rumors of a romance with the exquisite Garbo. This was the first time Novarro had been linked to any woman. He said of Garbo, "She's languid, naive, childlike—a perfectly wonderful person." Yet, he himself quashed the rumors of romance, as he did two years later when the papers hinted at imminent marriage to Myrna Loy. Meanwhile, as a distraction, MGM sent picture valentines to every woman who had ever written to Novarro, from Alaska to Australia.

Even *Mata Hari* didn't give Ramon the comeback that Thalberg had hoped for. Only a small loyal following went to see his movies. As a vote of confidence, Thalberg signed him to a new seven-year contract, hyping it to the press as one of the most extraordinary agreements in Hollywood. But Novarro's last three films for MGM were possibly his worst. He toiled valiantly to breathe life into weak scripts, but it was a losing battle. Rather than continue to displease his public, he voluntarily retired in 1934.

In the next few years he sang. He toured virtually every country in Europe, capping the trip with a sensational concert at the London Palladium. He attempted a movie comeback with the minor-league Republic Studios in a parody of his old self, *The Sheik Steps Out*. The studio was pleased and signed him for four more, but after the first, Ramon realized that the step down to Republic was just too demoralizing, and asked to be released from his contract. He had had enough.

He retired to the serenity of his 50-acre San Diego ranch, and claimed to be content spending his time painting, composing, writing, practicing yoga, and contemplating life. Occasional interviewers always remarked on his fabulous peace of mind. As late as 1947, he said he still toyed with the idea of entering a monastery. "I tried to become a Jesuit, but they said I was too old, and of course, they were right. Then I contemplated the life of a Trappist monk. Can you imagine an actor taking a vow of silence!" But under this tranquil surface brewed a secret, unspiritual side that Novarro had managed to hide through all his years of glory.

Novarro returned to character roles in Hollywood and eventually made a transition to television. His appearances on shows like *Dr. Kildare, Combat!, Bonanza, Walt Disney,* and *The Wild, Wild West* brought stacks of mail from still devoted fans. "The ladies are the same today as they were in 1925, except when they swoon over me now, somebody has to help them get up!"

After a bout with pleurisy, Novarro purchased a rolling Spanish estate at 3110 Laurel Canyon Boulevard, in North Hollywood. At sixty-nine, his smooth, muscular body had turned to flab, and his very poor health was aggravated by his most un-monkish inclination for gin, which led to a string of arrests for drunk driving. His famous jet-black hair was now gray, and his passionate brown eyes had grown pale and bleary. In the center of his living room stood the majestic bust of Novarro as Ben Hur, surrounded by souvenirs and photos of friends and films of the past, all holding court to the old crown prince of romance.

Novarro was still a romantic, but like many old men, he now paid for his love. Why hadn't the great ladies' man ever chosen a lady for himself? Why had he so deliberately squelched all the rumors of romance with Garbo and Loy? His checkbook held the answer. During the past six months, Novarro had written 140 checks to young male prostitutes. Poor gentle Ramon paid so often for affection that he had become well-known in hustlers' circles. His

At his ranch in 1955.

international fame as a lover had been reduced to a reputation as an easy touch for local male prostitutes. On October 30, 1968, he was expecting another young man.

Paul Ferguson was often in trouble during his youth in Chicago. A high school dropout and frequent runaway, he was arrested twice for assault with a deadly weapon and served time in a Wyoming prison for grand theft. The twenty-three-year-old looked like the tough punk James Dean symbolized in the fifties. And like Dean's most famous role, Ferguson was also a rebel without a cause . . . an angry young man who felt the world owed him a living. When he drank, this anger erupted into self-pity, violence, and revenge. His new wife was only beginning to see his dark side during their six months together in Los Angeles. They had very little money and few friends.

Paul convinced his seventeen-year-old brother, Tom, to join them in L.A. with the promise of easy work. Also a runaway, Tom had spent time in juvenile detention for petty theft and glue sniffing. But now in Los Angeles, neither Ferguson could find even a day's work, and they quickly exhausted their cash. Frustrated, Paul ducked his landlord and belligerently bullied his wife. She became fed up with his violent rages and left him.

Paul was desperate, and obsessed with getting the hell out of L.A. But for that, he needed money. He was reduced to grabbing at the last straw he could think of—hustling, male prostitution. It had gotten him out of prison alive; now it would get him out of L.A. He had heard about Novarro's reputation as an easy touch, but it was the rumor his brother-in-law, Larry, had repeated that came to mind now.

"Five thousand dollars in cash?" Paul had asked, incredulous.

"That's what they say . . . somewhere in his house."

"Well, Larry, you're his friend. Don't you know for sure?"

"I've never heard Ramon mention it and I never asked him." Paul despised Larry and all "faggots," but he clenched his teeth and called another hustler who he knew would have Novarro's number. This was the visitor Ramon so eagerly awaited.

The Fergusons hitchhiked to Novarro's around 5:30 p.m. Pleased to see them, he poured drinks all around. When Paul mumbled a request for cigarettes, Novarro phoned for a carton for each brother from a nearby drugstore.

Their drinking continued and the host entertained with fortune telling and stories of his career. The Fergusons couldn't have cared less; they'd never heard of Ben Hur, Ramon Novarro, or his old-time friends. Under the glow of gin, Novarro found Paul increasingly attractive, comparing his rough good looks to Clint Eastwood and Burt Lancaster. He even offered to get him started as an actor. Paul showed no interest, but Novarro persisted. With slurred speech, he called his publicity agent and, without naming Paul, set up a meeting for Friday. He wrote the appointment on a pad by the phone. Paul, bored, finished off a fifth of vodka and started on tequila.

Edward Weber, Novarro's secretary, happened to be in the drugstore when Novarro phoned and offered to run the cigarettes up to the house. He never saw the Fergusons. If he had, it might have changed their course. But Novarro didn't invite him in, and Weber, familiar with his habit, didn't push. "I left some dinner for you in the refrigerator, Ramon. Don't forget to eat something. I'll see you in the morning."

The three tried to eat, but were far too drunk. "I'm gonna get some air . . . take a walk or something," Tom stammered as he staggered to the patio door. Novarro took Paul to the piano. Forty years earlier he had sung these songs to enthusiastic crowds; but tonight, he romanced Paul Ferguson who was growing more touchy with each drunken note. When Novarro's hands wandered from the keyboard, he suggested they get more comfortable. Paul reluctantly followed him to the bedroom.

Tom returned, absently stumbling from room to room, looking for the others. He wasn't exactly sure how Paul was going to get money out of Ramon . . . maybe he'd threaten the old man, or rough him up some. He opened the bedroom door and froze at the sight of the two men, naked. "Get the hell outta here!" Paul screamed. Tom reeled backward, collapsing on the living room couch.

After a few minutes, he groped for the phone and called his girlfriend, Brenda, in Chicago. "I'm at a movie star's house," he bragged. "He's gonna make me and Paul stars." As the conversation continued, Brenda could hear screams. Somebody picked up the bedroom extension once, twice, a third time.

"What's going on there, Tom?"

"I better see what he's doing. I don't want Paul to hurt Ramon." Tom hung up, but stayed on the couch, still very drunk. He had been talking for forty-five minutes. The house was quiet again. He heard Paul call him. Tom grabbed a couple of beers from the kitchen and made his way back to the bedroom. "Hey, Paul, I brought you a . . ." but he was too stunned to finish. Paul was standing by the foot of the bed, his white shorts soaked with blood. Tom stared with disbelief. He saw blood everywhere—on the sheets, the floor, the walls, the ceiling. He gasped when he saw the nude Novarro, laying half off the bed, his face cut and beaten.

"Don't just stand there, get him into the shower," Paul ordered, "and don't let him near the phone."

Numb, Tom dragged the semiconscious Novarro to the adjoining bathroom. He could see three deep gashes on the back of his head. It seemed an eternity passed before the water in the shower finally ran clear. Novarro mumbled something. Tom listened closely and recognized a "Hail Mary." "Don't say anything more to Paul," he begged, hauling him back to the bed. Novarro moaned, and continued praying.

Paul had helped himself to Novarro's closets. With a fedora, a black vest over his blood-caked chest, and an ivory tipped cane, Paul pranced in front of a mirror, singing and howling with maniacal laughter. Horrified, Tom ran from the room.

Paul quickly tired of his bizarre amusement and walked out. Thinking this was his chance to escape, Novarro somehow pulled himself to his feet. Paul returned, enraged to see the old man standing before him. He grabbed Novarro's cherished cane and beat him with it, striking him over and over. His nose shattered, the flesh of his head and shoulders brutally split, Novarro collapsed to the floor in a battered heap. He would suffocate there in a pool of his own blood.

"No! No! No!" Tom screamed. Running to Novarro, he pressed his ear to his chest. There was no sound, no movement. "He's dead! He's dead!" Tom wailed.

"I didn't mean to . . . I didn't mean to kill him," Paul broke down. He shook Novarro's lifeless body as though he could undo his wretched act. He blamed everything and everyone. "I was so drunk," he whimpered, "and he made me so mad . . . when he touched me, I . . . God, I hate hustling. I hate it. All I wanted was his money. If only there had been work for us . . . I tried to find work. Why weren't there any jobs? . . . This is all Sophie's fault . . . that bitch. If she hadn't of walked out, none of this woulda happened." He began sobbing uncontrollably. Tom took over.

"Come on. Let's make it look like a robbery." Together they yanked the cord from the nightstand lamp, cinched Novarro's wrists and ankles, and dumped his body on the bloody bed. They ran frenetically through the house, overturning chairs, wiping fingerprints, and smashing the keepsakes Novarro had treasured for nearly half a century. Remembering that his name was on the phone pad, Paul tore it up and wrote "Larry" four times. He raced back to the bedroom to scrawl "Larry" under the body, then jammed the pen into the corpse's hand. Tom scratched Novarro's neck with a knife in a worthless attempt to simulate a woman's fingernails. He scattered a box of condoms around the room and scribbled the message on the mirror.

They ripped off their bloody clothes and threw on some of Novarro's. They turned out the lights and jerked the drapes shut, then fled through the patio door. But Paul came back. He couldn't resist one last macabre touch. Breaking the cane he'd used to beat Novarro mercilessly, he laid the shaft across his thighs and placed the ivory tip between Novarro's legs. He grabbed their blood-stained clothes and stupidly tossed them over a fence outside. The two brothers hitched a ride to Sunset Boulevard. It was 11:45 p.m. Six hours earlier their desperation had driven them to an equally desperate old man. Now Novarro lay murdered, victim of his own weakness and an easy prey for the mindless animals he had been so anxious to please.

Both Fergusons were convicted of murder and sentenced to life in prison. Seven years later, they were paroled.

WILLIAM DESMOND TAYLOR

Murder of a Perfect Gentleman

On a chilly February morning in 1922, Henry Peavey hurried through the courtyard toward William Desmond Taylor's apartment. He would let himself in and start his gentleman's breakfast just as he did every morning at 7:30. Mr. Taylor was a fine gentleman and an important director, and working for him made Peavey feel sort of important, too. This morning, the living room lights were on, and Peavey was surprised to think that Mr. Taylor was already up. Peavey, a soprano and avid needlepointer, took one step into the living room and began screaming. According to the *Los Angeles Times*, he ran out of the courtyard and onto fashionable Alvarado Street screaming all the way, "Massa Taylor is dead! Massa Taylor is dead!"

Neighbor Edna Purviance bolted upright in bed. Could she be hearing right? Bill Taylor dead? Chaplin's leading lady dashed to her window and saw Peavey, running like an hysterical town crier, tears streaming down his face. She grabbed her phone, but not to call the authorities. This was no time for police. Her first call was to Mabel Normand, premiere comedienne of the silent screen and possibly the last person to have seen Taylor alive.

On the night of February 1, Mabel had stopped at her favorite corner vendor for peanuts. From there, she called home for messages. Taylor had left word that he had two books for her, which she decided to pick up on her way home. Her chauffeur pulled in front of Taylor's bungalow court apartment at 7:00 p.m. The door was open, but Mabel heard Taylor's voice, talking on the telephone in a heated conversation, so she waited until she heard him slam the receiver down before she knocked. He was, as always, delighted to see her. Taylor ushered her into the living room where several of her photos hung beside pictures of stars he'd directed, including Mary Pickford, who had in-

The gentleman director.

scribed on her photo, "To the most patient man I ever knew!" They walked past the desk where Taylor had been preparing his income tax.

"Damn that Ed Sands," he said, referring to his previous manservant. "His forgeries are so good, even *I* can't tell which checks are his!"

Taylor rang for Peavey, and asked Mabel if she'd like some dinner, but she declined. Henry was happy to see Miss Normand again. She and Taylor had been very serious about each other, even announcing their engagement a few times, but Miss Normand always backed out. The one great love of her life had been director Mack Sennett, who, like Taylor, was an "older man." The workaholic comedy genius lost his lady when he canceled their wedding plans once too often, and she embarked on a whirlwind of parties, casual sex, and worse, some said. Taylor's maturity had a calming influence on her, but she drifted in and out of his life, unable to make a commitment. Henry thought Mr. Taylor was still in love with her, as he often saw him gazing at her picture for hours. This was the first time in almost two months that she'd paid a visit.

Upon inquiring, Peavey found that Taylor and his visitor would not need anything else before he went home for the night. He left the house at 7:20, ten minutes before his usual quitting time, stopping to chat briefly with Mabel's chauffeur outside.

Taylor, Hollywood's resident intellectual, gave Mabel two books, one by Nietzsche, the other by Freud. Taylor himself often spent his evenings reading. He was an elegant, worldly gentleman of forty-five, a phenomenon in the fast and loose Hollywood of 1922. Women adored his thin, wide lips and aristocratic nose, and he had a reputation as something of a ladies' man, especially amongst the younger ladies, like Mabel, who was only twenty-eight. But Mabel didn't stay long that night. As Taylor helped her with her coat, she thanked him for the books and asked him to call her in an hour or so. Leaving his front door ajar, he escorted her down the walk to her car. They said good-bye at 7:45. Mabel waved to him as her car pulled away. She sat in the back seat with empty peanut shells littered all around her.

Mabel told Edna that was the last time they saw each other—he had never called. Edna saw Taylor's lights on at midnight and knocked, but got no answer. There was no time to gab. Edna had other important calls to make, like the next one to Mary Miles Minter, the seventeen-year-old actress who'd been a blushing belle of the stage and screen for thirteen years. Her blonde curls and angelic face had made her Mary Pickford's closest rival. "If you've left anything in that house that you don't want anyone else to see," Edna warned her, "you better get it out now."

"No!" cried Mary, bursting into hysterical tears. Her schoolgirl crush had developed into a consuming passion, and some of Taylor's friends said he had complained about her persistence. Mary later claimed that they were engaged, just waiting until her eighteenth birthday to be married. Now she rushed to be with her beloved.

Peavey, who had by now regained some composure, called Taylor's doctor. The distinguished director suffered from a stomach ailment, and his doctor assumed that death was due to hemorrhaging in his stomach.

Charles Eyton, a prominent executive at Famous Players–Lasky Studio (later to be known as Paramount), was already under pressure to hide any breath of scandal because Fatty Arbuckle, one of the studio's biggest stars, was standing trial for the rape and murder of a contract starlet. In the pews and pulpits of America, people were railing against Hollywood's debauchery, sure that the colony would perish like Sodom and Gomorrah; and indeed it would not survive if these righteous folk made good their threats to shun the movies. Immediately after Peavey's phone call, Eyton and several other executives rushed to Taylor's bungalow, on a mission to remove anything "disagreeable," anything that could be sensationalized. They would not succeed.

Taylor's doctor telephoned the coroner, who made the most disagreeable discovery of all. When he lifted Taylor's body, which lay on the living room floor near his desk, he saw blood on the carpet. Death was undoubtedly due to hemorrhage, but the hemorrhage had been caused by a .38 calibre bullet. "They've killed him! They've killed Massa Taylor!" Peavey, as the papers of the day told it, was off again bringing the terrible news to the neighbors, one of whom finally informed the police.

Authorities arrived to find the scene of the crime a circus of activity. Studio

Taylor's living room—the picture is clear, but the murder is still unsolved.

execs who had already gotten rid of Taylor's bootleg whiskey were now rifling through his private papers, burning some of them. Mabel Normand and Edna Purviance were looking for love letters written by Mabel. Mary Miles Minter and her overbearing stage mother, Charlotte Shelby, arrived shortly after the police and couldn't even get in. "Let me see him!" Mary wailed to the officers who blocked her path. She pounded on their chests, pulled at her curls, tore her clothes, but they wouldn't let her have that one last look. In the center of it all lay Taylor, flat on his back, legs and feet neatly together, arms straight at his sides. With his coat buttoned, his hair neatly combed, he was the picture of unnatural composure. Police immediately eliminated robbery as a motive, thanks to the fact that he still wore his large diamond ring, and $1,000 in cash was lying around upstairs. Obviously they had a premeditated murder on their hands, but they'd have a tough job finding someone who didn't like Taylor, Hollywood's perfect gentleman.

"Bill Taylor was as fine and conscientious a gentleman as ever lived," said co-worker Frank Garbott. "The humblest extra on the set received as courteous treatment as the biggest star. He had no bad habits and he never had an enemy." With Taylor's death, Hollywood's entertainers, whom the sedate founding families of Los Angeles spurned as gypsies and trash, formed a true commune, a protective inner circle. The cops called it a "conspiracy of silence." No one seemed to have any idea who would murder poor Bill Taylor. The authorities spoke to Peavey, Normand, and Purviance, but the only worthwhile lead came from a neighbor.

Mrs. Douglas MacLean, wife of the actor, heard what could have been a shot just after dinner, about 7:50. Several of the other neighbors had heard it too, but dismissed it as a car backfiring. Faith MacLean, however, looked out the window. She saw someone leaving Taylor's apartment. It was a man, she said, of twenty-six or twenty-seven, about 5 feet 10 inches, 185 pounds, wearing a large dark coat, a cap pulled down over his eyes, and a muffler around his neck and chin. He also saw her, but remained casual, leaning back against Taylor's door as if to say good-bye. Then he closed the door, walked through the alley between the two homes, and disappeared. Seeing nothing strange about his behavior, she thought no more about it.

Police theorized that when Taylor walked Mabel to her car, the murderer must have slipped in the open front door, and awaited his victim behind a pillar in the living room. Taylor returned and sat down at his desk. The killer apparently yelled "Hands up!" because Taylor's arms had to have been raised for the bullet holes in his jacket and vest to match. From the pile of cigarette butts in the alley, police deduced that the killer had been waiting for some time for a chance to enter the apartment.

Then a few slim new leads developed. The MacLeans' maid recalled hearing footsteps in the adjoining alley when she was serving the second course, about 7:30. Two gas station attendants at nearby Sixth and Alvarado remembered a suspicious man, fitting the same description as the man Mrs. MacLean saw, asking for directions to Taylor's address at around 6:00 that evening, and a streetcar conductor recalled a similar man boarding near that corner at 7:55.

Strange, yet the police saw a contradiction—why would a person who committed such a well-planned crime leave such an obvious trail?

Peavey told the homicide detectives that a burglar had stolen jewelry and Mr. Taylor's special order, gold-tipped cigarettes two weeks earlier. Last week Peavey had found one of those cigarettes crushed out on the front steps, but Mr. Taylor had not ordered any more. Shortly afterward, pawn tickets for pieces of the stolen jewelry arrived from Stockton, up north, registered in the name of William Deane-Tanner.

The police checked out this name and discovered that William Deane-Tanner was William Desmond Taylor! In his previous identity, the respected director had been a well-known New York art connoisseur, husband and father who, one day in 1908, after seven years of marriage, simply disappeared. Mrs. Deane-Tanner, after years of futile searching, eventually obtained a divorce and remarried. Then in 1914, during his brief acting career, she saw her former husband in a film. When she contacted him, he invented a fantastic story of being shanghaied on lower Broadway and put on a vessel bound for Cape Horn. Mrs. Deane-Tanner only wanted child support, and Taylor willingly sent money for his daughter, Ethel Daisy. He left his entire estate to her in his will, to the amazement of his friends who were completely unaware of her existence or of his past. Coincidentally enough, Taylor's brother, Dennis, disappeared in exactly the same manner four years after William. Dennis's wife, in failing health, eventually moved to Los Angeles with her daughter and sought help from her wealthy brother-in-law. Though Taylor always denied their relationship, he helped to support them with a monthly allowance of $50 from a secret bank account.

The newspapers had a field day with the story. To think that Taylor had waltzed into Hollywood, a self-proclaimed director with no track record, and became an overnight success directing big money-makers like *Tom Sawyer*, *Anne of Green Gables*, *The Top of New York*, and several Mary Pickford vehicles! Then there was the matter of his leading ladies. No wonder Mary Miles Minter had been so anxious to get into Taylor's apartment that morning! Police found what she had been looking for—a lacy nightgown embroidered with the initials "MMM" and her note that said, "Dearest, I love you—I love you—I love you! XXXXXXXXX! Yours always, Mary."

Mary's fans were aghast to learn that she, the epitome of innocent maidenhood, had been involved with a man more than twice her age. The revelation destroyed her image, her reputation, and her career, but not before the papers learned that Taylor was also having an affair with Charlotte Shelby, Mary's mother. Reporters even speculated that the person seen leaving the crime might have been a woman in disguise . . . perhaps Mrs. Shelby, who quickly left on a European vacation that lasted three years. But police never seriously suspected her.

Police found Mabel Normand's love letters tucked in the toe of one of Taylor's riding boots. All of them began with "Dearest Daddy" and ended with "Blessed Baby" but revealed nothing more than that the two had been very close. Mabel got them back and promptly burned them, but her relief was only momentary.

The career of angelic, virginal Mary Miles Minter was ruined by gossip and rumors centering on a love note she'd written to Taylor, who was more than twice her age.

The search ended briefly when a prominent screenwriter confessed to the murder. He told police Taylor had seduced his wife and the wives of several of his friends. The confession proved false, but the press carried headlines of the "love cult" centered on Hollywood's perfect gentleman.

Finally, friends of the victim began coming forth with information. They hadn't considered it important before, but Taylor had mentioned getting harassing phone calls for months—hang-ups. He often heard noises in the house, occasionally found prowlers outside, and once had even chased away somebody with a pistol.

The immediate suspect was Edward Sands, Taylor's servant for two years.

During the scandalous aftermath of Taylor's murder, the silent screen's leading comedienne, Mabel Normand, was revealed to be a hopeless drug addict.

While Taylor was in Europe in 1921, Sands had forged thousands of dollars' worth of checks in his name, stolen his car, jewels, and wardrobe before completely disappearing. From time to time, Taylor would receive pawn tickets for the stolen items in his mail . . . always in the name of Deane-Tanner. Faith MacLean was positive, however, that the man she'd seen was not Sands.

If not Sands, who? Then again, who was Sands? In his Army papers, he was called Edward Fitz Strathmore. Nothing in this case was as it seemed. In fact, police had some reason to believe that Sands was probably not Sands *or* Strathmore, but Dennis Deane-Tanner, Taylor's long-lost brother! Men across the country were arrested and jailed for resembling Sands; all were released. Neither Sands nor Taylor's brother was ever heard of again.

Despite the studio's valiant efforts to hide it, authorities found out about Taylor's stock of illegal hooch. They also learned that Taylor had refused his last shipment because the goods weren't up to snuff. The supplier was reportedly "very unhappy," and police toyed with the idea that he might be unhappy enough to kill Taylor, but decided that wasn't likely. Then police uncovered a more dangerous connection to illegal substances—a connection that would ruin another career.

Taylor had been urging a police crackdown on local drug rings; in fact, he'd practically waged a one-man war against the vermin that were ruining Hollywood. He had fought with one of the dealers and on one occasion, actually knocked him into the street. Taylor was not motivated entirely by good citizenship. The object of his concern, it turned out, was Mabel. She was paying the ring a total of $2,000 a month for cocaine, plus the going blackmail rate. She got her coke inside the peanuts she bought from her favorite vendor. Mack Sennett released *Molly O*, perhaps Mabel's funniest film, about that time, but it played to empty houses, as did her subsequent films. Audiences wouldn't go to movies that starred a confirmed drug addict. Her career was washed up.

A sudden breakthrough came with the arrest of a Detroit hoodlum. He confessed to receiving $900 for driving two men and a woman to Taylor's, waiting outside, then driving them away. He told police, "a well-known actress who had it in for Taylor"—implying Mabel—had hired Harry "the Chink" Fields, a dealer, to do the job, but she herself had been along in the car. Fields was arrested in San Francisco with a .38 and lots of cocaine but no conclusive evidence. The "hired killer" theory seemed to make the most sense. A jealous lover in a crime of passion would have shot two, three, or four times, not once precisely through the heart. A professional would know he had only one chance. Hadn't all the neighbors said that if they'd heard a second shot, they would have acted? Taylor was most definitely stalked by someone so cool that even when he was spotted leaving the murder scene, he didn't panic. If he had, Mrs. MacLean would surely have called the police. Instead, the killer walked calmly to the streetcar whose arrival he had timed and disappeared into thin air.

After six months of pursuing love cults, "hop-heads," bootleggers, scorned lovers, a dual life, and disappearing servants, the police reached a dead end. Perhaps studio executives destroyed valuable evidence that morning, but William Desmond Taylor's killer was never found. Even the honesty of the investigation was suspect. Seven years after the murder, the district attorney involved was sent to Folsom Prison for accepting bribes. The man who took his place announced that a screen actress had killed Taylor and paid to cover up the crime, but as this was not official, the case remains unsolved.

"We know, of course, who committed the murder," said E. C. King, the investigator from the D.A.'s office, "but there is no evidence for the Grand Jury. The woman who killed him mentioned his murder to her chauffeur at seven in the morning—a full half-hour before Peavey found him lying dead—before anybody but the murderer herself knew that he was dead. We have had the woman in for detailed questioning, but she is a shrewd and cunning person and refuses to talk to us."

On the heels of Fatty Arbuckle's trial, the scandal was too much for the Hollywood kingdom's reputation. Tabloids in New York and Chicago reported that there was only one star out there in Sin City, California, who hadn't taken the drug cure and that even babies received nightly shots to keep them from crying. But a small, beady-eyed, elephant-eared man, Will Hays, Postmaster General in Harding's scandal-ridden administration, had arrived in Hollywood just in time to reassure America that an upstanding Presbyterian from Indiana was cleaning up the movies and weeding out the riffraff. By the end of 1922, the self-regulatory Hays Office was censoring the movies and overseeing the stars' private lives. Morals clauses were inserted into every actor's contract, and anyone who strayed from Hays's definition of "upright" was out of a job. Private detectives viciously competed to destroy careers, as formerly trustworthy servants were bribed to tell all about their famous employers. The Doom Book, a list of "dangerous" and unemployable actors, the first blacklisting, grew to outrageous proportions. The shot that killed William Desmond Taylor would reverberate for years.

D. W. GRIFFITH
The Master Forgotten

The lonely, bitter old man passed many an evening in a Hollywood bar, talking about the old days to anyone who gave him half an ear. "Directing was always a chore," he reminisced. "Believe it or not, I always considered it a temporary thing, a sort of springboard. My lifetime ambition has been to write." Few of the people who saw him in bars, or wandering Hollywood Boulevard, or hanging around the lobby of the timeworn Knickerbocker Hotel, recognized that he was D. W. Griffith, the single most important figure in American film history. Those who did were amazed that he was still alive.

David Wark Griffith was born in 1874 in Louisville, Kentucky, the son of genteel Southern folk who lost everything during the Reconstruction. He never forgot that he was an aristocrat, even with "the wolf pup of want and hunger" howling at his door throughout his young life. He quit school after the sixth grade. As a young man, he moved to New York to become a playwright, or, in platitudinous parlance, a starving writer. He couldn't afford to turn down the opportunity to make $5 a day as a bit player at Biograph Studios, but he was ashamed that the wolf pup had reduced him to being a movie actor, so he hid behind the name Lawrence Griffith. In 1906, when he married actress Linda Arvidson, he told her, "In a way, it's very nice, but you know . . . we can't go on forever and not tell our friends how we are earning our living."

Biograph offered Griffith the chance to direct a film in 1908, assuring him that if he were unsuccessful, he could always continue as an actor and scenario writer. It was the end of the career of Lawrence Griffith, actor. *Adventures of Dollie*, his first film, which starred his wife, was so successful that Griffith directed every Biograph feature for the next year, a remarkable 190 one-reelers.

The lonely master.

Dollie was also the beginning of Griffith's sixteen years of partnership with the skillful and talented cameraman Billy Bitzer.

Griffith, from the start, made films that were far more dramatic and far more technically advanced than anything American audiences had seen before. He claimed to have introduced the close-up, distant views, the switchback, sustained suspense, the fade-out, and restraint in expression, but that was not really true. All of these things were being practiced in Europe where they were also experimenting with color, sound, optical effects, movement of camera, and feature length work. Griffith himself was shot in close-up as an actor, before his directing days. He *was*, certainly, one of the first Americans to consciously employ these techniques, refining them and breaking the barriers of creative possibilities. His vision was boundless. He sermonized to Lillian Gish and a small group of actors, "You are taking the first baby steps in something predicted in the Bible," and he called film the universal language. "When silent film reaches perfection," he continued, "it could, combined with music, speak to the world without the use of words. Wars come about because people cannot clarify their issues. In the future, the difficulties could be filmed for all to see and understand and even bring about the millennium."

In short, Griffith made the movies come alive. His films at Biograph appealed to their primarily working class audience by lacing a Victorian ethic and an intrinsic sympathy for the sufferings of the poor with Griffith's own love of irony, of Fate, and coincidence. He always had compassion win out over vengeance.

Griffith's dynamic ideas also led to a new, more subtle style of acting. With the camera finally close enough to show meaningful expression, actors learned to smile, frown, and cry at his command. He unleashed a powerful new force in film—emotion. Audiences soon began to recognize their favorite performers. The faces that D. W. Griffith carefully selected became the world's first real movie stars: Blanche Sweet, Mae Marsh, Donald Crisp, Lionel Barrymore, Douglas Fairbanks, Wallace Reid, Richard Barthlemess, Mack Sennett, Mabel Normand, and his most famous discoveries, Lillian Gish and Mary Pickford. "We pick the little women because the world loves youth and all its wistful sweetness," he declared. He understood how far he was ahead of all other filmmakers in his realization of the potential of film. His innovations had tremendous worldwide impact on the entire film industry, and particularly on directors Erich von Stroheim and Mack Sennett. "He was the first to realize he was a genius," Sennett said of his idol.

Griffith and Arvidson separated in 1911, and she left for Hollywood to star in a film. Their differences were irreconcilable, and they would remain apart for the duration of their marriage. Remaining at Biograph making two-reelers, Griffith grew increasingly unhappy as more sophisticated four- and five-reel films were being made in Europe. The studio made Griffith general director in an attempt to placate him, but its limitations were still too frustrating. In 1913, he moved over to Reliance-Majestic, taking Bitzer and most of his stable of actors with him. He left behind 450 films made under the Biograph banner.

At last, he was allowed to create without restrictions. The ambitious Grif-

Griffith (right) at work with his cameraman Billy Bitzer (circa 1916).

fith's first independent film was a mammoth project. A year and a half in the making, with a running time of three hours, *The Birth of a Nation* opened in 1915 to sensational controversy and packed houses, even at an unheard-of $2 a ticket. President Woodrow Wilson requested a personal screening, making it the first film shown in the White House. "It's like writing history with lightning," the President said afterward. Originally titled *The Clansman*, it starred Henry B. Walthall, Lillian Gish, Mae Marsh, Donald Crisp, Wallace Reid, and Raoul Walsh as John Wilkes Booth. Director John Ford claims to have been one of the Ku Klux Klan horsemen. The story took the audience through the destruction of the South in the Civil War, the Lincoln assassination, the bitterness of the Reconstruction, and the resurrection of the White South, through the birth of the KKK. For Griffith, it was his personal vindication of the Old South that he'd heard about on his father's knee. Many citizens' groups, however, greeted him with violent charges of prejudice, declaring the movie to be "a flagrant incitement to racial antagonism," with its slovenly depiction of Negroes and heroic portrayal of the Klan. Griffith was hurt and confused by the criticism. He told Lillian Gish, "Why, to say that I am against the Negro is like saying I am against children, as they were our children, whom we loved and cared for all our lives." He truly meant no harm; he just hadn't kept up with the times.

Griffith went heavily into debt to finance his next epic, *Intolerance.* At a cost of $2,500,000, it ran over thirteen reels. It was really four different movies, but Griffith attempted to interweave four widely separated historical dramas about man's inhumanity to man. (Two of the stories were released individually in 1919 as *The Fall of Babylon* and *The Mother and The Law.*) The Babylonian story, for which Griffith constructed spectacular sets, complete with eight life-size elephants, deals with the fall of Babylon to Persian conqueror Cyrus the Great. The Judean story—the life of Christ—and the French story based on the 1572 Massacre of St. Bartholomew's Day, in Paris, were comparatively underdeveloped. The fourth story was set in a modern American mill town and the slum area of an American city. In this sequence, a completely captivating Mae Marsh portrays The Dear One, not merely as an individual, but as an expression of the spirit of faithful womanhood itself. It was a typical example of Griffith's personal expression, this time his unsophisticated, highly romanticized view of women. Critics commented that his girls were always "fluttering," and even Mary Pickford admitted, "Mr. Griffith always wanted to have me running around trees and pointing at rabbits, and I wouldn't do it." Miss Pickford did not appear in *Intolerance,* but the cast boasted Lillian Gish, Erich von Stroheim, Bessie Love, Constance Talmadge, and featured Alma Rubens and Wally Reid in bit parts.

Although it earned Griffith the title of "The Master," *Intolerance* was a box office failure. Audiences found it rambling and, on the eve of entering World War I, didn't accept Griffith's pacifism. In the twentieth century, he seemed naive and moralistic. "The simple things, the human things, are important in pictures," he told the press. "There are only a few basic plots. The most important thing is humanity." *Intolerance* ruined him financially, but won high critical praise. Its reputation went as far as Moscow, and Lenin had it imported in 1919. Eisenstein, Pudovkin, and other young Russian film students showed the influence of Griffith in their later work.

Trying to recoup his losses, Griffith bounced from studio to studio until 1919, when he, Mary Pickford, Douglas Fairbanks, William S. Hart, and Charlie Chaplin decided to stop a merger between producers and distributors that would have destroyed their artistic independence. The result was a new studio run by the artists, appropriately named United Artists.

"On that night," said Chaplin in his autobiography, "the five of us sat at a table in the main dining room of the Alexandria Hotel. The effect was electric.

J. D. Williams * unsuspectingly came in for dinner first, saw us, then hurried out. One after another, the producers came to the entrance, took a look, then hurried out, while we sat talking big business and marking the tablecloth with astronomical figures . . . very soon, a half-dozen members of the press were at our table taking notes as we issued our statement that we were forming a company of United Artists to protect our independence and to combat the forthcoming big merger. The story received front page coverage."

Griffith went back to the East Coast to shoot his next films, *Broken Blossoms*, a tragic story of unrequited dreams and love, starring Lillian Gish, Richard Barthelmess, and Donald Crisp; and *Way Down East*, second only to *Birth of a Nation* at the box office. *Way Down East* set the tone for perilous acting roles; in the famous runaway ice floe scene, Miss Gish was exposed to terrible physical hardship. For three weeks, she lay on the ice slab twenty times a day while her hair froze and her eyelashes turned to icicles. The hand that she trailed dramatically through the freezing water troubles her still.

Despite the success of both films, Griffith, with his customary extravagance, ran up such a debt on production costs that both films lost money and ultimately forced his break with United Artists in 1924. He joined forces with Adolph Zukor at Paramount in New York, but what he gained in the financial security of studio backing, he sacrificed in artistic freedom. Without his Griffith-trained cast and crew or the power to choose his subject matter, his self-confidence took a brutal beating. He directed three rather mediocre films, two with W. C. Fields *(Sally of the Sawdust* and *That Royale Girl)* before Zukor dissolved his contract.

In 1927, Griffith went back to Los Angeles and United Artists, but he found that most of his original power had been usurped. The Hollywood film industry had changed greatly during his eight-year absence. He had trouble adjusting to the new studio system. His first three films for U.A. showed his uneasiness. Then in 1930, he directed his first talking picture, *Abraham Lincoln*, starring Walter Huston. Critics labeled it "corny" and, as usual, accused Griffith of lacking his former originality, but the epic biography was a box office success, providing his career with a badly needed boost. However, United Artists refused to give him any further financial backing.

Griffith hoped to restore his reputation as an independent producer with a movie aptly titled *The Struggle*, which he co-wrote with Anita Loos and John Emerson. The Master bet his last dime on this somber study of alcoholism— once again, out of step with public temperament. In the throes of the Depression, moviegoers wanted light and uplifting entertainment, and they so totally ignored this gloomy picture that it was withdrawn from the theaters after a run of only nine days. (After that, the film was recut without Griffith's consent. Only the cut version survives.) The disappointment was the final blow to Griffith, and he entered a long period of seclusion. With his assets frozen through many debts, he was forced to sell his U.A. stock, severing his only remaining tie to the industry. Though he lived another seventeen years, his name would never again appear on a film credit.

* The president of First National—producers and exhibitors of all of Chaplin's films.

This is not to say that he was completely estranged from the movies. England's Twickenham Film Company requested his supervision on their sound version of *Broken Blossoms*. Griffith traveled to London, but disagreed strongly with the cast selection. After they screened his original, he decided it could not be improved with sound and left the project. In 1939, the Motion Picture Academy dusted off the aging Master, dapper and distinguished as ever in his tux, trotting him out to accept an honorary Oscar for "distinguished creative achievement as director and producer and invaluable initiative and lasting contributions to the progress of the motion picture arts."

That same year, Hal Roach hired him to produce *One Million, B.C.*, and stories say Griffith directed some of it as well. However, the two men had so many disagreements that Griffith insisted his name be removed from the credits. His old friend Mae Marsh said that he called her to play the mother of starlet Carole Landis but later called her back with the bad news, "They refused that. They refused to have the other people I wanted in it. They're not taking any advice of mine. First, I was asked to direct it; then I was asked to advise. They're not letting me do either; I think I will not be able to stand it."

"He quit," said Marsh. "We had lunch and he said he was very sad. That was the last time he was in any studio that I know of."

When *Gone with the Wind* was released in all its glory, Griffith's indignation was evident. "Chaplin said I got the same effect in *The Birth of a Nation* with a close-up of a few corpses," he snapped.

He returned to his first love, writing, usually reworking old scripts he'd written, and using the pseudonyms Gaston de Tolignac, Captain Victor Marie, Roy Sinclair, and Irene Sinclair. Once again, he was unsuccessful as a writer. At last given reason to seek a divorce from Linda, he married the young star of *The Struggle*, Evelyn Marjorie Baldwin, but the marriage didn't last, and a series of lawsuits began that would plague him for the rest of his life.

He spent his final years in a string of hotels, finally settling in The Knickerbocker, a once-majestic building that was now as faded as its forlorn tenant. He lived as a recluse in a room full of stacks of yellowing, unfinished scripts. His only pleasure was his daily constitutional down the Boulevard of Broken Dreams, where he was just another anonymous face.

On July 22, 1948, the seventy-three-year-old Griffith was found slumped over his piles of scripts, victim of a stroke. He died of a cerebral hemorrhage early the next morning. The Master, who left an estate worth between $30,000 and $50,000, would have been further embittered by the moving tribute the industry held to mourn the loss of one of its founding fathers, the "Shakespeare of the Screen."

"The whole industry owes its experience to Mr. Griffith," Chaplin stated.

"Through his genius," spouted C. B. DeMille, "he gave the screen mind and soul . . . his passing is a heartache."

Norma Talmadge expressed deep sadness at Griffith's death. "His great art was equaled only by his great charm and personality."

Blanche Sweet remembered Griffith in a way that would have pleased him most. "I shall never think of him as dead," said the fifty-three-year-old Griffith discovery. "I'll see his master touch in every picture ever made."

WALLACE REID
Derailed

"Our cartoonist was an ex-vaudevillian, always the life of the party. That day in January, 1923, he came into the office, his face as somber as the mask of tragedy. 'Wally Reid just died.' We all quit for the day. In every studio in Hollywood, too, all work stopped," a reporter for the *Los Angeles Mirror News* recollected about "Good Time Wally" 's shocking death at thirty-one from drug addiction. "Many believed Reid was going to win, even up to the day of his death . . . If grief and fury alone could have done it, the dope evil would have been slaughtered that day . . . The national furor that followed was so tremendous that if any dope peddler had been found anywhere, he would have been ripped to shreds in maniacal grief."

Everyone loved Wally Reid. When he made the Doom Book because of his morphine addiction, even Will Hays was moved to tell the public that ". . . the unfortunate Mr. Reid should be dealt with as a diseased person—not to be censured, shunned." No lurid headlines tainted him. "It was the ideals back of that handsome face," wrote Adela Rogers St. John, "corresponding so completely with the beauty and fineness of his outward being, that earned him the love of his fans . . . His death grieved and bewildered and shocked the whole world."

For Wally, morphine was an occupational hazard. He'd always thought that acting wasn't "quite a man's job," but for him, the physical labor of stardom was tougher than going to war.

Born in St. Louis to a theatrical family, Wally grew up backstage in theaters all over the Midwest. His mother, Bertha Westbrook Reid, starred in the melo-dramas written by Hal, her husband, who was considered "erratically bril-

'Yankee Doodle Dandy''—the charmed ife of America's #1 male star would end in gony at thirty-one.

liant," as both a writer and a husband. He'd have spurts of great creative productivity and familial devotion, then suddenly heed the call of his womanizing habit and disappear for a while. Wally worshipped his father nevertheless, and to his dear mother, the twelve-year-old Wally had inscribed on a gift, "To she who stood by her two erring boys with the patience of Job and the forgiveness of the Savior." The Reids split up off and on and eventually divorced when Wally was an adult, but he never took sides and remained close to both of them.

Wally first appeared on stage in his parents' act when he was four. Little "Cotton-Top" amazed his parents by reciting whole monologues from the show. He had no playmates, so he entertained himself, reading a great deal and playing with the musical instruments. He mastered the violin and piano, and eventually went on to play every string and woodwind instrument by ear.

The Reids moved to New York when their child prodigy was ten. There he discovered his own "secret caves" to hide in and read *Tom Sawyer* and *The Last of the Mohicans,* but he came out to play frontiersmen and Indians with the other boys in the neighborhood. His parents wanted the best education possible for him, so off he went to military school, where he excelled in football, basketball, and painting. He planned to study medicine at Princeton and passed the entrance exam, but he was suddenly . . . bored. The seventeen-year-old was eager to taste everything life had to offer. He talked it over with his father's good friend William "Buffalo Bill" Cody, who had sought out Hal Reid in New York to write a play for his show. Buffalo Bill said the Wild West would do young Reid some good and invited him out to Cody, Wyoming. Within a few weeks, Wally was gainfully employed as the clerk at the Hotel Irma, owned by Buffalo Bill's sister, where for hours he'd listen to the old-timers swapping yarns around the potbellied stove. In 1909, the West was still untamed, and the tenderfoot Reid quickly learned to ride, shoot, and survive on the plains. He roamed Wyoming for almost a year, working as a hand and living off the land until his father asked him to come to Chicago and join him at Selig Studios, where he was now writing and directing scenarios.

At Selig, Wally's athletic prowess and Adonis physique got him hired as a stunt man, specializing in diving and swimming tricks. He became pals with rodeo star Tom Mix, who did all the horse stunts. Wally's insatiable curiosity was still at work. The fledgling picture business fascinated him, and he was determined to master every aspect of it. From Selig, he went back to New York, where Vitagraph and Reliance hired him as one of the first mood musicians. He serenaded the actors on the sets so that they could emote in the proper atmosphere. He worked as a cameraman, writer, director, and character actor. Then the West promised him more adventure, and he turned his sights to the rapidly prospering Hollywood.

Wally loved the sights of Hollywood—movie shacks sprouting in the midst of the citrus groves, the hordes of flamboyant hopefuls roaming the dusty streets in search of stardom. He got himself signed on at Nestor Studios as a director, but the studio heads took notice of his wholesome good looks and immediately drafted him for the male lead in *His Only Son,* opposite the darling of the Nestor lot, sixteen-year-old Dorothy Davenport, a dark-eyed beauty descended from a long line of actors. Reid was happier behind the camera; he always resented getting work based solely on his looks rather than his ability. He sulked openly and Dorothy snubbed him in return. The third day on the set, the cowboy actor Hoot Gibson decided to play a practical joke on the dour newcomer. For a scene where Reid was to ride a horse, Gibson and the crew saddled up a wild, unbroken stallion. As Dorothy, an excellent horsewoman, emerged from her dressing room, she was astonished to see Reid sticking like glue to a bucking bronco. He rode the beast to a dead stop. The joke backfired. Everyone, including Dorothy, looked on Wally Reid with new-found admiration, while Gibson became a laughingstock for the remainder of the shoot. Later, he and Wally became close friends.

A year after the bronco escapade, while Wally was directing Dorothy in *Lightning Bolt* at Universal, they got married after work one night. Thunderous cheers and popping guns greeted their arrival on the lot the next morning, and newspaper headlines trumpeted, "Universal Film Director Marries Leading Lady." It was, by Reid's own account, "the happiest time of my life," despite the fact that his mother bitterly opposed the union and cut herself off from them for six years. Dorothy was the only girl for Wally. He never considered, never even looked at another, although women were always chasing him.

In 1914, D. W. Griffith offered Wally a new challenge so exciting that he gladly agreed to act again. Griffith wanted him to replace ailing Henry B. Walthall in the lead in his new controversial project, *The Clansman*, which would be known to history as *The Birth of a Nation*. But at the last minute, Walthall recovered, and Reid was offered the small part of Jeff, the blacksmith. He was furious, but he accepted his consolation prize and let all his anger out in the way he played the role. Ironically, the critics and audience alike thought him a standout. Before the filming was over, Wally had a second role—because he was so beautiful, Griffith used him as the Christ figure in *The Clansman*'s final tableau. The crew commenced with the filming of that scene before dawn, and Reid, half-naked, nearly froze hanging outside on the cross. Someone ordered shots of brandy to warm him up. By the time the perfectionist, Griffith, was satisfied with the shoot, his "Christ figure" was thoroughly soused. Wally was able to hide it, of course, and his adoring public never suspected anything was amiss.

After *Birth of a Nation*, the studio wanted him on the receiving end of the camera only. "My damn face kept me from [being] a writer or director," was the way he saw it. He was the leading actor at Paramount for the next seven years, without a break. As leading ladies, he had the Gish sisters, Bebe Daniels, and Mae Murray, among others. In Cecil B. DeMille's *Carmen* (1915), he played the "vamped" lover Don Jose opposite the much-celebrated Geraldine Farrar, the Metropolitan Opera star who often sang with Caruso. By that time he was earning an untaxed $3,000 a week, fifty-two weeks a year.

Wally bought a choice acre of land between Sweetzer and DeLongpre Avenues in what is now West Hollywood, just below Sunset Boulevard. His gargantuan $23,000 home, the first in Los Angeles to have a swimming pool, included rooms for film, billiards, music, a chemistry lab, a huge library, and a "pit" in the garage where Wally indulged his passion for race cars. He still couldn't resist a thrill, and he was often seen tearing through Hollywood at breakneck speed in his fire-engine-red roadster. His custom-made horn played "I'm a Yankee Doodle Dandy."

On-screen he was always the embodiment of the ideal American youth— and offscreen he was equally wholesome, filled with love for the red, white, and blue, and anxious to serve his country when World War I broke out. But Paramount was not about to lose its number-one star to the trenches. "As inspiration and entertainment for millions of people," the studio heads told him, "you are far more important here in front of the camera than behind a single rifle on a battlefield." They also pointed out that he was the sole support of his mother-in-law and his wife, who had given up her career to be mother to their newborn son, William Wallace Reid, Jr. "Your first duty is to them." With all the money he made, Wally still had no head for finances, and he spent his money or gave it away as fast as he made it. If he left his family, he'd be abandoning them with no savings. Reluctantly, he stayed behind. But every time he passed a man in uniform, he cringed inwardly. The fact that he was staying behind made him feel like a phoney and a hypocrite. His self-respect suffered a blow from which it would never recover.

Meanwhile, his career was hotter than ever. "No man has ever been so besieged by the attention of women," the fan magazines gushed. Every day he turned away girls who hid in his car or bribed studio guards for a peek at his dressing room—anything, just to be near him.

At home, "Good Time Wally" was known for his "open-door" style. The party in his sprawling home never stopped. He and his wife adopted a daughter, Betty Ann. To his friends, Wally's life seemed idyllic, but Dorothy began to worry about his grueling schedule. Working endlessly, at times on two films at once, he made 177 films during his twelve-year career. He never had a moment to relax, but if he was tired, his sturdy physique never showed it. Everyone thought that Wally Reid was Peter Pan.

The beginning of the end came in 1919 when he was filming *Valley of the Giants.* Reid was aboard the train carrying the cast and crew to their location in the High Sierras when it jumped the track. Though he was badly injured, Wally staggered through the wreckage to help the women to safety and was himself one of the last to receive medical aid. He suffered damage to the base of his spine and a severe gash on his head, which would later cause him blinding headaches. The stoical troupers went on with the filming, however, and the company doctor freely prescribed morphine to ease Wally's pain.

Wally had never known defeat until he tried to kick the morphine. When he realized he had to have it, he began to drink, heavily, hoping one would hide the other. It only made things worse. "He was a cause of constant anxiety to me," said Gloria Swanson, his co-star in DeMille's *The Affairs of Anatol* (1921). "I heard endless rumors that he was an addict, and although I never saw him take drugs, his behavior never seemed quite right. He gave me the jitters."

Paramount, which made $2 million a year on his films, kept Wally on a treadmill, despite the rumors, churning out a series of light adventure films

Cecil B. DeMille (seated at table) in a conference with members of his Affairs of Anatol *cast. (Left to right) Elliott Dexter, Wallace Reid, Theodore Kasloff, and Gloria Swanson.*

that the public adored and their hero despised. To see him in these movies is to chronicle his rapidly deteriorating health. The red-blooded American Adonis was growing more and more weak and emaciated. In fact, he hardly seemed to know what was happening around him. He managed to keep going through the motions until he collapsed on the set of *30 Days.* Director Henry Hathaway grimly remembered, "He sort of fumbled about and bumped into a chair. Then he sat down on the floor and started to cry. They propped him up in the chair [to continue filming] but he just tipped over. Finally, finally, they called the ambulance."

Reid entered a sanitarium in December of 1922. Always the champion, he told DeMille, "I'll either come out cured . . . or I won't come out."

"The King of Paramount," handsome Wally Reid was America's ideal.

Dorothy Davenport bravely told the story to Wally's stunned fans. "Wally is desperately ill, the victim of a disease . . . the disease of drug addiction." The press and public were assured that this was no Hollywood joy ride and poured out their heartfelt sympathy for Wally's struggle. Every day the headlines brought news of his courage and determination. The *Los Angeles Examiner* ran off a special copy just for Reid, in which they deleted the story of his addiction and institutionalization. He was never aware that the public knew. This was the type of loyalty that Reid inspired.

Somewhere, though, the good times had screeched to a halt for Wally. He was humiliated over his cowardice in war, his contempt for his frivolous acting roles, and finally, his failure to shake off the hard stuff. The sanitarium did not wean him away from his habit; they stopped it cold turkey. Dorothy, keeping a constant vigil at his bedside, watched her strapping husband shrink to 120 pounds in a month. Wally lapsed in and out of a coma, but when he came to he'd smile weakly at her, and say, "Tell them we're going to make it, Mama . . . I'm clean . . . we're going to win."

On January 18, 1923, he cried out in agony, "God . . . I . . . Please!" and stopped breathing. Ten thousand people attended his funeral.

Soon afterward, Dorothy appeared at a Hollywood awards banquet that was broadcast on the radio. As she stepped up to the microphone, she raised her head and proudly proclaimed, "Hello everybody. This is Mrs. Wallace Reid." The line was used again in *A Star Is Born*. She called herself "Mrs. Wallace Reid" for the rest of her life. She flew to Washington, D.C., to participate in a conference on narcotics to contribute what she intimately knew. When she returned to Hollywood, she appeared in two antidrug films for Thomas Ince: *Human Wreckage* and *Broken Laws*, both of which she helped finance. She went on to produce other moral message films against drugs, venereal disease, and prostitution throughout the 1920s. She turned to writing in the forties and finally retired altogether in 1968. She never remarried.

JIM THORPE
The Fall From the Heights

Jim Thorpe became an international hero when he won both the pentathlon and the decathlon at the 1912 Olympic Games in Stockholm—a feat that has never been equaled before or since then. The air in Stockholm was filled with the strains of "Yankee Doodle Dandy." As a royal tribute, Sweden's King Gustav proclaimed him the greatest athlete in the world and presented him with a chalice in the shape of a viking ship. Thorpe, a man of few words, told Gustav, "Thanks, King."

Burt Lancaster played him in *Jim Thorpe—All American*, a 1951 movie. As a stiff-faced Thorpe, Lancaster vaulted from victory to defeat, from the world's greatest athlete to a broken man driving a junk truck. At the end of the movie, he recaptured some of his glory when he was honored at a dinner hosted by the state of Oklahoma. In real life, Jim Thorpe was wasting away on the ragged edge of Hollywood.

Jim and his twin brother, Charlie, were born in 1888, in a one-room log cabin on the banks of the Canadian River, near Prague, in Indian territory that is now Oklahoma. His mother, following the tradition of naming her children for the first thing she saw after giving birth, called him Wa-Tho-Huck—Bright Path. He was the great-grandson of the famous Chippewa chief Black Hawk. Thorpe's grandfather was an Irish fur trader and explorer who had wooed Black Hawk's daughter away from her tribe. The twin boys grew up among their people, the Sac and Fox, and by the age of three, were swimming or roaming on horseback over the 160-acre farm their father had acquired during the Oklahoma Land Rush. At nine, Charlie was stricken with spinal meningitis. When he died, the Sac and Fox believed that Jim became endowed with the

Jim Thorpe—All American

physical strength of two. Perhaps this is the explanation for the amazing feats he would accomplish.

On a crisp fall morning in 1907, Jim was impatiently watching the tryouts for track and high jump at Carlisle Indian College in Pennsylvania. He was wearing heavy boots and street clothes, but on a sudden impulse, he dashed forward, clearing the high bar and continuing to race like the wind around the track. Coach Glenn "Pop" Warner looked up in astonishment as Thorpe easily outdistanced every runner on the track. "I saw the promise of a great future," recalled Warner, who immediately put Thorpe on the varsity football team. By the end of the 1908 season, the *Washington Post* was calling him "the most talked about athlete in Pennsylvania."

That summer, as part of Carlisle's system of half-study, half-earning, young Jim went south to do farm work. When he was invited to play baseball there, he naturally jumped at the chance. A friend explained that when you join the Carolina League, you can make sixty bucks a season—$2 a day.

"I can play baseball and get paid for it, too? When do I start?" It seemed like a simple enough decision.

After playing the 1909–10 season with the Carolina League, he returned to Carlisle's football team, where Pop Warner was now calling him "the greatest football player of all time." "Big Jim" not only ran 70 yards for a touchdown against unbeaten Harvard, but before the day was out, he'd also kicked four field goals. He ran over West Point for a 97-yard touchdown and was personally responsible for twenty-two of Carlisle's twenty-seven points against Army's paltry six. At the end of the 1911 season, Thorpe's performances won him the selection as half-back on Walter Camp's honorary All-American Team and Pop Warner's promise to groom him for the coming Olympics.

During his career at Carlisle, Jim Thorpe set records in running, jumping, swimming, shooting, skating, baseball, tennis, hockey, lacrosse, shot putting, and pole vaulting. He also excelled in basketball and boxing. After his incredible performance at the Olympic Games, he was the most talked about athlete in the world. After the games, Thorpe married and returned to Carlisle for their 1912–13 football season. Again named honorary All-American he was, not surprisingly, the nation's most sought-after college athlete.

But by January of 1913, a dark cloud was settling over Thorpe's "bright path." Sportswriter Roy Ruggles Johnson exposed Jim's "fling" in pro ball to the Amateur Athletic Union, which certifies the amateur status of American Olympic contestants.

"I didn't play for the money that was in it, but because I liked to play ball . . ." he explained. "I was simply an Indian schoolboy, not wise to the ways of the world."

The A.A.U. would not accept Thorpe's explanation. Revoking his amateur status, they ordered him to return all of his medals and trophies. Further, they stripped his records from the books and declared two other contestants winners of the decathlon and pentathlon. Though the world rushed to Thorpe's defense, the committee stuck firmly by its decision. Thorpe obediently sent his medals to his nearest contender, Sweden's H. K. Wieslander. "I do not know what your rules are in regards to amateurism in the United States,"

Wieslander wrote the A.A.U., "but I do know that Thorpe is the greatest athlete in the world."

If the committee considered him a professional baseball player, then that was what he'd be. Jim signed a three-year contract with the New York Giants, but "from the very beginning," reported the *New York Times*, the greatest athlete in the world "ran like a deer in the outfield, fielded well, but was absolutely helpless against the curved pitching of the big league stars." The last two years, Thorpe was assigned to the Giants' farm team in Jersey City. He was traded three times before his ignominious professional baseball career ended in 1919.

By 1920, he found a way to bounce back from disappointment. Jim organized and was elected president of the American Professional Football Association, which two years later became the National Football League. He was called "the terror of the grid-iron," and he led the Canton (Ohio) Bulldogs to two undefeated seasons. Thorpe was known for his spectacular open-field running. Once he was free with the ball, the opposing team found it easier to stop a freight train. He went on to play well for New York and Florida, but retired from football in 1929, when the rules were changed to effectively curb his natural advantages.

He wasn't so fleet of foot anymore. His playing days were over, and Jim found life a sport for which he was unprepared. By then he was divorced, remarried, and the father of seven children. He took to drifting aimlessly across the country, accepting almost any work to survive. He dug ditches for $4 a day, became a carnival sideshow attraction, and eventually wandered into Hollywood, where he became a bit player in western movies and short football features. His biggest roles were in *Green Light*, a 1937 film starring Errol Flynn, and as Swift Arrow in the 1931 serial *Battling Buffalo Bill*, which starred Rex Bell.

By the time he started working the movies, he was close to fifty and rapidly declining. His best friend was now a bottle. "He had an Indian's weakness for liquor and an Indian's inability to hold it," a former teammate said. His once-formidable physique had grown bloated and flabby. With frustration facing him in every direction, he applied to the A.A.U. for reinstatement of his medals and records but was denied.

Thorpe turned back to his people. He became active in Indian affairs and toured the country, lecturing on the culture and traditions of the Native American and the significance of sports in modern life. In 1943, the Oklahoma legislature joined his appeal to the A.A.U. for reinstatement. The answer was still no. A short time later, Thorpe, now fifty-five, had his first heart attack.

During World War II, "Old Jim" joined the merchant marine. After his discharge, he settled in Los Angeles, alone, in an apartment at 5162 Melrose Avenue, a modest street not far from some of the film factories but populated by has-beens and never-weres. He married his third wife, Patricia, in 1945. She set to work putting his life back in order.

In 1950, the nearly forgotten name of Jim Thorpe returned to the headlines. An Associated Press poll voted him the greatest male athlete of the first half of the twentieth century, in a landslide victory over Babe Ruth, Jack Dempsey,

Jim Thorpe presents Hedda Hopper with a headdress of her own.

The world's greatest athlete—from Olympic Games to kids' games.

and Ty Cobb. The same poll declared him the greatest football player of 1900–50, over the legendary Red Grange. The recognition brought him no material rewards, because the now sloppy and overweight Thorpe had long ago sold the rights to his life story to Hollywood for a flat fee. The simple Indian boy had been outwitted again. The press hyped Thorpe's position as technical adviser on *Jim Thorpe—All American,* not explaining that for his "advice," he received $250. The next year, when he was hospitalized for cancer of the lip, the papers revealed that he was penniless. More than $2,000 came in from loyal fans.

After his second heart attack in 1952, Old Jim and Patricia moved to a trailer park in Lomita, a little north up the Pacific Coast Highway, where Thorpe planned to rest and fish. Another legislative group petitioned the A.A.U. on his behalf, but again the union refused.

"I cannot decide whether I am well named or not. Many a time the path has gleamed bright for me, but just as often it has been dark and bitter indeed," he told a friend about that time.

An unusually cold wind was blowing in to the trailer park from the ocean on March 29, 1953. Old Jim, passing another bleak and lazy day, sat down to an early supper at three o'clock that afternoon. Fifteen minutes later, neighbor Colby Bradshaw heard Patricia screaming hysterically, and he raced to the Thorpes' trailer. Jim was having another heart attack. Bradshaw applied artificial respiration for half an hour, until the County Rescue Squad arrived. At last, sixty-four-year-old Thorpe came to. He looked around slowly and quietly spoke to Patricia and Bradshaw. A sigh of relief was barely on their lips when a second massive attack killed him.

On October 13, 1982, twenty-nine years after his death, the International Athletic Committee voted to reinstate Thorpe's amateur standing. On that day, his Olympic feats were restored to the record books, and the medals he earned seventy years earlier were presented to his daughter Charlotte. She has donated them to the U.S. Olympic Hall of Fame.

CLARA BOW
Losing "IT"

Sixteen-year-old Clara Bow could escape from her unhappy cold-water tene-
ment home in Brooklyn for a little while whenever she opened *Photoplay*,
Motion Picture Classic, or *Shadowland*, her favorite movie magazines. She
spent hours imitating Gloria Swanson, Mary Pickford, and Norma Talmadge,
and more hours fantasizing about how glamorous their lives must be.

"You're as pretty as any movie star," Robert Bow, her mild and distant
papa, assured her. He was more than willing to help his baby enter *Motion
Picture* magazine's 1921 "Fame and Fortune" contest.

Sarah Bow, her mother, felt differently. She had lost two infant daughters,
and Clara's difficult birth had almost killed both mother and child. Sarah was
left an invalid, and her mental agony grew worse every day, along with her
religious fanaticism. One scorching summer night, Clara was startled out of
her sleep by the touch of cold steel at her throat. She opened her eyes to find
her mother holding a butcher knife. "You'd be better off dead than an actress!"
she screamed. Clara lay sobbing while her mother launched into a demented
tirade about morality and such. She'd seen these fits before, but had never
been in such mortal danger. Gulping spasmodically for air through her tears,
Clara tried talking to her wild-eyed mother to calm her down. Hours passed
before Sarah Bow slipped into a trancelike state and the knife fell from her
hand. Clara huddled in the closet, whimpering in utter terror, until her father
came home the next day. From that time on, she never slept through the night
again.

In an incredible stroke of luck, *Motion Picture* magazine selected "Little
Miss Bow" as winner of their contest. Her prize was a part in a movie. Six
years later, all the world knew her as "The Brooklyn Bonfire," "The Ultimate

"The Ultimate Jazz Baby," Clara Bow—the twenties' "IT" girl.

Sincerely
Clara Bow

Jazz Baby," and America's "It" girl, a phrase writer Elinor Glyn coined to mean all that and something more. "There are only three in Hollywood who have 'It,' " Glyn declared. "Clara Bow, Tom Mix's horse, and the doorman at the Ambassador Hotel."

Clara positively glowed with the effervescence of the new, jazz-crazed generation . . . her bouncy energy and red-haired, tomboy beauty epitomized the Roaring Twenties. She was the emancipated working girl on screen, playing manicurists, waitresses, usherettes, dance hall hostesses, and shop girls, always with her provocative combination of childlike innocence and wanton sex. As *Variety* put it in 1923, "She lingers in the eye after the picture has gone."

It was 1927: the peak of Coolidge prosperity, as Lucky Lindy soared into the hearts of two nations and Eddie Cantor sang about "Makin' Whoopee" from center stage of Ziegfeld's Follies. "The rapid success of Clara Bow," said one Los Angeles paper, "has furnished Hollywood with almost as much conversation as the recent economy wave." Bow had women everywhere bobbing their hair, going without undergarments, and giving their lips the "bee-stung" look. Her fan mail inundated Paramount—in fact, Clara Bow got more mail per week than the average American town of 5,000. She dominated the fan magazines that had once mesmerized her. "Clara Bow—Beauty, Brains, or Luck?" "The Mystery of Clara's Chinese Den," "How to Get THE LOOK." Fans could read all about her speeding along the coast in her Kissel convertible which she painted red to match her hair. Next to her in the front seat were seven Chow dogs and an occasional monkey, also red. Fun-loving, generous, the darling of every film crew, the twenty-two-year-old star was a loyal pal to everyone with whom she worked, from the lowest extra to the highest exec. She felt more at home with working people than with the high-flung socialites who courted her; she found their gatherings stuffy and overbearing, and inevitably would whisper to her date, "Let's scram . . . this party is takin' the snap out of my garters."

She did her best to convince the studio that "pal" Gary Cooper was more than just a cowboy actor . . . in private, she confided to a friend that he was one of the few men who could satisfy her all through the night, "a great lay." The laconic actor was wild about her, and she helped launch his dramatic career as the young pilot in William Wellman's flying epic, *Wings*, the best picture of 1927. But he was just one of an infinite number of men in restless Clara's life. The combination of her insatiable, athletic, carnal appetite and her insomnia sometimes drove her into the arms of two, three, or more men a night. She was, at one time or another, engaged to *Gone with the Wind* director Victor Fleming and to King of Broadway Harry Richman. "That wonderful woman gave me the most wonderful days of my entire life," the thoroughly smitten Richman reminisced. Among her many other lovers were Richard Arlen and Buddy Rogers, her *Wings* co-stars; John Gilbert, whose "upper-crust" friends chided him endlessly about her; Charles Farrell; Frederic March; Gilbert Roland, who was her first serious romance; Eddie Cantor, her co-star in *Kid Boots*; boxer Slapsie Maxie Rosenbloom; and even Bela Lugosi,

Little Miss Bow—the Brooklyn Bonfire.

who kept a nude portrait of Clara in his home long after their affair had ended. About the only man in Hollywood Clara didn't sleep with was Al Jolson. To his endless frustration, he could never figure out why, but the "It" girl did whatever she wanted. In 1925, Yale football star Robert Savage attempted suicide by slashing his wrists when Clara rejected his marriage proposal. "I am engaged to Gilbert Roland," she told the press. "The whole thing is ridiculous . . . I only knew [Robert] a week. He tried to sweep me off my feet with his speed, but he is just an episode in my young life." Savage told reporters that Clara had kissed him so passionately that his lips bled and ached for days. Papers across the country published his poems to her.

> A haunting voice came in the twilight whispering soft and low,
> Telling of a beautiful creature, telling of Clara Bow.
> And I lie in my bed by the window to happily, happily scan
> The heavens so star-filled above me, grateful indeed I'm a man.

"All I can say about Bob is that as a lover, he's a wonderful poet," the kiss-and-tell Bow responded.

The owners of 2,700 theaters voted Clara Bow their Favorite Cinema Star, and she worked hard for the title. Paramount had her churning out an endless string of films—twelve in 1924, fourteen in 1925, eight in 1926, six in 1927. Sometimes more than acting was required in the line of duty. On the set of *Ladies of the Mob*, Clara, Richard Arlen, and William Wellman were all wounded by ricocheting bullets, as in those days the ammunition was live. By night, the High Priestess of "It" partied in the Blossom Room of the elegant Roosevelt Hotel or at the Coconut Grove in the Ambassador. Or she might hole up in her Beverly Hills home—modest by celebrity standards, but palatial for the girl from the slums of Brooklyn—immersed in an all-night poker game.

"I think wildly gay people are usually hiding from something in themselves," Clara confided in a personal interview. ". . . The best life has taught them is to snatch at every moment of fun and excitement, because they feel sure fate is going to hit them over the head with a club at the first opportunity." She was only twenty-two when she prophesized her own collision with fate.

Clara couldn't sleep, so she feverishly burnt the candle at both ends. Between pictures, she sometimes suffered "little nervous breakdowns." She was always on edge. When her pent-up tensions threatened to explode, she found solace in binge eating or binge sex. Each little collapse fueled her fear that she might end up as unstable as her mother, and made her more nervous.

Clara had a devoted pal who paid her bills, kept the house running, and rushed to her side any time of the day or night—she was Daisy DeVoe, a former studio hairdresser. Clara had grown close to Daisy at Paramount, and had asked her to work as her live-in secretary in 1928. For two years, Daisy was like a sister. She had full run of the house, and Clara included her in all the parties and poker sessions. Then one day, Rex Bell, Clara's cowboy lover, discovered that Daisy had indeed been sharing everything, including Clara's bank account. Missing were $35,000, clothing, furs, jewelry, and silver, as well as love letters and telegrams. "She had a bureau drawer full of them," DeVoe testified later. Shocked and hurt, Clara fired Daisy who, in retaliation, threatened blackmail. Clara's fans knew she was wild, but they had no idea how many men had shared her sleepless nights. When Clara refused to play the victim any longer, Daisy made good on her threat, selling her version of Clara's nocturnal adventures to a tabloid paper.

Bow's loyal friends in the publicity department had labored long, hard hours to help her out of situations that might have violated her morals clause and invited the wrath of the Hays Office. By the time Daisy got to the papers, she'd already given the studio publicists a run for their money. Clara had been named as correspondent in the divorce of a wealthy Texas doctor, and had eventually paid the alienated wife $30,000. Later, she ran up enormous gambling debts in Reno. She picked a very bad year for scandal—it was 1930. Coolidge prosperity had crashed, and as Hoovervilles went up, her fans, now waiting on bread lines instead of movie lines, took a very dim view of her extravagance. The studio mill couldn't protect her from Daisy DeVoe.

"I was more than a secretary to her," DeVoe told a crowded courtroom in January of 1931, after Clara pressed charges. "I was almost a sister to her. I did everything for her. I hennaed her hair, fitted her clothing, paid her bills, bought her liquor . . . I did just everything."

"If she wanted to buy whiskey," Clara countered, "she bought it and I knew nothing about it. That's why I'm so sore. I trusted her. I never looked at the books."

"It was her own fault," Daisy went on. "If she had paid attention to business, I never would have taken a dime from her. She put me in a position to take anything I wanted . . . I was going to tell Clara about it later on . . . It's hard to see a girl like Clara with everything and no respect for anything."

The jury found this logic warped and decided in Bow's favor, and because of the plaintiff's appeal for leniency for her former "best friend," DeVoe received only an eighteen-month sentence. But the damage to Clara's reputation was irreparable. Her fans lost their tolerance for "two little Hollywood girls" who could lose a total of $350,000 in money, furs, and gems in two years without noticing it was gone.

Everything caught up with Clara at once—the frenetic pace, the booze, the pills to sleep, the abortions in Tijuana, the clap, and now the scandals and betrayal by her trusted friend and her once-adoring public. The Brooklyn Bonfire was burned out. Her nervous energy turned against her—she was completely unable to cope. She collapsed, and went to a sanitarium in Glendale. In June her contract at Paramount was "terminated by mutual consent for health reasons."

Throughout her ordeal, Rex Bell stood loyally by his sweetheart. "If she had been Minnie Zilch instead of Clara Bow," he said, "perhaps this never would have happened to her. But the emotional strain of her early years was just too much for her nervous system." When she was released, he whisked her away to his Nevada ranch, where he cared for her and quietly married her. As her spirit returned, Clara had some of the cows dyed red.

"In retrospect, perhaps I should have paid Daisy and saved myself many heartaches," she told reporters. "I took it on the chin and my health suffered." After a European honeymoon with Rex, Clara announced a comeback. She had just celebrated her twenty-fifth birthday.

"There are many 'rumor stories' about the new Clara Bow floating around Hollywood. Because she will not see reporters or interviewers, it has been said that she is pulling a Garbo. Another story has it that she has a fear complex— that she is frightened of people. The sob sisters would have you believe that

Hollywood has broken the spirit of Clara Bow . . . ," intimated one fan magazine.

"No more hot-cha," Clara answered back. "I'm young, but I'm getting older. I'm going to lead a quiet life just like a nice married girl."

But serenity still eluded her. She suffered a fit on the set of *The Secret Call*, and broke a mirror over the director's head. Rex, always there when she needed him, stopped her in the nick of time from cutting her throat with the broken glass. She returned to the Glendale sanitarium and the film was reshot with Peggy Shannon, a less memorable but also less tempestuous actress.

Call Her Savage (1932) and *Hoopla* (1933), her last two films, were talkies for 20th Century–Fox. She had sung a few songs in earlier films, but with the "all talking" pictures, the constant retakes and the limitations on movement took all the fun out of work for her. The old Clara Bow was always bouncing —now she had to be demure to stay in range of the hidden microphone. "Many months of suffering have given her an added dignity and new ability. Her performance is more polished . . . more rounded . . . she goes Jean Harlow a close second in revealing her anatomy," Louella Parsons said in praise of Clara

The "IT" cafe at Hollywood and Vine.

in *Hoopla,* but she was definitely not the box office draw she had been. Surprisingly, she no longer cared, and permanently retired from the screen in 1933.

The Bells opened the "It" Cafe at Hollywood and Vine in 1937. Clara enjoyed playing hostess, though many called it therapy. The cafe became a popular hangout for servicemen, but they never saw Clara because, by that time, she'd retired to raise two sons. The boys in uniform would have been disappointed anyway; her figure was growing ever more matronly, and at one point she weighed almost 200 pounds.

Retirement did nothing for her emotional pain. By 1950, she needed a constant companion. She and Rex separated, but never discussed divorce. He would never have let that happen. Off and on, Clara returned to Glendale, before finally settling in with Mrs. Estella Smith, her nurse for the next sixteen years. Clara became a recluse in a small, plain house in the middle-class community of Culver City, where she could be close to a sanitarium and her doctors. She passed her days oil painting, watching television, and occasionally writing letters to her old Hollywood friends. For years, she sent a Christmas card to Louella Parsons, always inscribed in the same shaky script, "Do you still remember me?" A few old timers, like Richard Arlen, visited her once in a while before she became permanently unsettled in menopause. After that, she never left her home, except to attend Rex's funeral. He was elected lieutenant governor of California in 1954, and was running for governor in 1962 when he was struck down by a heart attack. Clara went home and planned her own funeral, choosing as her pallbearers her old friends and lovers —Harry Richman, Richard Arlen, Buddy Rogers, Jack Oakie, and Maxie Rosenbloom. She would, of course, be buried next to her Rex.

Forever the insomniac, Clara died from a heart attack while watching *Dr. Broadway* on *The Late Show,* September 26, 1965. Not long before her death, she told a friend, "It wasn't ever like I thought it was going to be. It was always a disappointment to me."

MACK SENNETT
I Thought They Stayed Forever . . .

"I believe I have associated with more fools than any man living . . . a blessing for which I thank God," wrote Mack Sennett in his 1954 autobiography.

In 1900, twenty-year-old Sennett had a cockeyed notion to sing grand opera. He carefully presented a letter of introduction from the family lawyer, Calvin Coolidge, to the great stage actress Marie Dressler. Miss Dressler was amused by the gawky 6 feet 1 inch boy standing in her dressing room. She referred him to theatrical impresario David Belasco.

"Go home," Belasco told the eager Sennett. When he refused, Belasco suggested he get stage experience in burlesque, "With your gall, you'll get in anywhere." Sennett followed this advice and began his illustrious career—as the back end of a horse.

Burlesque took Sennett to the chorus of several Broadway musicals, but the need for steady employment sent him to Biograph Studios where he could earn as much as $5 a day as a bit player. Working with Lionel Barrymore, Mary Pickford, and Blanche Sweet, Sennett co-starred in many one-reelers directed by the great D. W. Griffith. "Griffith was my day school, my adult education program, my university," said the worshipful Sennett, who scrutinized the director's techniques, absorbing all he could about the craft of motion picture making. He wrote several scripts for him, but found that Griffith neither shared his interest in comedy, nor was amused by his obsession with policemen as comic characters. Mack discovered early on that "the reduction of authority and the downfall of pretension . . . is the basis for all true comedy."

Sennett met the most important person in his life at Biograph. Just before Griffith brought him along for a month's stay in California, Mack took the curvaceous, teenage Mabel Normand for a ride on the Staten Island Ferry. Awkward as a schoolboy, the thirty-year-old presented her with a $2, genuine

"The Old Man."

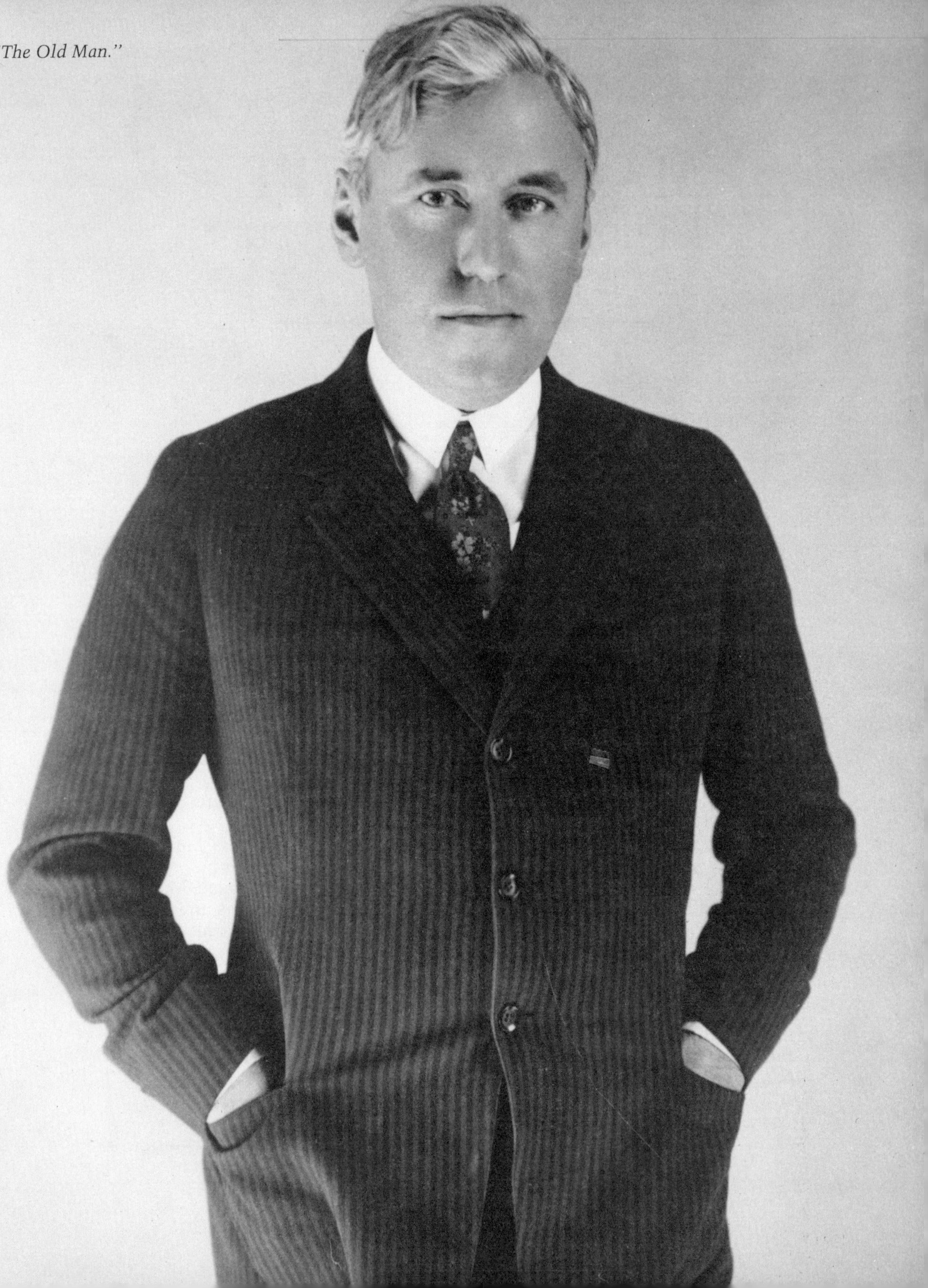

diamond ring that he'd been scrimping to buy. Of all the expensive jewels he would give her in the years to come, none would ever be more precious to her.

In California, the illness of one director, combined with a lot of begging, got Sennett his first chance to direct. His first picture, *One Round O'Brien*, was based on an idea offered to him by a friend, who had stolen the story from a magazine. Biograph was slapped with a $2,500 plagiarism suit. From then on, Sennett used only his own ideas.

The fast talking, hard-drinking Irishman hustled back to Los Angeles after convincing two New York bookies, to whom he owed $100, to invest $2,500 in Keystone, the new company he'd formed. Mabel, Fred Mace, Sterling Ford, and Henry "Pathé" Lehrman all left Biograph to go west with Mack. They weren't in Los Angeles for thirty minutes before Sennett set up his camera and started shooting. Seeing a Shriners' parade approaching, he jumped to take advantage of a free spectacle.

"We've got ourselves a whopper of a crowd scene—all free!" the quick-thinking director shouted to his troupe.

"What's the story?" Pathé asked.

"Got no story," Sennett replied. "We'll make it up as we go along. Pathé, run to that department store and buy a baby doll. Ford, put on an overcoat and make like an actor. I'll set the camera up over here."

"Who am I?" asked an excited Mabel.

"A mother," Mack answered.

"I would be the last to know," she teased. "I'm a poor working girl, betrayed by the big city, searching for the father of my child," she wailed, grasping the baby doll. "This characterization requires a shawl."

"Get her a shawl," Mack screamed as the parade drew nearer. Her costume complete, Mabel proceeded to run up and down the line of marchers, pleading, stumbling, holding out her baby. The Shriners reacted with horror, dismay, and complete embarrassment. One kind soul dropped out of step and tried to help her. With that, Ford leaped in, screaming at the innocent Shriner until the police moved in. Ford insulted them and took off, and the police did something that delighted Mack—they chased Ford. Sennett dubbed them the original Keystone Cops. The troupe went straight to their little studio in Edendale, shot a few more scenes and some close-ups, and had their first comedy.

One morning Sennett got a tip that the city would drain a small lake in Echo Park. The crew raced out there and filmed Mabel with a screen lover sinking to the bottom of the lake in a small boat. Back at the studio, Sennett inserted a shot of a villain pulling a plug and, with trick photography, speeded up the draining sequence. Audiences were amazed at the spectacle which cost Sennett absolutely nothing. No other studio could touch Keystone for slapstick comedy.

The workaholic Sennett made 140 pictures his first year, expanding the studio to 28 acres and turning his hair white in the process. At thirty-two, Sennett had a new nickname, "The Old Man."

One afternoon in 1913, as a prank, the impudent Mabel threw a custard pie into Ben Turpin's face. Sennett saw it as "a fine, wish-fulfilling, universal

Mabel Normand—Mack's best girl and the silent screen's comedy queen.

idea, especially in the face of authority, like a cop or mother-in-law." In no time at all, he had cops and doty mothers-in-law being hit by pies doing figure eights around telephone poles. "Comedy is a satire on the human race. It always has been. That is what clowns have been up to ever since kings kept fools. Our specialty was exasperated dignity and the discombombulation of authority."

The Old Man sure had an eye for clowns. Over the years, he discovered Charlie Chaplin, Wallace Beery, Marie Prevost, Carole Lombard, Ben Turpin, Chester Conklin, Fatty Arbuckle, Edgar Kennedy, Harry Langdon, Gloria Swanson, W. C. Fields, and Bing Crosby. In 1914, he put his old friend Marie Dressler in her first film, *Tillie's Punctured Romance*, with Normand, Chaplin, Conklin, and Fields. "The secret of Sennett's success was his enthusiasm," Chaplin wrote in his autobiography. "He was a great audience and laughed genuinely at what he thought funny. He stood and giggled until his body began to shake. Under his direction, I felt comfortable, because everything was spontaneously worked out on the set. Thus grew a belief in myself that I was creative and could write my own stories. Sennett indeed had inspired this belief."

The Sennett Bathing Beauties—the girls who never got wet—were a brilliant publicity creation of 1914. Mack dressed the girls in so little that even some of the Keystone employees thought they were too risqué. He paraded them at the beach and posed them for publicity pictures with his top comedians, being sure that the men could not be cut out. Then he sat back as every paper carried the photos on their front pages. "When the studio received hundreds of letters of protest from women's clubs," chuckled The Old Man, "I knew we had done the right thing."

"Mabel Normand's presence graced the studio with glamour," Chaplin fondly remembered. "She was lighthearted and gay . . . kind and generous; and everyone adored her." No one adored her more than Sennett. Mack and Mabel were a team. As Sennett's name became synonymous with comedy, Normand had blossomed under his direction, into the screen's premiere comedienne, as well as a gifted director. He lavished her with gifts and jewels, and only she could melt his gruff exterior with just a look.

Sennett at work on a Chester Conklin short at Keystone Studios, 1915.

"She was as beautiful as a spring morning," Sennett sighed. Although they set a date to marry almost every year, Sennett could never seem to tear himself away from work long enough for a wedding. They argued and made up a dozen times, but by 1915 Mabel tired of the struggle. When she gave up, a little of her spirit was lost in the defeat. Sennett, though he never stopped trying, just wasn't able to rekindle the flame, and the new path Mabel chose would lead her to a dark, lonely end.

Normand grew restless, convinced she was capable of more subtle artistry. Sennett set up The Mabel Normand Feature Film Company and directed its first feature, *Mickey*. He thought it was the best film she'd ever made . . . no slick gags . . . no pies in the face . . . and no theater would book it. He pushed the film for over a year, but in the meantime, a disappointed Normand had signed a five-year contract with Goldwyn. When *Mickey* was finally released, Sennett noted that ". . . the money rolled in so fast, we had to hire educated men to count it." As if trying to make up for lost time, Mabel, separated from The Old Man for the first time since she was sixteen, by that time had abandoned herself to a whirlwind social life of all night-parties, bootleg booze, and, rumor had it, drugs. She began to be a problem at work, showing up late or not at all. Goldwyn was only too happy to "loan" her to Mack for a picture.

Mack gasped in horror when he saw his beloved again. She was thin and ill, all her sparkle gone. They made *Molly O* together anyway, at a cost of $1,500,000, but Sennett's timing, which was so flawless in the cutting room, was disastrously unlucky in the theaters. He released the film in January of 1922. Early on the morning of February 3rd, Mabel, who hadn't phoned him in the two years since they finished *Molly O*, called him.

"Are you awake, Mack? It's Mabel." He could hear distress in her voice.

"Mabel: I'm trying to get awake . . . just a minute."

"I have to hang up quickly. I think people are listening in. There's something peculiar about Bill's death." Mabel was referring to director William Desmond Taylor who had been found dead in his apartment early the day before. "Somebody shot him . . . shot him in the back. He was murdered."

"Wait a minute, Mabel, I . . ."

"Mack—Mack, I'm in serious trouble. I was the last person seen with him." There was a long pause as Mack tried to take in what Mabel was telling him. He could hear clicks and hums on the line and suddenly understood what she meant about people listening in. Sennett assumed their conversation was being tapped by the police.

"I'll see you first thing in the morning . . . let's try not to talk now. I'm sorry, and you know I'll do all I can—"

"There's nothing for you to do, Mack," she interrupted in a deadly calm tone that belied her hysteria. "I just wanted you to know . . ." Sennett heard the click of her receiver.

For Mabel, it was a clear-cut case of guilt by association. As the trial went on, digging up scandal after scandal, the press and hundreds of citizens' groups persecuted Mabel. *Molly O* disappeared from the theaters. Finally, the investigation revealed her cocaine habit—all she could take. Mabel collapsed.

Mack managed to recoup the $1,500,000 by rereleasing *Molly O* at the end of the year. He built a new studio in the San Fernando Valley, The Mack Sennett Studio, but it was a sad place for him without Mabel. He enticed her back for two more films. The first, *Suzanna,* was a successful historical costume comedy. Enough of her old bounce and effervescence returned for critic Robert E. Sherwood * to write, "Once a year, she steps forth to remind us that she is still the first comedienne of the silent drama. . . . It is Mabel Normand's presence in the cast which saves it from being just another one of those things. You can't imagine this irrepressible gamin doing anything stupid, or dull, or obvious on the screen. . . ."

But by the time the movie was finished, Mabel was exhausted. She sailed off on a European vacation and came back with a shattering cough. She needed a long rest before the next film, *The Extra Girl.* Mack could see that Mabel had changed. Her spirit was drained. He told people that she was ill, but they knew the truth . . . she was a drug addict. He would have done anything, given her anything, but he was too late. He had let their moment slip away. Sennett would never marry nor would he ever forgive himself for not taking care of Mabel. Once again, he planned an ill-timed release date for *The Extra Girl.*

Mabel had remained formal to him throughout his New Year's Eve bash, marking the end of 1923. She left early with Edna Purviance for the apartment of the playboy son of a Colorado millionaire, Courtland S. Dines. During the evening, Normand's new chauffeur, Joe Kelly, fought with Dines, wounding him twice with Normand's gun.

During the ensuing trial, Joe Kelly was revealed to be Joe Green, a cocaine addict and recent prison escapee. Pleading self-defense, Green was acquitted. Miss Normand's involvement was never questioned, but in the wake of the Taylor murder, it was more than her faltering popularity could stand. *The Extra Girl* was never released and Sennett never saw or spoke to her again. Seven years later, at thirty-six, she died of tuberculosis.

Sennett continued alone. By the mid-twenties, his estimated worth was $15 million, including 500 acres of Los Angeles real estate and three homes, where the two-fisted drinker threw many legendary parties. But his Midas touch was tarnishing. He lost $250,000 in gold mines with no gold. He bought the old Brown Ranch, a mountain near where the Hollywood sign would eventually sit, paying $152,000 for 304 acres, and not a level inch among them. After building a road to the top, he shaved off 60 feet of bedrock for four level acres where he planned to build the grandest abode of all. However, the land was so snake infested that he had to purchase 500 hogs to kill the snakes. When they finished off the snakes, they ate everything else in sight until they were soon dying of starvation. Sennett was forced to buy garbage all over Los Angeles just to feed his herd of ornery hogs. He never built his dream house. It was worthy of a Keystone comedy, but Mack wasn't laughing.

When the Mack Sennett Studio foreclosed, he continued producing and directing shorts for Paramount. With some difficulty, he managed to adapt to the new talking pictures, producing several W. C. Fields shorts and a series of musical shorts with Bing Crosby. He even experimented with an early color

* Later a Pulitzer Prize–winning playwright.

process, but the King of Comedy's style was antiquated now, no matter how hard he tried to keep up with the technical advances. Audiences were now demanding plot development over sight gags. The birth of the double feature and the growing popularity of Disney's animated slapstick killed Sennett's brand of two-reel shorts. He did a short stint with Educational—a big step down for him—in 1935, where he made *The Timid Young Man,* his only film with another waning comedy great, Buster Keaton, before retiring from the industry.

When Paramount declared bankruptcy in the 1930s, Sennett was wiped out. He lost the mountain, the real estate, the houses, everything. A bitter and lonely man, he retired to the Canadian farm he'd bought for his mother. He inherited it when she died three months later, and discovered a gusher. The land was full of oil and asbestos; Mack was rich again!

In 1937, he went back to Hollywood to accept a special Oscar dedicated "to the master of fun, the discoverer of stars, sympathetic, kindly, understanding, comedy genius, Mack Sennett, for his lasting contributions to the comedy techniques of the screen, the basic principles of which are as important today as when first put into practice." But while he was visiting, the IRS practiced its own basic principles, draining his oil income for payment of back taxes. He had to sell the farm and find a job. Twentieth Century–Fox offered him an associate producer position in 1939, but the lack of creativity was like a prison sentence to him. The frustrated Old Man sat behind his big desk all day and dreamed of more exciting days packed with action, surprises, clowns, and pretty girls. He finally walked out, never to work in the picture business again.

Sennett spent the last ten years of his life wasting away in near poverty at the Garden Court Apartments on Hollywood Boulevard. His home was another relic; in the twenties and thirties, the Garden Court had been Hollywood's most luxurious residential hotel, home to Louis B. Mayer, John Gilbert, and Mae Murray. Beyond the marble-floored ballroom, glamorous guests had climbed the mahogany staircase to reach the ornate suites, each complete with original paintings, Oriental rugs, and baby grand piano. Now, both Sennett and the Garden Court were growing decrepit. Mack was a virtual stranger in a town he'd once been brash enough to call his own. He drank heavily and bent the ear of anyone willing to listen to his stories. On rare occasions, he had a drink with a fellow resident, a young actress just getting started—Marilyn Monroe.

The autobiography that he wrote with Cameron Shipp was a love story—of his love for comedy and his love for one woman. Shortly after the book came out, Shipp surprised Mack by starring him in a segment of Ralph Edward's TV show, *This Is Your Life.* Though many of The Old Man's friends were there to cheer him, the one most dear to him was gone. Sennett went home to his apartment—alone with his 48,000 Mabel Normand clippings, yellowed and dog-eared from his continuous perusal. "I thought the audience stayed forever and kept on laughing," he told Shipp.

Sennett moved to the Motion Picture Hospital in January 1960. On November 5, a few days after he'd had urological surgery, the laughter stopped for Mack Sennett forever.

PEG ENTWISTLE
Jinxed

Four thousand electric globes emblazoned the name "Hollywoodland" across the side of Mt. Lee, high above the city. Built in 1923, to advertise an exclusive 500-acre real estate development that Mack Sennett and other investors had bought, it was the largest sign in the world. Its letters stood five stories high and stretched a city block across the barren mountainside. In the thirties, the bright lights of Hollywoodland were used by pilots for navigation. Local residents could see its shimmering declaration of glamour from every breadline and soup kitchen in town. Later the sign was shortened to "Hollywood," and today it remains a monument in the midst of the sprawling hills.

Lillian Millicent "Peg" Entwistle lived literally in the shadow of the sign and gazed up at it for hours from the front yard of her Uncle Harold's rustic Beachwood Canyon home. She was a blonde Hollywood hopeful, with finely chiseled cheekbones and a Mona Lisa smile and an impressive track record on stage. Peg was considered an overnight sensation at only seventeen when, after her debut with a Boston Repertory Company, she received a recruitment invitation from the prestigious Theater Guild of New York. For more than five years, Peg scored triumph after triumph on the New York stage. Bette Davis, who was preparing for her own Broadway debut, was one of her greatest admirers. However, when Peg left New York in 1932, it was to flee a disastrous season. Eight consecutive failures had shaken her confidence. She decided to move in with her uncle, her only living relative, and to make a fresh start in Hollywood.

She arrived in April. It didn't take Peg long to get a good role; she played supporting actress to the delightful Billie Burke in a play aptly titled *The Mad Hopes*. But the play closed after a short run. To Peg, it was one more defeat.

Built in 1923, the Hollywoodland sign mesmerized Peg Entwistle. She rode horseback almost daily on the trails surrounding it.

Her spirits lifted several weeks later when RKO Studios optioned her for a role in *Thirteen Women*. Her chance to turn the tide of failure, to make it big, had finally come—maybe her only chance. She was only twenty-four, but Bette Davis was the same age and already under contract at Universal, and most of the leading actresses weren't much older. Peg felt that her time was running out. She sat on pins and needles during the film's sneak preview in August, and was devastated when the reviews panned it. RKO delayed release until the film could be recut. Though she'd made a nice showing in her small role, RKO unceremoniously dropped Peg's option. It confirmed her deepest fear— the jinx that had pursued her on Broadway had dogged her footsteps all the way across the country. "She tried to get money to go back to New York, and Broadway, her first love, but she was unable to raise anything," Harold Entwistle later told the press.

On September 18, Peg took action. After dinner, she told Uncle Harold that she felt like taking a walk up the wooded drive to the Hollywoodland drugstore to buy a book. Then she thought she'd visit a friend. Harold just nodded —Peg was giving a believable performance as a composed young woman in a

She longed for fame and achieved it in a way she never dreamed.

flowered silk dress. She set out on her walk, straight up the long, winding, side road that leads to the sign.

She stopped at the "H," removed her jacket, and carefully laid it on the ground next to her purse. Inside her purse she had placed a note: "I am afraid I am a coward. I am sorry for everything. If I had done this a long time ago, it would have saved a lot of pain. P.E." She gripped the rung of the electrician's ladder and slowly pulled herself toward the top of the 50-foot letter. Halfway up, one of her well-worn shoes slipped off and fell to the ground. She stood at the top of the letter and stared out at the city stretched beneath her—Hollywood, land of a thousand shattered dreams. Hollywood had summoned her only to beat her down, to toy with her dreams and deny her proper citizenship. Now it seemed to beckon her with its arms open, with millions of glittering lights calling for the grandest of finales. With one quick movement, she leaped toward those lights, plunging to the rocks and thorny bush below. It was not until several days later that a hiker spotted the mangled body.

The headlines reported the "spectacular suicide of an unidentified woman, about twenty-five, blonde, blue-eyed, and moderately well dressed." When Harold read about the note signed "P.E.," he rushed to the morgue and sadly identified his niece's body. "Although she never confided her grief to me, I was somehow aware that she was suffering intense mental anguish. . . . It is a great shock to me that she gave up the fight as she did," he said. As for the rumor that Peg had killed herself over an ill-fated love affair, her uncle said she had not been romantically involved with anyone since the breakup in 1929 of her two-year marriage to actor Robert Lee Keith.

In October, *Thirteen Women* was rereleased, again to poor reviews. Ironically, Peg's friends felt sure her performance was strong enough to have brought her the success she was so desperately seeking.

BELA LUGOSI
The Curse of Dracula

"I am Dracula . . . I bid you welcome." Universal Studios' Valentine's Day present to 1931 filmgoers was Bela Lugosi, a man born to play Dracula, "the strangest love story ever told."

"He was pure sex on the stage," said actress Carroll Borland, who played *Dracula*'s Lucy Harker in the stage production. "You could sense his tremendous sexual attraction and power, and it was as much a part of Lugosi's character as it was Dracula's. It was impossible to separate the two."

The actor and the vampire were alike in many ways. Like Dracula, Lugosi was born in the mysterious hills of Transylvania, his soul filled with its folklore and superstition. He carried on the Count's tradition of being a ladykiller, too. He had an aura that few women could resist.

"He has some sort of power over your emotions. It's like he could just will you to go to bed with him," remarked a girlfriend of fellow Hungarian Joe Pasternak, Lugosi's close friend.

Before he came to Hollywood, Lugosi was known in Hungarian theaters as a sensual romantic type. He played Armand Duval in *Camille*, Count Vronsky in *Anna Karenina*, and a lascivious Romeo. He was one of Budapest's leading actors at the time of the collapse of the Austro-Hungarian monarchy and the creation of a short-lived, but bloody, Communist regime. Lugosi had formed an actors' union and bravely led their meetings and protest marches until 1919, when he was forced to flee for his life to Germany. He and his young wife, hiding under straw at the bottom of a gypsy cart, passed through all the checkpoints but were spotted running across a dark field toward an open cockpit plane. The Lugosis had to dodge flying bullets as they scrambled through the darkness into the rear cockpit, but they made it and flew to safety. He would never see his homeland again.

Lugosi once walked with pride down his beloved Hollywood Boulevard. Later, he frequented a Boulevard shoe repair that was a front for drug pushers.

Once he was safely settled in Germany, Lugosi, along with fellow exile Michael Curtiz, found themselves looking for work in a country already up to its liederhosen in unemployed actors. (Curtiz would also find great success in America eventually, most notably as the director of *Casablanca*.) Bela did manage to work in several German films, including his first touch of the sinister in the title role of F. W. Murnau's *Dr. Jekyll and Mr. Hyde* (which he called *Dr. Warren and Mr. O'Connor* to avoid royalties). Murnau was the first to bring Dracula to the screen in *Nosferatu* of 1921, but by then Lugosi had divorced his wife and gone to America.

In New York, he joined "The Nest," a company of Hungarian performers. His debut on the American stage came in 1923, opposite Estelle Winwood, in *The Red Poppy*. He wasn't proficient in English yet, and he memorized his lines phonetically. Later he scored great reviews in Norman Bel-Geddes's *Arabesque* (1925), playing the Bedouin sheik. He also appeared in *Silent Command* and *Daughters Who Pay*, two films for 20th Century–Fox, but his schedule was not so hectic as to prevent him from marrying a second time. As a suitor, he was an amorous charmer, but the marriage license transformed him into a jealous, paranoid husband who kept a constant watch over his property, who happened to be a woman with liberated, suffragette leanings this time.

"His wife . . . was like a slave," recalled Estelle Winwood. "He barked orders at her while we talked shop, and she jumped up and down like a marionette doing everything he told her to do without a word." For Bela, she was the perfect picture of domesticity.

"Success in marriage depends entirely on the woman" was his philosophy. "It is up to her to get along with the man. It is not in his nature to be able to adjust to her . . . [she] cannot be happy in business or in being independent. Women need a master, to be led. Her place is in the home taking care of the man and the children. . . . If she does her work well, she has more than enough to keep her busy." In other ways, he pampered his caged little bird—hiring servants to do the cleaning, dining out often, encouraging her artistic expression (*not* on the stage!). But in return, he demanded her undivided attention twenty-four hours a day. She must never interrupt, must sense his every mood. It's remarkable that the marriage lasted an entire two years.

Lugosi got his vampire fangs in 1927, when *Dracula* came to Broadway. Jean D. Williams, the director of *Rain*, believed that Bela was "the only actor in America suitable for the part," and was responsible for his getting the role. Williams was never so right. Lugosi held audiences spellbound through a record 265 performances in 1927. He radiated such eroticism that many critics proclaimed him the new Valentino. A bizarre series of accidents backstage didn't hurt the Transylvanian actor's reputation either. Many people believed he was responsible for sudden illnesses in the company, unseen forces knocking people over, and stage lights working by themselves. Bela was amused by it all, and always left his fans wondering where Dracula ended and Lugosi began.

He continued to play Dracula for two years in road shows that eventually led to the Biltmore Theater in Los Angeles. The press announced that doctors and nurses would be in attendance to serve the weak-hearted during the show. Among the thousands who came to see him was the jazz baby, Clara Bow, who fell victim to his devastating charms. Their romance remained at the boiling point for a number of months until Lugosi's possessiveness and old-fashioned ways became too much of a hindrance to the "It" girl. Lugosi, already close to fifty, doted on younger women, guarding them as his precious link to agelessness itself. But, naturally, he never tried to adapt to the independent temperament of American women. His third marriage ended after four days, when he discovered that his wife's drinking would prevent her from attending to his daily fresh-squeezed orange juice, the cleaning of his pipes, jumping on command to light his cigars, and all his other macho demands. No, he needed a woman trained in the old European ways to satisfy him.

After his phenomenal success as Dracula onstage, one would think that he would have immediately been offered the film role, but Lugosi wasn't even considered. Hollywood's King of Horror, Lon Chaney, Sr., was originally cast in the film, but his death from cancer forced Universal to hunt for another actor. John Carradine, Conrad Veidt, and Paul Muni all vied for the cape, but Lugosi finally won the role. "It was a take-it-or-leave-it contract," revealed Evan Hoskins, his publicity agent, "offering him five hundred dollars per week for the seven-week shooting schedule. Of course, there was no such thing as royalties in those days. . . . He knew there were five hungry actors waiting to get the part, so what could he do but accept the terms. . . . Every revival of the picture was a reminder to him that he could have been a wealthy man."

Nevertheless, the picture made him the new Master of Terror from the moment the Count descended the dark, massive staircase to introduce himself to movie audiences. There were glorious days ahead for Lugosi, whose "live for today" credo relished the red-carpet service and first-class treatment that came with the title of "Star." He thought nothing of spending $100 just for breakfast. Every day, he strode proudly down Hollywood Boulevard to purchase his newspapers and beloved cigars. By night, he shunned the rowdy spots, preferring quiet, intimate evenings of waltzing and dining at the elegant Roosevelt Hotel. His social circle, however, was restricted mostly to the Hungarian community that also made Hollywood its home. At one of their parties, he met Lillian, a seventeen-year-old girl who became the fourth Mrs. Bela Lugosi.

"Dracula Weds Beauty," the headlines announced in 1933. Lillian was overwhelmed by the fifty-one-year-old man from the start. Bela adored the suppleness of her youth. She was so fresh and impressionable, he could easily mold her into his vision of the perfect mate. The couple often dined at the Gypsy Camp Restaurant or the Hungaria House, where the strains of gypsy violins could bring tears to Bela's eyes. They carried on until dawn, feasting on the food and wine of their homeland, until the owner would insist on closing. Undaunted, Bela would bring his friends and the orchestra back to his home. They'd close the heavy drapes to keep out the sunlight, and toast the beloved land of their birth, singing and dancing until the musicians' fingers bled from the frenzy.

Bela Lugosi lived in elegance at his peak in the thirties.

Bela's career flourished, and he and his bride enjoyed the good life. However, thanks to his own shortsightedness, he was forced to share his crown as Master of Evil with Boris Karloff. Lugosi was called for the part of Frankenstein's monster, but he was insulted when he read the script and discovered that the monster had no lines at all. "Any half-wit extra who knows how to grunt could do it," he said, disgusted. Director James Whale brought in Karloff after seeing his brief scene in *The Graft*. Karloff imbued Frankenstein with an emotion and depth Lugosi had not even considered. Dracula had created his own monster—now he had a first-class rival. He kept busy, however, with *Murders in the Rue Morgue, Island of Lost Souls, The Black Cat,* and *The Raven.* He longed for more versatility, but he didn't tamper with success. The horror film was riding the crests of popularity, and he was working all the time.

Then, in 1936, the horror genre suddenly began to fizzle. Lugosi found himself out of work, with only a few scattered offers. He hadn't bothered to save or invest his earnings, and by 1937 he was desperate. To add to his financial woes, Lillian was pregnant. When their son was born in 1938, they had long since given up their luxurious home in the Hollywood Hills for a modest little nest in the San Fernando Valley.

The popular appeal of horror films bounced back in 1939, prompting Universal to dust off some of their old sets for *Son of Frankenstein*. Aware that Lugosi was in no position to argue over money, they offered him a measly $500 a week, further instructing director Rowland V. Lee to keep Lugosi's part to one week. Lee, who had great respect for The Master, enlarged the role of Ygor so that Lugosi would work the full eight weeks alongside Karloff and fellow Hungarian Peter Lorre.

Later that year, Bela played his only comic role in *Ninotchka*, the movie that showed Greta Garbo laughing. Because the major studios generally ignored him, he began appearing in scores of terrible films that further diminished his image. Offers from Broadway having stopped long ago, the Lugosis now packed their car for the summer, making the long drive from one small town to another, to appear in cheap stock productions and even a Las Vegas revue. Giving interviews in coffins, always wearing his tuxedo and cape, he eventually became a derisive caricature of himself.

Lugosi began drinking heavily during his long stretches of unemployment. More and more, he relied on medically prescribed morphine for a World War I injury and resulting duodenal ulcer. Lillian helped to wean him of his addiction, reducing his dosage until he eventually got just the bare needle. When he was finally well again, she told him she was leaving. After twenty years of marriage, Lillian had had enough of Bela's unrelenting, unfounded jealousies, and enough of all those years on the road when she had to be at every rehearsal, every performance. "He kept me under his thumb twenty-four hours a day. Even when I went to the dentist, he would call up and make sure that's where I was." His fourth divorce was the most traumatic event of his long life. When she and fifteen-year-old Bela, Jr. left, Lugosi lost all faith in himself. He could be seen wandering Hollywood Boulevard, like himself in steep decline, a desolate, embittered soul. Almost immediately, he turned back to drugs.

The Hungarian "ghoulash," clowning in his later years.

"Bela Lugosi Surrenders Self as Drug Addict." The Los Angeles papers shouted the news in 1955. Lugosi had simply walked into Los Angeles County General Hospital and given up the struggle. It was no coincidence that the day he chose was Lillian's birthday. In a move calculated to gain sympathy and revenge, Lugosi exaggerated his three-year battle with drug addiction to a war lasting twenty years. The seventy-three-year-old did not, however, exaggerate the amount he used. "When I switched to methadone, I injected two ccs every two hours. When I went to bed, I injected two ccs of Demerol and also took barbiturate capsules so I could sleep for eight or ten hours. So—and only so— could I work. During the twenty years, my habit cost me thousands of dollars. I cannot estimate how much. I only know I spent money on it when I didn't have money to eat. Half a century I worked, but now I have only my old age pension—just enough for my rent—not enough for my food. . . . I used to inject the methadone in my legs, but I lost fifty pounds—from 180 to 130— and my limbs became just strings of muscle. When I could no longer find a place to inject . . . that was the end."

In great physical pain, Lugosi was still proud, and struggled to maintain his dignity as he fought his addiction. Nonetheless, an aura of unspeakable sadness had enveloped him. Exaggerations aside, committing himself was the most courageous step of his life, and he hoped it would inspire others with similar problems. Letters and telegrams offering Bela emotional and financial support poured in from the likes of fellow countrymen Paul Lukas and Joe Pasternak, and Frank Sinatra, who merely wanted to repay Bela in some way for the "many hours of wonderful entertainment" he'd given him. Another fan wrote letters of great sensitivity every day, signing them only "a dash of Hope."

On August 5th, Lugosi walked out of the hospital . . . cured. Though his appearance was skeletal and world-weary, through his victory, his spirit was renewed. "My life is about ended, but it is a great thing to be able to say that while I have life, there is Hope." He set about finding his "dash of Hope."

The woman was Hope Lininger. Ever since she had first seen him in *Dracula* when she was a child in Pennsylvania, she had spent her life trying to get close to him. Working her way across the country, she eventually landed a job in Los Angeles as a film cutter at RKO Studios. Lugosi quickly found her and at the end of their very first visit, he proposed. Lininger, in her late thirties, unhesitatingly agreed to become his fifth wife. Hours before they were married on August 25th, he begged Lillian to come back to him but she would not.

The couple moved into a small apartment on Harold Way in Hollywood. It wasn't a happy marriage. Her youth, which had attracted him, now served as a constant reminder of his own advanced age. Then too, he bitterly wondered if there was something wrong with her for marrying him. Hope quickly discovered the obvious, that Lugosi was no longer the dashing romantic figure with whom she had fallen in love. She often taunted her very superstitious husband who, among other folk habits, insisted on sleeping with a glass of water by his bed "to ward off evil spirits." To torment him, she would threaten to remove it while he slept.

Lugosi worked at what was offered: talk shows, a play, and three low-budget horror films. His dream was to remake *Dracula* in color and stereophonic sound, but he was in no condition to undertake it. Drugs had so debilitated his mind that he could barely remember the lines. In two of the last three films, *The Black Sheep* and *Plan Nine From Outer Space*, he played a deaf-mute to get around that problem. He was anxious to begin work on a third film, *The Final Curtain*, but it was not to be. When Hope returned home on the evening of August 18, 1956, she found him on the bed, clutching the script, an incredible look of peace on his face. He had succumbed to a heart attack.

As he stipulated in his will, Lugosi was buried in his tuxedo and cape. The Hungarian's final journey, however, took as strange a turn as any mountain road in Transylvania. As the funeral procession made its way from the mortuary toward Holy Cross Cemetery in Culver City, the driver of Lugosi's hearse suddenly paled. Preparing to turn right, the hearse inexplicably veered left, across Vine Street's oncoming traffic and down Hollywood Boulevard. This had been Lugosi's favorite stretch, where he bought his cigars, his cigarettes, the daily papers, and his drugs. Afterward, the frightened driver could not provide his supervisor with an explanation for the unexpected detour. "I don't know what happened," he mumbled, walking away. "I just don't know."

RUSS COLUMBO
Sob Ballad

Ruggiero de Rudolpho Columbo was a child prodigy, singing and playing the violin on stage by the time he was four. His moderately well-to-do parents moved their twelve children from Philadelphia to Los Angeles in 1913 so that Russ, the youngest, could study with a master. Under the clear blue skies and swaying palm trees, young Russ was caught up in the excitement of being near the movie stars. With his violin, the romantic teenager got even closer to them; he worked as a mood musician on the otherwise silent sets. Russ left high school in 1925 to tour as a concert violinist, but the glamour of Hollywood lured him back. He was determined to be a part of it.

He got the break he wanted singing with Gus Arnheim's Band. He was a big hit in their live radio broadcasts from the elegant Coconut Grove, and his stardom was buoyed along by his friendly rivalry with another young crooner, Bing Crosby. The press regaled the competition as "The Battle of the Baritones." Russ had the advantage of being a singing Valentino. He was slender, six feet tall, a fiery Latin with wavy black hair and a sexy voice that made him the king of the "sob ballads." The seductive way he rolled his eyes while performing "Prisoner of Love," his own composition, became a trademark. He began to indulge his Latin lover appearance with a weekly $200 hair and sunlamp treatment.

At the opening of the Roosevelt, Hollywood's first grand hotel, Columbo was a sensation singing with Professor Moore's band, and the studios started to notice him. Between 1929 and 1930, he made six films, including *Wolfsong* and *The Texan*, both with Gary Cooper. By the end of 1930, he had no sooner opened his own night spot, the Club Pyramid on Hollywood Boulevard, than he was persuaded to make his stage debut at the Paramount Theater in New

Russ Columbo, the leader of the band, had just signed with NBC for his own coast-to-coast radio program.

York. He captivated the Eastern audiences, and was invited to open the sophisticated new supper club at the Waldorf-Astoria. NBC wasted no time in signing the twenty-two-year-old balladeer to a contract that quickly vaulted him to one of "the Big Three of Radioland." Carl Laemmle, the president and founder of Universal, followed Columbo's meteoric East Coast success, and within a scant ten weeks had him signed. Russ had conquered Hollywood.

Now he was one of Hollywood's most eligible bachelors. His first serious romance began the following year, the result of his performance at the premiere of Pola Negri's film *A Woman Commands*. The thirty-eight-year-old Polish vamp, who had collapsed six years earlier at the funeral of her greatest love, Valentino, was so deeply moved by Columbo's resemblance to him and

The Coconut Grove of the Ambassador Hotel, circa 1930—"where stars twinkle and clouds drift and the moon waxes and wanes."

by his sensual voice that she presented him with the bizarre Oriental ring Valentino had once given her. "I fell head over heels for her," Columbo confided, "but for her, the romance faded quickly." Apparently, he was just a passing fancy. In her 1970 autobiography, she doesn't even mention him.

Negri was probably the only woman to resist his charms, especially after the release of *Broadway Through a Keyhole* and *Moulin Rouge*, featuring Russ and Constance Bennett. The songs he penned with Con Conrad—among them, "You Call It Madness, I Call It Love," "Let's Pretend There's a Moon," "When You're In Love," "Too Beautiful For Words," "Is It Love?" and "You Captured My Heart"—filled the airwaves and rang out from the country's most popular nightclubs.

He was a national sensation, and he had a lifestyle and bank account to prove it, although he hadn't even had a major role in a movie yet. The home he shared with his parents was a mansion in Outpost Circle Drive, an exclusive Hollywood neighborhood. He carried his cigarettes in a $1,500 diamond-studded case, and practiced his music on a $20,000 Stradivarius violin.

In 1933, Carole Lombard, recently divorced from William Powell, healed the heart that the siren Pola had wounded. Though Russ continued to see other women, including Sally Blaine, Lorretta Young's sister, he and Carole became an inseparable pair in the gossip columns. Russ coached her for two songs in *White Woman* and was, in turn, allowed to study acting technique as an observer on her sets. Study paid off when he landed his first starring role in *Wake Up and Dream,* and a $10,000-a-week contract. When the movie was finished, he made plans for more lessons, this time in opera. "At twenty-six, I find that I have just about everything I want from life," he told interviewers, "and am pretty happy about the way things have worked out for me."

On the balmy night of August 30, Russ and Carole attended a preview of his film, and both were thrilled with it. "You're going to be a star," Carole predicted. But it was a short-lived triumph.

Two days later, Russ drove to the modest Hollywood home of Lansing V.

A sexy Russ Columbo recording "Wake Up and Dream" at Universal, shortly before his tragic death.

Brown, a successful portrait photographer who'd been his best friend for more than a decade. They spent some time with Brown's parents before going into the adjoining room to look at Brown's collection of antique guns. It was just after 1:00 p.m.

They sat at opposite ends of a mahogany table, toying with cap-and-ball dueling pistols. Brown had snapped the triggers on these 125-year-old guns hundreds of times. "Watch this trick," he said, holding a match in front of the raised pistol hammer. The hammer lowered, lighting the match as Brown had planned, but to his unexpected horror, the fire set off a percussion cap that had apparently been in the gun since the Civil War. The ball slug fired, ricocheted off the tabletop, and struck Russ just above his left eye. In a split second, his eye shattered as the lead ball tore through to the back of his skull. Russ went down with a scream.

At the sound of the shot, Brown's parents burst into the room. "Call an ambulance!" their son shrieked, but Columbo never regained consciousness. He was dead within two hours.

The shooting, which was ruled accidental, could have been even more horrible. Investigators found that the matching pistol Russ had held was also loaded.

Carole, who had been vacationing at Lake Arrowhead over the Labor Day weekend, came back that evening, planning to dine with Russ. She was devastated by the news. "His love for me was the kind that rarely comes to any woman," she told the press. Sally Blaine, who was at his bedside when he died, was similarly grief stricken, but it was Carole who attended the funeral with Russ's family. Inside the church, 3,500 friends and fans fought for seating room, while 1,000 more waited outside. The women outnumbered the men twenty to one, but all stood in shocked silence broken only by sobs as his coffin, draped in a blanket of gardenias from Carole, was carried in by her brother Stuart, Gilbert Roland, Zeppo Marx, director Walter Lang, and Russ's old "rival" Bing Crosby.

The one woman who didn't attend the bleak affair on that sunny afternoon was Russ's mother. Julia Columbo, nearly blind and in very poor health, could never have stood the shock, so the family kept it from her. For the next eleven years, they carried out a massive charade, "a compassionate conspiracy." For three of those years, Carole faithfully visited Mrs. Columbo and told her stories about Russ traveling abroad, on a successful tour of European capitals. Each week, Carole and the family read the fragile old lady postcards and letters "from Russ," complete with simulated postmarks and filled with newsy accounts, tender sentiments, and reports of his success. Each month, he "sent" home a check, which they had drawn from his royalties and his insurance policy. "After a certain amount of time had passed, we could have told her . . . she was well enough," her husband, Nicolo, said after her death in 1944, "but we couldn't see the point in upsetting her." The hoax worked so well that in her will, she bequeathed part of her estate to the son she believed to be the toast of Paris and London.

As she breathed her last, Mrs. Columbo asked her children to " . . . tell Russ . . . I'm so happy . . . so proud."

THELMA TODD
Who Killed Hot Toddy?

Every weekday morning at 10:15, housemaid Mae Whitehead would drive her employer's car from the hilltop garage to the chic oceanside restaurant just at the foot of the hill. The sight of her chocolate brown Phaeton convertible was the familiar sign that meant Thelma Todd's Sidewalk Cafe was open for business. But today, Monday, December 16, 1935, was different. Mae knew that Miss Todd had still not come home from a party on Saturday night, not even to change her evening gown. Perhaps she was enjoying a weekend fling. Mae did wonder why the garage door was partially open. As she entered the dark garage, she saw that the car door on the driver's side was also open. And there, slumped in the front seat, wearing her now rumpled formal, was Thelma Todd. "Wake up, honey," Mae whispered gently. When she saw blood on Thelma's upper lip, she ran to call the police.

Within hours, reporters from across the nation were flocking to Hollywood to cover the shocking death—probably a murder—of the vivacious thirty-year-old "Ice Cream Blonde." It was hardly a fitting end for a comic actress. "She was a favorite with everyone on the lot, from the lowliest employee to the highest," producer Hal Roach said. "She was always joyous and happy and thoroughly enjoyed her work."

A former schoolteacher and model, Thelma launched her acting career after she won the Miss Massachusetts title in 1924. "Hot Toddys" 's infectious gaiety and impeccable timing made her the perfect foil for the comedy greats of the day. She starred opposite Charlie Chase in a series of one- and two-reelers directed by Chase and by the brilliant Leo McCarey, who also directed her in several shorts and two features with Laurel and Hardy, *The Devil's*

"Hot Toddy"

Brother and *The Bohemian Girl. Speaks Easily,* Buster Keaton's farewell to MGM, allowed Toddy to show off her dazzling wit and long, long legs. She added spice to vehicles for Jimmy Durante, Joe E. Brown, Harry Langdon, and, perhaps most memorably, the Marx Brothers in *Monkey Business* and *Horsefeathers.* In all, she appeared in eighty films during her ten-year career, but what won her a loyal following and the nickname "Queen of the Comedy Shorts" were two series she starred in under the masterful guidance of Hal Roach. In the first, Thelma was always ready with a flip remark and a quizzical expression for her scatterbrained sidekick ZaSu Pitts. In 1933, chubby deadpan Patsy Kelly replaced gawky ZaSu, but Toddy could answer her with just the arch of an eyebrow.

A big blonde with "the face of an angel and the body of a goddess," Thelma had men buzzing around her like flies—director Roland West being one of the swarm. Back in 1931, an infatuated West was convinced that the wide-eyed Thelma was capable of great dramatic work. He starred her in *Corsair,* changing her name to Allison Lloyd "in order that no taint of comedy might cling to her skirts." Hal Roach, furious at West's disdainful remarks, announced that in Thelma's next short with ZaSu, he would call her "Susie Dinkleberry,

Thelma, Chico, and Groucho in Horsefeathers.

so that no taint of drama will cling to her pajamas." Roach didn't need to worry; Thelma's fans didn't like the change of name or style. She never made another drama and West never made another film. That, however, was not the end of their working relationship.

Thelma Todd's Cafe, opened in 1935, quickly became a fashionable gathering place for her industry friends. A week before her death, she installed a cocktail lounge in preparation for a busy New Year's Eve. Above the cafe, in her second-floor apartment, lay hundreds of Christmas presents that she'd bought for friends. Behind the cafe, a steep 100-yard incline led to her garage and Roland West's palatial home, aptly named Castillo del Mar—Castle by the Sea. West's ex-wife, silent screen actress Jewell Carmen, who was a close friend of Thelma's, now lived in this hillside abode. West, who was Thelma's partner, and according to some, her lover, also lived down the hill in an apartment above the restaurant. Hot Toddy was completely tied to West financially, but friends said she had recently dropped hints that she planned to leave him, perhaps by the new year. But poor Thelma never lived to see 1936. Coast to coast, the nation read the baffling story—how police estimated her death at 4:00 a.m. on Sunday, but at least nine people claimed to have seen or talked to her as many as eighteen hours after that.

Thelma spent Saturday afternoon at the dentist having a tooth filled. She returned home to prepare for a lavish party Ida Lupino and her parents were giving in Thelma's honor at the Trocodero. When her chauffeur, Ernest Peters, arrived, she was dressed to the nines, with her hair meticulously marceled. Toddy was considered one of the best-dressed stars in Hollywood, and tonight she was dazzling in a blue-and-silver sequin-spangled gown, wrapped in a mink coat. Before she left, West told her, "I'll be locking the restaurant at two o'clock . . . better be back by then."

"I'll be back at five minutes after," she replied. At the coroner's inquest, West testified that they often teased each other that way. Indeed, she told Peters to pick her up from the party at 1:15 a.m., because she had an appointment at the Cafe at 1:55.

The party began with an embarrassing incident. Agent and notorious playboy Pat DiCicco, who was Todd's husband from July 1932 until their divorce in 1934, had bumped into Ida Lupino a few days earlier and insisted on an invitation. Ida first checked with Thelma, who not only said yes, but reserved the seat next to her in the private dining room. That chair remained empty as, all through dinner, DiCicco danced with a date in another room. When she approached him, he explained it had all been a joke . . . that he never intended to go.

"I know he was serious when he spoke with me. I know it!" a furious Ida Lupino told her. Thelma reassured her that it was okay, and returned to dance, dine, and be her usual hilarious self. Everyone agreed she was the life of the party. "She told me she was having a dynamite affair with a man in San Francisco," Lupino later testified. "She said it was the most wonderful affair she'd ever had and she hoped I could meet him soon."

Around 1:45, just ten minutes or so before the meeting for which she had told her chauffeur she must be home, Thelma excused herself from the party

Thelma Todd's Sidewalk Cafe. The "Ice Cream Blonde" had planned to open restaurants in Palm Springs and in her home town of Lawrence, Massachusetts, before death cut short her dream.

and went to the ladies room. "When she came in, she was happy, smiling—like always," remarked the attendant. "She made a phone call and was very secretive about it. She kept it real confidential." The authorities later asked the attendant if she thought Miss Todd might have been calling Pat DiCicco in another part of the club. "I couldn't guess *who* she was talking to, but after the call, she was upset. I asked her if I could get her anything. She said she was fine, but I could see she wasn't."

Some of Thelma's friends noticed her mood change, too. Theater owner Sid Grauman asked if he could help. "Yes," Thelma answered, "would you call Roland at the cafe and tell him I'm on my way?"

"Sure, Thelma," Sid said, but Thelma remained at the party until 3:30. Even the hat-check girls, familiar with her usual effervescence, noticed that she seemed disturbed.

Ernest Peters noticed it too. " 'Faster, drive faster,' she told me," he recounted to the police, "even though I was already doing sixty-five miles per hour. Then she told me she was in constant fear for her life. We arrived at her home at four a.m. It was my custom to escort Miss Todd up the steps to her door, but that night she told me it wouldn't be necessary. She said, 'I must owe you quite a bit. Send me a bill.' " It appeared that she was preparing to leave West and closing out her debts to a number of people. Recently, she'd also paid up her dressmaker, telling her, "I'll probably be broke soon." As Peters drove away, he saw Thelma disappear in the direction of the steps. On that raw, windy, foggy night, it was the last move anyone could be sure Thelma Todd made.

Five hours later, two men in a downtown cigar store immediately recognized Miss Todd when she ran in asking them to dial a phone number for her. "She seemed dazed and upset. Before I could dial the number for her, she ran out. I'm sure it was Thelma Todd," the proprietor told police. He watched her run across the street, her spangled gown reflecting the early morning light. She joined a heavyset man who was holding her mink coat, as they briefly sat on the steps of a church. At the inquest, the storekeeper identified her evening gown.

Jewell Carmen was positive she had seen her friend Thelma in Hollywood, driving her Phaeton past the corner of Sunset and Vine, around 11:15 Sunday morning. "There was a dark, handsome, well-dressed stranger with her and," she noted, "Thelma looked tired." People were wondering—was it a pleasure drive, or had Thelma Todd been taken for a ride?

Mrs. Wallace Ford, wife of the well-known character actor, had planned a large soirée that Sunday afternoon. "Thelma called around four to see if it was all right to bring a guest. I ventured a few guesses as to whom it might be, but she would not even let on if it was a man or a woman. All she said was 'You'll drop dead when you see who it is.' She also said that she was dressed in evening clothes and was that all right. I've talked to Thelma hundreds of times on the phone. I know her voice."

Another woman corroborated Mrs. Ford's testimony during the coroner's inquest in that jammed, standing-room-only courtroom. Even in Hollywood, a beaded formal and mink coat attract attention at 4:00 in the afternoon. Sara Carter was positive it was Thelma Todd she had seen in a drugstore phone booth. Because of her clothes, she thought it must be late, but no, it was only 4:00 . . . 4:04 to be exact.

Miss Todd never went to Mrs. Ford's party. On that clear, cool winter afternoon, she was driving with another beautiful woman—or so swore Santa Monica official J. A. Clough, who had been driving through Beverly Hills with his family that Sunday. "Look! There's Thelma Todd," he pointed, as her Phaeton passed them on Wilshire Boulevard. "Miss Todd was driving, wearing the mink coat. Next to her was a lightly built, rather short, beautiful blonde girl. We were on our way home; it was just starting to get dark . . . about four-thirty."

The last person to recognize Thelma Todd was the manager of a Christmas tree lot in Santa Monica. She and a man matching Jewell Carmen's description, about twenty-five, black hair, heavy eyebrows, selected a tree to be silvered about 11:00 p.m. The manager remembered an intimate scene, "They were laughing and giggling . . . they talked about putting something over on someone, then they laughed again. They seemed to have been drinking." The couple told him they would return shortly for the tree. Perhaps they got

Garage where Thelma Todd's body was found. Psychics have been overcome by noxious fumes here and past residents have heard a car engine running when they knew the garage to be empty.

something to eat, as the autopsy showed that Todd had eaten within two or three hours of her death. At any rate, she never went back for the tree. No one saw her again until Mae opened the garage door eleven hours later.

Thelma's body was slumped forward in the driver's seat, her coat and gown spattered with blood. The tooth she had had filled Saturday morning had been broken in her mouth, and there were questionable marks on her throat. Whether or not these were bruises was never determined. "The body was beautiful even in death," lamented the press ". . . with the face showing no sign of terror or struggle." Her evening bag lay on the floor at her feet—inside were two extortion letters.

Todd had been receiving such letters for a long time. "Our San Francisco boys will lay you out. We'll wreck that Santa Monica cafe of yours," crudely signed with an ace of hearts. There was one arrest. A man confessed to an elaborate fantasy life with Miss Todd and was subsequently committed to the psychopathic ward in Bellevue. The letters did not stop, however, and Todd became increasingly upset. She received so many that Mae systematically bundled them up, sending them to the police without even showing Miss

Todd. Strong rumors were circulating that mobster Lucky Luciano had tried to convince Thelma to open an illegal gambling operation above the cafe. A short time after she refused, the threatening notes began—but Toddy courageously held her ground. The description of the dark, handsome stranger driving with her fit Lucky Luciano perfectly.

That description also fit Pat DiCicco, who flew to New York immediately after his ex-wife's body was discovered. When the police "urged" him to return, he told them that he thought West was responsible for Thelma's death. He theorized that West had caught her in the garage on her way to a rendezvous—and no, she was not going to meet him, absolutely not. West probably struck her in anger, and, knocking her unconscious, left her there to teach her a lesson. He did not believe that West had meant for her to die.

West told the authorities that he locked the restaurant just after 2:00 a.m., Sunday, as he said he would. He did not like Miss Todd being late. When this had occurred in the past, she had gone to sleep at her mother's. That was why he hadn't worried about her, or reported her absence, all day Sunday. Thelma's friends didn't believe him. Their suspicion was that West knew Thelma was supposed to be "hit" by Luciano's boys that night, with his part of the bargain being to lock her outside. No charges were ever brought against him. He retired, retreating from Hollywood forever.

Police investigated a suicide angle, which they rejected, and an accident theory which didn't hold up either. The cause of death was definitely established as carbon monoxide poisoning, with blood on the upper lip being a common reaction. If the cafe was locked, she might have climbed the 208 stone steps to the garage, and, alone in the darkness, started the motor. She might have gone there to sleep, starting the motor for warmth. There was one thing wrong with this idea: investigators found Todd's shoes to be "as good as new." A policewoman made the climb to the garage in an identical pair of shoes, and hers were scuffed and scraped when she reached the top. It seemed apparent that someone did keep an appointment with Thelma at the cafe.

And then, suddenly, everyone stopped talking. Jewell Carmen abruptly announced that she was no longer sure if it had been Thelma Todd in that chocolate Phaeton. Todd's mother, who had screamed murder from the beginning, now told authorities that her daughter's death was surely a suicide. The Christmas tree salesman lost his memory, too. Mae Whitehead was accosted by a man who told her to "keep her mouth shut," and a waiter at the Trocodero was threatened with kidnapping. Police dropped the investigation.

Months later, police from Ogden, Utah, contacted Los Angeles authorities about a man there they were certain had murdered Thelma Todd. After two letters, they received a terse reply: Thelma Todd was a suicide. Several principal witnesses had withheld the solution—they wanted the public to believe it had been an accident. The case was closed . . . there would be no further investigation.

Forty years later, Patsy Kelly was touring in *Irene*. After a performance in Ohio, a tall, dark man who said he was from Florida went backstage. He'd been to California once and had something to give her. He slipped a ring into Miss Kelly's hand, and as he walked away said, "That was Miss Todd's."

JEAN HARLOW
You Always Hurt the One You Love

Police were not the first to arrive at Jean Harlow's Beverly Hills mansion on Labor Day, 1932. MGM chiefs Louis B. Mayer and Irving Thalberg, anxious to protect the image of their twenty-one-year-old sex goddess, had already sleuthed around the place, looking for incriminating evidence as to why Harlow's husband, Paul Bern, the prominent MGM executive, had shot himself.

The Berns had quarreled the night before, and Jean had spent the night at her mother's. It was Thalberg who told her that Bern, who was his closest associate, was dead. She collapsed into Thalberg's frail arms.

Mayer had pocketed Bern's suicide note, but eventually his colleagues persuaded him to surrender it to the authorities. Newspapers all over the world demanded an explanation of the note's sensational implications, and reporters set up camp on Jean's mother's doorstep. Any other Hollywood star would have been ruined by such a scandal-ridden suicide, but Jean Harlow was secure in her position as the "foremost U.S. embodiment of sex appeal." The truth was, underneath the sugar-coated studio ballyhoo, the platinum-haired goddess had been imprisoned in a disastrous in-name-only marriage. Her death five years later was a direct result of her nuptial nightmare.

The "Platinum Venus" had eloped at sixteen to escape the boredom of her Midwestern girls' boarding school. She and twenty-one-year-old Charles McGrew ran off to Los Angeles, followed shortly by Mama Jean and her second husband, Jean's stepfather, Marino Bello. Several months later, "Baby Jean" broke into films as an extra and a bit player. Charlie Chaplin used her in *City Lights* and producer/director Hal Roach cast Jean to glamourize several Laurel and Hardy shorts, most notably *Double Whoopee*. Jean was to slither out of a limousine while the comedy team fumbled clumsily at the door. When the

The formula Harlow gown—loose top, tight bottom, in white, Jean's favorite color. She did all the rest.

seventeen-year-old emerged, she was wrapped in a clinging white gown that clearly revealed she was wearing absolutely nothing else. Mama Jean smiled proudly from behind the camera at her gorgeous baby. When Roach found his voice, he yelled, "Cut!" Then, inspired, he added, "Find Jean a *black* dress!" In a few short years, Roach would regret that he did not save the first take of the voluptuous bit player. That piece of motion picture history was left on the cutting room floor and thrown away.

In 1929, she divorced McGrew and won her first featured role in *The Saturday Night Kid*, which starred Clara Bow. Clara thought the movie was "just terrible," but she took a liking to Jean. More than once she moved the blonde beauty to the front of a scene, telling her, "You're too pretty to be way back there." Very few, if any, other female stars ever felt confident enough to do anything like that, but Clara was cut from a different mold. Jean never forgot the kindness, though the film did nothing for her career. Clara had picked her own successor.

The knight in shining armor who rescued Harlow from obscurity and enabled her to inherit Bow's crown as America's reigning sex queen was Texas millionaire Howard Hughes.

Hughes started filming *Hell's Angels*, his World War I saga with the astonishing flying sequences, in 1927. A million dollars later, none of the film was usable—silents were out, and Hughes needed a whole new screenplay tailored for a talky. The biggest problem was his Swedish leading lady, Greta Nissen,

Clara Bow (second from left) embracing Jean Harlow on the set of The Saturday Night Kid, *flanked by Jean Arthur and Lorna Love. Harlow went on to inherit "IT" from Bow.*

whose heavy accent made her an impossible choice for the role of an English girl. Agent Arthur Landau discovered Jean hanging around the Roach lot with nothing to do and brought her to Hughes who made her his new star and signed her to a three-year contract. However, it would take even longer than that for Jean to recover from the injury she suffered during the film's final sequence. The damage was wreaked by the intense lighting needed to shoot in color, which was still in the experimental stages. "I had a number of close-ups to do. For these shots big batteries of lights were arranged on each side of the camera. I had to face these, looking directly into them. The heat was terrific, but I didn't realize how terrific until later," she said.

Her eyes were severely burned, and for almost four years, she lived in constant fear of losing her sight. Jean silently endured the pain—not even her closest friends knew about her suffering until doctors pronounced the danger passed. "I blame no one. It was an accident, pure and simple," she told the press, who cheered the actress's stoicism. The glamour queen was also a real "trouper."

Hell's Angels made her popular. Even in staid old London, they called her "sexquisite." Though critics considered her talents debatable, no one argued with Jean's sassy sex appeal or rakish sense of humor. Writer Adela Rogers St. John remembered her at a party. "She walked in and a cry went up from every woman in the room, 'My God! There's Harlow—Where's my husband?' To my consternation, I found myself liking the girl! There was a directness, a simplicity, a hearty good humor and a joy of life about her that were irresistible and totally unexpected. She kept us in hysterics with a story about a funny looking man she'd seen on the subway."

Jean amused the press, too. "Miss Harlow, do you wear brassieres?"

"That sounds like a near-sighted question to me," she retorted. Everyone was laughing except the brassiere industry, whose sales promptly "sagged." On the other hand, Harlow almost singlehandedly saved beauty parlors during the Depression, as women poured in to platinize their locks.

The electricity between Harlow and another rising newcomer, Clark Gable, was unmistakable in her next film, *The Secret Six* (1931). The wisecracking duo, billed as "The pair born to co-star," became close friends, delighting fans in five more films together. Later that year, she even began winning the critics' approval with convincing performances opposite Jimmy Cagney in *Public Enemy* and Spencer Tracy in *Goldie,* their first of three films.

Tracy was genuinely fond of Harlow, ". . . a square shooter if ever there was one." He met with her early on the *Goldie* set to help her with her lines. One morning he interrupted their rehearsal. "Jean, why are you acting so god-damned phony?"

She stared at him.

"You're good—really good. When you're just being yourself, you have a great laugh, a great way of talking, and a great way of shaking your fanny. But as soon as you start to act, you put on this phony diction and a phony walk like you're trying to be the goddamned Queen of England. Just be yourself."

A grateful and determined Jean worked diligently, improving so quickly that MGM bought her contract from Hughes for $60,000. Thalberg and Paul

Spencer Tracy and Jean Harlow were very fond of each other, working in front of the camera and off camera as well.

Bern continued the grooming process, softening her cheap, flashy side. They convinced her that "less is more" and taught her to be subtle and sophisticated, without losing her natural gift for wisecracking comedy.

With her trademark tinted scarlet for *Red-Headed Woman*, she rivaled Mae West for the Hays Office's bad girl of 1932. The czar of virtue declared that the film violated the "Sinners must pay" code. Anita Loos's story about a gold-digging stenographer who wins in the end so enraged the London censors that they banned it completely, and the film has never been released in England. It was a cause célèbre that made Jean the hottest box office attraction in the world. She was only twenty-one.

There weren't many men in Hollywood who hadn't made a pass at her by then. Louis B. Mayer never forgave her for turning him down. But Paul Bern was interested in her mind. He encouraged her to read and listened to her ideas. He was forty-two—twice her age—a soft-spoken little man with thinning hair. They were an unlikely romantic team, but Jean was attracted to this stable, dignified, mature man who treated her with a fatherly devotion.

"I met Paul Bern one night three years before our wedding at the home of a mutual friend and from that time onward, his friendship, his sane wisdom, and his understanding were the greatest influences in my life. He was the one man in Hollywood who had confidence in my ability to play another sort of girl and who understood my ambitions to go forward rather than die a screen death," she told Adela Rogers St. John.

Until he was twelve, Paul Bern's childhood was haunted by his brothers' and sisters' cries for food. As an adult, he was so sensitive to other people's unhappiness that he was known around the studio as "Father Confessor," "St. Francis of Hollywood," and "The Man with the Gentle Eyes." He got his start in Hollywood working as a scriptwriter for the distinguished directors Josef von Sternberg and Ernst Lubitsch, then took to directing himself before Thalberg appointed him producer and story consultant in 1926. Thalberg trusted Bern's insight so completely that he placed him in charge of all of Greta Garbo's movies.

Jean and Paul were married quietly on July 2, 1932, before a small gathering: Mama Jean and Marino, Thalberg and Norma Shearer, Arthur and Beatrice Landau.

In the early morning hours following the ceremony, Jean called Landau, hysterical.

"Come and get me! I'll be waiting outside," she sobbed.

Landau rushed over to 9820 Easton Drive, deep in the wild Benedict Canyon area of Beverly Hills. He brought Jean back to his house, where she tearfully told the Landaus the sickening details of her wedding night.

After the guests had left, the newlyweds had continued celebrating until both were happily drunk. When they retired to the all-white master bedroom, Jean began undressing for her first amorous encounter with her husband, but Bern seemed preoccupied, distracted. The closer she tried to come, the further he retreated.

"Paul, what's wrong?" the young bride asked her oddly elusive mate. It was then that Bern revealed his terrible secret. He told her he would not be able to

The "Love Goddess" loved posing, and her admiring fans couldn't get enough of publicity shots like this one.

"Father Confessor" Paul Bern, MGM executive, reacted keenly to the unhappiness of others. His own problems remained a dark secret, only hinted at in his cryptic suicide note.

consummate their marriage. His sex organ, the size of a child's, rendered him impotent. Drunk, Bern pathetically threw himself at her feet, begging for understanding . . . for Harlow to work her screen magic on him.

"You're a sex goddess—you can help me!" he pleaded.

"I'm no goddamn goddess!" she yelled back. Believing that she had at last found a man who loved her for herself, not her glamorous image, she was furious at Bern's betrayal. "I'm just a woman—an ordinary woman! What the hell are *you!*"

With an alcoholic rage to fuel them, they railed mercilessly against each other's failures. Jean's taunts pushed a humiliated Bern over the edge. He threw his bride to the floor, biting her legs so savagely, he drew blood. With uncontrollable fury, he grabbed a cane, beating her over and over until, exhausted, he passed out.

Harlow carefully lowered her blouse. "Look at my back," she told the Landaus. She showed them five long welts stretching from her hips to her shoulders, and more marks across her buttocks. They gasped when she revealed bloody teeth marks on her inner thighs.

"Oh my god," Landau whispered.

"Arthur, I never want to see him again."

Landau was on the phone with MGM executives until dawn, deciding what must be done. The spotlight was on, and scandal had to be avoided at all costs. It was decided that Bern and Harlow would remain together in the house on Easton Drive until after a suitable time—six months or so—when they would quietly divorce. The charade began immediately with their formal wedding reception the next afternoon. Most of her friends were dressed to the hilt, but Jean's casual manner allowed her to get away with wearing loose-fitting green pajamas and to coyly maneuver her way out of painful embraces. She gave the performance of her life . . . the happy, blushing bride.

For two months, the couple lived together, their hatred growing daily. When the bruises healed, Jean, desperate to escape, buried herself in *Red Dust*, a scintillating reteaming with pal Gable. It was sheer humiliation for Paul, who managed to drag himself to the studio once or twice a week, only to see his wife going off to the embraces of a real man—movie or no movie. Especially when he found out she wasn't wearing anything in that barrel in the shower scene! He comforted himself with the realization that she was no longer worried about her back. Back at home, she fell into an exhausted sleep in her locked bedroom in a house Bern had mortgaged to the hilt. She was handling everything; he couldn't even pay his bills. He tossed and turned in the den, never sleeping, despising her . . . himself . . . his life. Bern was completely shattered. Finally, one night, he found the courage to sleep in the master bedroom.

Harlow cringed as he turned away to remove his robe. She was sure he couldn't be stupid enough to try anything. When he turned to face her, words caught in her throat. Strapped to his body was a huge leather penis. A chuckle escaped from Jean. Their eyes met and suddenly both were shaking with waves of laughter. Jean helplessly clutched her sides, tears streaming down her cheeks as Bern pranced and danced, pretending to fish, to conduct an orchestra, and to ride a horse. He collapsed, convulsing with laughter, rolling onto the bed next to Jean. Suddenly, they were in each other's arms, sobbing from their hearts for the hopelessness of their love. Releasing weeks of pent-up conflict, Bern ripped the grotesque object from his body, ferociously hacking at it with a pair of scissors. Jean, kneeling by him and crying quietly, flushed away the pieces.

Bern's bizarre tarantella was more like a death dance—the death of his self-worth. Two days later in the predawn hours of September 4, 1932, after a fight with Jean that sent her packing to Mama, he shot himself once in the head. His nude body was discovered face down in front of Jean's full-length bathroom mirror. He held one gun in his hand and had placed a second gun on her dressing table where Mayer found his note.

Dearest Dear,
Unfortunately this is the only way to make good the frightful wrong I have done you and to wipe out my abject humiliation.

I love you,

Paul

You understand that last night was only a comedy.

After wild speculation, the press discovered what they believed must be behind Bern's "abject humiliation"—the overly generous man had ruinously mismanaged his finances, being forced to borrow money from Jean, who inherited his mountain of debts days later. The coroner revealed the full story— Harlow's celebrated union was in name only. Other than telling the press that the love the couple had shared transcended sex, Harlow said nothing. Despite the scandalous publicity, Jean was once again the stoic and her fans rallied to support the "grief-stricken widow."

Victor Fleming, director of *Red Dust*, told interviewers, "She came back to carry on. She knew darn well that Paul's absence had left the studio in an awful hole. She knew how it had depended on Paul. So she came back sort of to make up as much as she could for all the trouble. She's a trouper. She went through it all."

In shock and under great pressure from the unrelenting eye of the press, Jean had misjudged her strength that first day back. "She has more guts than most men," Clark Gable said. "She went on working—trying not to hold us up—then all of a sudden crumpled down on the floor in a dead faint—scared me to death."

Harlow was not the only woman to suffer because of Bern's death. When Dorothy Millette heard the news the following day in San Francisco, she boarded a steamer and flung herself into the Sacramento River.

Millette, an aspiring actress, had met Bern years earlier at the American Academy of Dramatic Arts in New York. They fell in love and lived together as common-law man and wife until Dorothy was stricken with what doctors diagnosed as incurable amnesia. Bern's brother, Henry, described her symptoms for the press. "You could talk to her for half an hour and realize the keenness of her mind. Mention religion, and the conversation was over . . . she became maniacal about religion." Heartbroken, at great expense, Paul placed her in a Connecticut sanitarium, promising to care for her for the rest of her life. He moved to Los Angeles to make a fresh start.

In the summer of 1932, Dorothy Millette's memory cleared and she could not comprehend that more than a decade had passed. Hearing that Bern was married and living in Los Angeles, she wrote she was coming to join him.

Bern fought desperately to stall her until he could think of a way out, pleading for her to understand that the scandal of bigamy would ruin Jean's career and might possibly result in jail for him. She heard only that he did not want to be with her. Bern, who was emotionally exhausted by then, relented. "Go to San Francisco. I'll meet you there later." Dorothy waited. Weeks passed, and she finally announced to him that she was flying to Los Angeles over Labor Day weekend.

The night following his tormented "dance," Bern staged the quarrel that predictably sent Jean to her mother's. Later, neighbors noticed a limousine deliver a veiled woman to the house. They could hear Bern and the woman arguing by the pool, and a short time later the limousine returned, taking the woman away.

Millette had refused to see Bern's predicament. A wretched Bern agonized over his utter uselessness. Trapped between a wife who despised him and a woman whose demands would ruin even the pitiful remnants of his life, he saw only one alternative. After a proper period of mourning, Harlow, free at last, ended the sham with gusto. The sex symbol without a man made up for lost time with several drunken sexual binges in Northern California, all of which MGM managed to keep out of the papers. She cruised around town in her Cadillac V-12, tastefully hung with Hollywood Fire Department signs. At Agua Caliente Casino, she held the unofficial record with thirty-four straight passes . . . that was with dice.

Meanwhile, Jean's stepfather convinced her that he could manage her career more effectively than Landau. Bello's outrageous salary demands resulted in nearly a year's suspension of Jean's contract, at a time when she could little afford to be out of work. Bern had left enormous debts, and even Dorothy Millette's heirs, suing for half of his $10,000 life insurance benefits, received $2,000.

One year and two weeks after Bern's death, Jean earned herself a higher spot on the Louis B. Mayer doghouse list when she eloped with her camera-

The "Sexquisite" Harlow.

man, Harold Rosson, who was sixteen years her senior. Mayer not only resented her for scorning his advances but also believed that a married sex symbol was box office poison. She and Rosson flew to Yuma, Arizona, with the pilot doubling as their only witness. A year later, Harlow told a judge that her husband ". . . was jealous of my friends, of my time, and of my position—of everything I had. He belittled my profession. . . . It got so bad, this jealousy of his, his sarcasms, that it affected my health and my work. I could stand it no longer—so we parted." No one was happier than Mayer when they divorced. Later in 1935, her philandering stepfather left her mother. At his departure, Mama Jean suffered a complete emotional collapse. In her warped grief and jealousy over her famous baby, she turned to Christian Science for solace.

Yet somehow, except for her period of suspension, Jean kept making movies. Fox and Warner Brothers suffered multimillion-dollar losses and Paramount filed for bankruptcy in the early Depression years, but MGM, with its stable of "more stars than there are in Heaven," boasted an $8 million profit. She made another hit with Gable in Anita Loos's *Hold Your Man* (1933) and played a star surrounded by a lovable but freeloading family, a whitewashed version of herself, in *Bombshell,* her personal favorite, the same year. Her scenes opposite surly Wallace Beery in the all-star *Dinner at Eight* were considered to be her best work ever. To broaden her range, MGM starred her in the 1935 musical *Reckless.* They used doubles for her singing and dancing, but the plot had a familiar ring: a Broadway star's career faces ruination in the wake of her husband's scandalous suicide. Her leading man, William Powell, was amicably divorced from another sexy blonde comedienne, Carole Lombard. Powell, forty-three, and Harlow, twenty-four, fell in love. Their first public "smooch" was captured by a photographer and their fans thrilled to the news, "Harlow and Powell Kiss." *Time* magazine put her on its cover.

She was maintaining a grueling six-day schedule—up at 5:45 a.m. and at the studio by 7:00—making film after film to pay off debts; not only Bern's now but also the bills her stepfather had run up in her name before he ran away. Jean was now happily reinstated with Landau and anxious to pick up the pieces of her tumultuous life. She made *China Seas* with Gable, Wallace Beery, Rosalind Russell, and Robert Benchley. She went right into *Riffraff* with her old buddy Spencer Tracy, and during a party on the set Jean and Powell announced their engagement. "I have made up my mind that I shall not marry until I am as independent as it is humanly possible to be," she told the columnists. She was driving herself with relentless disregard for her health.

In December 1935, during *Wife vs. Secretary,* again with Gable and Myrna Loy, Jean collapsed from fatigue and overwork. Mama Jean nursed her at home, but Harlow's condition was more serious than she would admit. Her film crews were accustomed to her frequent breaks to go to the bathroom, a further result of Bern's wedding night beating which had damaged her kidneys. Just as she had silently suffered with her eyes, Jean told no one about the pain in her lower back. Unaware herself of how serious her condition was, Jean put off seeing a doctor and after a few days' rest was back at work.

Nineteen thirty-six was Harlow's year. Though she and Cary Grant were box office pleasers in *Suzy*, it was in *Libelled Lady*, paired with Spencer Tracy and opposite the powerful screen team of Powell and Loy, that Harlow was at her peak. Powell winced during Jean's love scenes with Tracy, who played them up to tease him. "Must you be so realistic, Spencer?"

"Of course, Bill," Tracy would answer. "It's all for art, you know." Jean giggled in the background. For insurance, Powell gave his fiancée a 150-karat, $20,000 star sapphire for Christmas. The happy screen collaboration resulted in a smashing comedy nominated for Best Picture.

In January Jean embarked on a publicity tour with her *Personal Property* co-star, Robert Taylor, who was the only MGM star receiving more mail than Jean. She flew to Washington, D.C., for President Roosevelt's Birthday Ball and lunched with the First Lady. The exhausting tour, where they sometimes made twenty-two personal appearances a day, caused both stars to become ill, leaving Jean with a tough bout with the flu.

Four months later Harlow became seriously ill with an inflamed gall bladder. "I'm just a mess, Bill," she admitted to Powell, who urged her to take a

Reporters gather at the Beverly Hills home of Paul Bern and Jean Harlow hours after news of his suicide.

rest and see a doctor. However, *Life* magazine's recent cover girl was in the middle of yet another film, *Saratoga*, with Gable. Her hard work had paid off. Jean was, at last, out of debt, happily in love, and the darling of the critics and public alike. At only twenty-six, she was embarking on the most fruitful and stable period of her young life. Then on Saturday, May 29, 1937, on the set of *Saratoga*, Jean collapsed in Gable's arms.

She was exhausted and assumed she just needed another rest over the weekend. She went to Mama Jean's, despite protest from her co-workers that she go to a hospital. Her already damaged kidneys, severely weakened by the gall bladder attack, were beginning to fail, but no one, not even Jean, knew what was happening.

Mama Jean, in her twisted state of mind, saw this as her big chance to put everyone in her debt. She would heal her Baby Jean through simple prayer, while assuring Jean's friends that she was recovering quickly. When she was not back on the set by Tuesday, her friends decided to see for themselves.

Landau, Gable, Frank Morgan, Powell, director Jack Conway, and producer Bernie Hyman forced their way into Mama Jean's home. She led the men to Jean's bedroom, triumphantly pointing toward her daughter. "Doesn't she look better now?" They stared in horror at the beautiful Jean, who lay semi-conscious, moaning and belching, nauseated, and burning with fever. Her back, chest, and shoulders were wracked with pain. Her pulse was dangerously erratic. Mama Jean's idea of "better" was killing her daughter. Adhering devoutly to her Christian Science principles and blinded by her jealousy of her daughter, she refused to allow a doctor to see Jean, who was now too ill to speak for herself. Landau and Hyman tried frantically to reach Bello and Jean's father for permission for surgery, but neither one could be located. With time running out, they searched for another way around the stubborn Mrs. Bello.

Studio researchers scoured books on Christian Science until at last they discovered a paragraph stating that nurses could be present in extreme cases. Mama Jean finally yielded to the men's pleas but frustrated the nurses' every effort at basic care, constantly remaining in the room and even sleeping there as Jean lay dying.

By Sunday, June 6th, the situation was desperate. Jean's closest friends stood by helplessly frustrated, watching her slip away. She needed massive sedation now for the pain, as her kidneys were literally being torn to pieces by a diseased gall bladder. One of the nurses could smell urine on her breath.

"Please, Mama Jean—your baby is sick!" Landau implored. "She's got to go to a hospital!"

"She is not sick!" Mama Jean snapped angrily. "She's just pretending to make a fool of me. She won't admit what I've done for her." Mama Jean would not budge.

Hyman and Powell grasped at a final straw to save Jean's life. Together they raced to the beachfront home of Louis B. Mayer—the one person Mama Jean feared. Still no fan of Harlow's, at first he refused to help.

"She's dying!" Hyman yelled hysterically. Mayer, startled by Hyman's intensity, called Mama Jean and ordered her to send Jean to the hospital.

The ambulance screeched through Los Angeles to Good Samaritan Hospital. Harlow was too weak now to undergo surgery. A team of doctors could only administer two emergency blood transfusions during the night, in an attempt to clean the poisons that had spread throughout her body. By morning, she was comatose. Her breathing was weak and shallow. She suffered the convulsive spasms of cerebral edema. Doctors called in the inhalator squad of the fire department, whose ensignia had once frivolously bedecked Jean's car. Setting up an oxygen tent and tanks, they began pumping, as Jean's friends and family kept a vigil near her bed. Mama Jean tried endlessly to rouse her. Powell spoke to her but broke down. The rescue squad worked feverishly, but at 4:37 a.m., they stopped. Jean Harlow was dead. William Powell ran out of the room. Mama Jean had to be sedated. A nurse led a devastated Arthur Landau and Bernie Hyman to a small office where, privately, all three cried.

MGM closed down on the day of Harlow's funeral, while every other studio observed one minute of silence in memory of their fallen queen. *Saratoga*, only half finished, was shelved until, at the insistence of Harlow's loyal army of fans, it was completed using a double.

Her needless death at twenty-six was the result of being "used" in the grand Hollywood tradition. Yet, unlike most classic Hollywood stories, she had not been used by agents or producers but by family. Those whom she had loved and who loved her destroyed her.

F. SCOTT FITZGERALD
A Boat Against the Current

"When he moved, it was as if he secretly enjoyed the ability to fly, but was walking as a compromise to convention," wrote Zelda Sayre of the brilliant boy-wonder with the yellow hair and lavender eyes. Success and love came early to F. Scott Fitzgerald. He was only twenty-three when his first book was published. *This Side of Paradise,* the "novel about Flappers written for Philosophers," was the voice for the reckless, defiant youth of the 1920s, the new generation. He met the radiant and witty Zelda while he was doing his stint in the service. First Lieutenant Fitzgerald, then twenty-two, was stationed in Montgomery, Alabama, with the Infantry, and it was there, one hot summer night in 1918, at a country club dance, that he met the golden-haired Southern belle and knew that he had to have her. The Yankee ardently pursued and won her, and together they embarked on what he called "the romance of the century." They drank endlessly, would do almost anything on a dare, and set the mad pace for all children of the Jazz Age to imitate. "They didn't make the twenties," Lillian Gish remembered. "They *were* the twenties."

Zelda's every breath inspired him. With his hand firmly gripping the pulse of the "Lost Generation," Scott's phenomenal success continued with *The Beautiful and the Damned, The Great Gatsby, Tender Is the Night,* and several volumes of short stories. He dedicated all his books to Zelda, the heroine of all he wrote. In 1921, she gave birth to a daughter, Frances Scott—Scottie.

Hollywood wanted him, of course. Scott, at the peak of his glory, made his first trip there in 1927, when United Artists hired him to write an original screenplay for Constance Talmadge. On this trip he also met Irving Thalberg, from the MGM corner, another young man with a record of meteoric triumphs. Thalberg left a lasting impression on the celebrated writer.

Beautiful boy, spokesman for a generation.

It hardly mattered that UA rejected Scott's idea for a Talmadge vehicle. He and Zelda lived the life of luxury in their private bungalow at the elegant Ambassador Hotel. It was Hollywood's heyday, and they were enthusiastic participants in the glamorous whirl, living, as Scott described it, amidst, "the sound of clinking waiters . . . a time when he bought his ties and had to ask if gin would make them run."

As time passed, both Scott and Zelda paid an enormous price for their fun. Zelda began to get tired of living in her husband's shadow. She may have been the inspiration for everything he wrote, but what she really wanted was her own artistic success. When passages from her diary and letters she'd written to Scott appeared in his novels as his work, it was a swift blow to her self-esteem. "In fact," she wrote in one of several magazine articles, "Mr. Fitzgerald seems to believe that plagiarism begins at home." She turned to painting and dancing and grew wispy and nervous. The endless parties and three abortions stole the sparkle from her gray eyes and gnarled her graceful hands. Time had been no kinder to Scott. His strong physique had become soft and flabby and there were deep circles under his bloodshot eyes. The first two fingers on both hands were stained to the palm with nicotine. He agonized over a deep creative block and drank enormous amounts of gin, although which problem stemmed from the other is difficult to say. When drunk, he viciously lashed out at Zelda's attempts at independence which, in his insecure state of mind, he saw as acts of competition and betrayal. So literally did he suffocate her spirit that Zelda began to suffer from severe asthma and excruciating outbreaks of eczema that left her once beautiful skin pitted and scarred. She entered a sanitarium for the first time in April of 1930.

Fitzgerald's deepest fears—the fears of failure, loss of love, the end of youth—came crashing in on him. Zelda would remain institutionalized for great stretches of time for the remainder of her life and a piece of Scott was lost with her forever. His fires cooled, his pride slipped away. When he returned to Hollywood in 1931, he was a very different man.

For those who remembered a proud, cocky Scott, drunkenly tearing up the town, the new Fitzgerald was a shock. Many said that it was depressing just to be around him. Thalberg hired him for the screen adaptation of *Red-Headed Woman*, a vehicle for Jean Harlow, but Fitzgerald couldn't get a grip on it. His old friend Anita Loos took over and Fitzgerald returned East, more uncertain of himself, of his future, than ever. He was, as he had once noted, a man "on the lose."

The East proved no different. Though tremendous debts weighed heavily on his once regal shoulders, Scott's real trouble was not money, it was writing. He seemed unable to write anything worthwhile—"one of the champion false starters of the writing profession." There were occasional spurts of genius in the many short stories he wrote for magazines, but less than half of them were accepted for publication, and most of those were written with an undercurrent of financial desperation. More than life itself, he wanted to redeem his literary reputation, but he seemed doomed, like Jay Gatsby, to drift as "boats against the current . . . borne ceaselessly into the past." So many of his contemporaries, like Loos, Donald Ogden Stewart, Dorothy Parker, Alan Campbell, Lillian

Hellman, William Faulkner, Ogden Nash, and Robert Benchley, had succeeded in Hollywood, but he just didn't seem able to grasp his old vitality. In 1937, he joined their ranks to give it one last try.

Hollywood was full of many new faces, too, members of the new generation, many of whom had never read F. Scott Fitzgerald. Among them was the gossip columnist Sheila Graham, who called anyone she thought was old-fashioned "an F. Scott Fitzgerald type." He'd foreseen the thirties generation years ago. He'd predicted that after the craziness of the Jazz Age, there'd be disappointment and despair, and an overthrow of old values, or as he put it in *This Side of Paradise*, youth "grown up to find all gods dead, all wars fought, all faiths in men shaken." Now he had to face the thirties, an era he didn't seem to belong to.

The social scene gave him some relief from his failures at the typewriter. The Garden of Allah, an exotic hotel on Sunset Boulevard that was a gathering place for Eastern writers, became Scott's new home. It was there, at a party in

The Garden of Allah Hotel. Once the mansion of the exotic actress Alla Nazimova, The Garden provided lodging for three decades of Hollywood celebrities, such as Gloria Swanson, Valentino, Dietrich, the Barrymores, Errol Flynn, and Garbo. Bogart and Bacall honeymooned here.

Robert Benchley's suite, that he met the dazzling, divorced Miss Graham, at a party honoring her engagement to the Marquess of Donegall, a wealthy playboy. Scott was fascinated by this gorgeous woman, who told him all about her elite but adventurous background. Raised in London, she told him, she'd gone to finishing school in Paris, had a London debut followed by presentation at court and a marriage to a retired British Army major twice her age. Graham found Scott "most appealing, half young, half old. The thought flashed through my mind that he should get out into the sun." A short time later she was "shacking up" with Scott at the hotel and reading his books, and the Marquess became only a memory.

Sheila had saddled herself with the job of nursing a pale shell of a man who trembled and cowered, painfully insecure in the presence of old friends. He tried to start over and learn screenwriting with all the enthusiasm and curiosity he could muster. He studied a myriad of films for style, structure, and dialogue, convinced that success lay in duplication of past formulas. He worked for several studios on various scripts, including *Madame Curie* and *Gone with the Wind*, but to his bitter disappointment, his work was rewritten beyond recognition. His name appears in the credits of only one film, *Three Comrades*, and even that movie bore little resemblance to his original script. At one point, he was moved to write his daughter, at Vassar, "You don't realize that what I am doing here is the last tired effort of a man who once did something finer and better."

Sheila moved him away from the heavy drinking at the Garden of Allah, but he just drank alone. During the arguments that followed his binges, Fitzgerald hammered unmercifully at Sheila's story, chipping it away piece by piece until she broke down. She had been born Lily Sheil and had been raised in the slums and orphanages of London. She worked as a maid, a clerk, and a showgirl until, at seventeen, she married the major. Eight years later, in 1933, she moved to California, and in 1935 began her Hollywood column. Alongside Louella Parsons and Hedda Hopper, Graham became a powerful force in filmdom's gossip machine. She was a self-sufficient working woman, the opposite of ethereal Zelda. For Scott she was an anchor, but he loved her with a mixture of gratitude and resentment. He needed her strength, but Fitzgerald, the inveterate snob, felt she lacked Zelda's nobility; in his mind she was a "step down," but in keeping with his new station.

Eventually, Scott realized that he would be lost without Sheila. She gave generously of herself, helping with his work and battling with him for his life. Yet, life with Scott wasn't easy. When she found a gun in his dresser drawer, he tackled her to the floor to get it back. Sheila threw it across the room and screamed, "Take it! Shoot yourself, you son of a bitch! See if I care. I didn't pull myself out of the gutter to waste my life on a drunk like you!" But like Gatsby's "boat," she was always drawn back to him, even a year later when he threatened her life in a drunken rage.

In public, he made a drunken fool of himself more than once. At a party at the Thalbergs, he got crocked and insisted that Ramon Novarro play the piano. Scott went on singing, verse after verse, until John Gilbert started to hiss and jeer. Other guests joined in the hissing, trying to shut the singer up. At last,

Schwab's Pharmacy (circa 1940). The world-famous "drugstore of the stars" where writers and actors have gathered for fifty years.

Norma Shearer escorted the stumbling Fitzgerald out. Drinking kept him away from work for weeks at a stretch. He went to Dartmouth with Budd Schulberg in February 1939, assigned to observe the Winter Carnival for a script but went on a bender, instead, of dangerously excessive boozing that landed him in a hospital with pneumonia. Schulberg wrote *Winter Carnival* without him, as well as *The Disenchanted*, a "fictional" account of a young screenwriter's trip to Dartmouth's Winter Carnival with a declining genius. Fitzgerald summed it up, "Then I was drunk for many years, then I died."

Back in Hollywood, spiritually and financially depleted, he continued to drink. Sheila thought surely he must be trying to kill himself, a reflection Scott may have shared. With no offers of work, he collected Zelda in North Carolina to embark on a Cuban holiday, which curiously prompted him to note, "Suicide and wife arrive in Cuba." The trip was such a total disaster, with Fitzgerald drinking the entire way, that Zelda was forced to place him in a New York hospital where he remained for two weeks. It was the last time they would ever see each other.

Scott returned to Hollywood and to Sheila, who took him back and tended to him through several more weeks in bed. When he was strong enough to get up, he began to worry about money to live on. Though he'd been well paid his first year and a half in Hollywood, it had taken that long just to pay off his staggering debts. He survived by writing a series of short stories for *Esquire* magazine. In March 1940, his sagging spirit got a boost when he sold the screen rights to "Babylon Revisited," one of his earlier stories. It was about this time that he moved to 1403 Laurel Avenue, just around the corner from Schwab's drugstore in West Hollywood. "It's just big enough so that I don't look poor, which is very important here," he wrote Scottie. He felt his work on the screenplay for *Babylon* did much to restore his reputation in the industry, and two job offers that followed also gave him tremendous financial relief.

Along with his confidence, Fitzgerald's health seemed to bounce back. He entertained small groups of old friends, among them S. J. Perelman, Ogden

Fitzgerald—before the crack-up.

Nash, Frances and Albert Hackett, Nunnally Johnson, and Nathaniel West and his new wife, Eileen, whose sister immortalized her in the play *My Sister Eileen*. (The Wests were killed tragically in an auto accident just outside of Los Angeles the day after Fitzgerald's death.) Scott frequented Musso and Frank's restaurant and Schwab's, favorites of L.A. writers, not only for the food but for the credit they extended. Most important, he began working on his dream, a novel about Hollywood, *The Last Tycoon*. He was changing with the times—no more debutantes and Ivy Leaguers pursuing endless wild sprees. With this novel, he was dealing seriously with a profession for the first time. He drew his heroine this time from the strong, self-reliant character of Sheila rather than his childlike Zelda. Irving Thalberg was the model for Monroe Stahr, a man who was powerful, intense, and hard-working, the opposite of Gatsby and Scott's other leading men.

"I have long chosen Thalberg as a hero," he wrote his editor, "because he

Musso and Frank's Grill (circa 1926). The oldest restaurant in Hollywood, the back room was the hangout for Eastern writers who not only enjoyed the ambiance but also the credit extended. The thirties and forties saw William Faulkner, John O'Hara, Christopher Isherwood, Dashiel Hammett, William Saroyan, Nathanael West, Aldous Huxley, Lillian Hellman, Thomas Wolfe, and James Agee as regular patrons.

is one of the half-dozen men I have known who were built on a grand scale."
Thalberg, who had suffered with a heart ailment all his life, had died in 1936,
at age thirty-seven. *The Last Tycoon,* based on his rise to power, could have
been written only by someone intimate with studio life on a day-to-day basis.
Though Fitzgerald was again writing a novel and not a screenplay, he had
succeeded in learning Hollywood's system.

Fitzgerald was showing a sober side, literally. The party was over, and life
had become suddenly serious. Both Fitzgerald and Stahr were unable to dis-
entangle themselves from their careers, and both men were in love with only
two things: the memory of their wives and death. In October 1939, Scott wrote
to Scottie, ". . . I have begun to write something that is maybe great."

In late November 1940, Fitzgerald was in Schwab's buying a pack of cigarettes when he suddenly keeled over, dizzy and faint. He had just suffered a
heart attack. Though he recovered, he was no longer able to climb the steps
to his apartment, so he moved into Sheila's ground floor abode, a block from
his own. With no interruptions, he continued working on his novel, dictating
to his secretary from bed or writing there on a wooden desk he'd made.

He wrote Zelda in December that his latest cardiograms showed his heart
was mending, but it would be a long process. "It is odd that the heart is one of
the organs that does repair itself," he said. To Scottie he wrote, "My novel is
good." He kept working.

On November 20, after completing an especially rough passage, he decided
to escort Sheila to a press preview of *This Thing Called Love* at the Pantages
Theater. Afterward, as they left the theater, he staggered. Sheila caught him
just before he fell. "I suppose people will think I am drunk," Scott, still proud,
whispered, "but I feel awful . . . like I did in Schwab's." Because the doctor
was due at the apartment the next day, they decided not to disturb him. Scott
managed to sleep soundly through the night.

According to Sheila, the next day Scott patiently waited for the doctor while
making notes in a Princeton alumni magazine on next year's football team.
He loved listening to the games and always made it a point to catch them. He
glanced at the clock and saw that it was just after 2:00. Suddenly, he gasped,
jumped to his feet, then fell to the floor, dead. Several years later at a dinner
party, Hedda Hopper told a different story. A friend had told her that Fitzgerald
met with death while in the throes of passion. Sheila supposedly called this
same friend for help in moving him to a more respectable room.

He had already written his own epitaph: "Drunk at 21, wrecked at 31, dead
at 41." He was dead at forty-four.

Tycoon, published in its unfinished state, was heralded as Fitzgerald's most
mature work, ". . . far and away the best novel we have had about Hollywood,
and it is the only one which takes us inside," said the foreword by Edmund
Wilson. The literary world suddenly regretted its neglect of him, and mourned
the loss of one of its most imaginative minds. Of the few who paid respects at
the funeral home, Dorothy Parker thought of another epitaph that Fitzgerald
himself had written—this one for Jay Gatsby. Leaning over the casket, looking
at her old friend who was now cold and gray, she muttered, "The poor son of
a bitch."

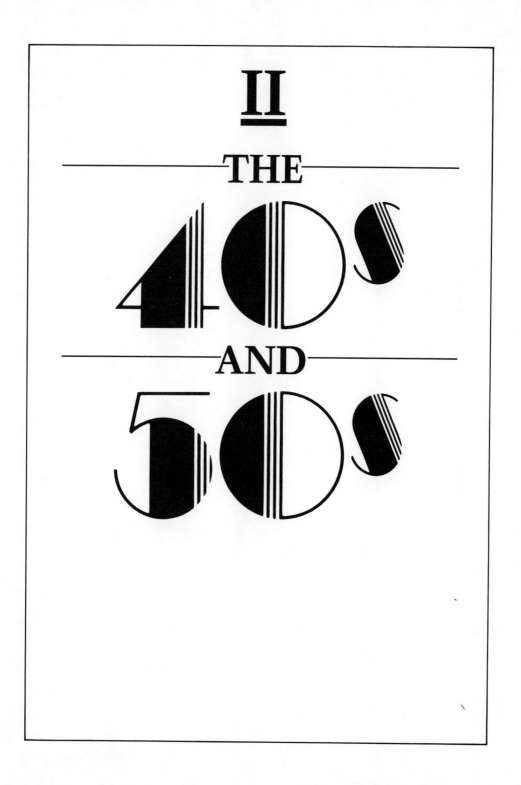

II

THE

40s

AND

50s

ROBERT WALKER
Split Image

Robert Walker and Jennifer Jones used to pose for the press as the perfect American couple, he with his specs and boyish-Greenwich-Village-poet look, she in a frilly apron, with their two sons beside them. His Hollywood career was moving along decently; hers was even better, with the guiding hand of wizard producer David Selznick. After the happy couple split up, Jennifer married Mr. Selznick, and Robert became known as "the bad boy of Hollywood," famous for his drunk-driving arrests and nervous breakdowns. By 1949, at the age of thirty, he was so unhappy and out of control that he entered the Menninger Clinic. The doctors examined his shattered life for almost a year and decided that his troubles had started long before his arrival in Hollywood.

The battleground of his broken home in Utah left deep scars on him as a child. He had what school counselors called behavior problems, so his parents decided to send him to a San Diego military academy for a strict education. Even at the academy, Walker showed great potential as an actor. After graduation, he set off to try his luck in New York.

He was accepted into the prestigious American Academy of Dramatic Arts in 1938. There he found friends, a niche, and love. Within a year, he married fellow student Phyllis Isley, who later changed her name to Jennifer Jones. Their honeymoon brought the ambitious couple to Hollywood, where Phyllis's saucy ingenue beauty and talent got her leads in several minor films. *Gone with the Wind* producer David O. Selznick was enchanted enough to sign her to a long-term contract. But Walker, who landed only a few bit parts, was unhappy in Hollywood. They returned to New York.

While Phyllis interrupted her career to give birth to Robert, Jr., and Michael,

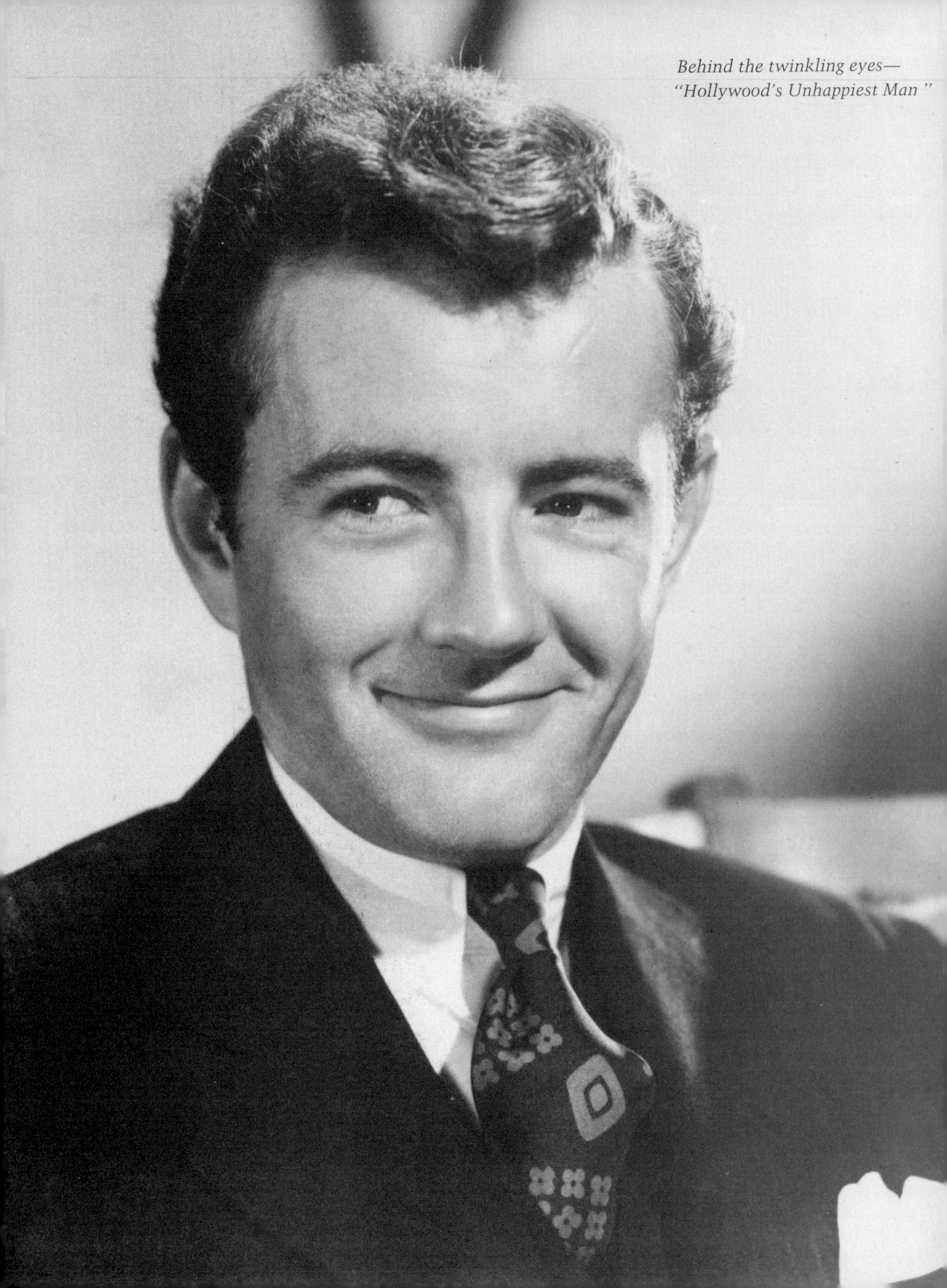

Behind the twinkling eyes—
"Hollywood's Unhappiest Man"

Robert got a role as a regular in a radio series. Steady work went a long way in restoring his confidence, so he packed up the family for another go at Hollywood.

Once again, Phyllis blossomed in Hollywood, with Mr. Selznick grooming her. It was he who told her to change her name. As Jennifer Jones, she starred in *Song of Bernadette* in 1943, and won an Oscar. Walker, who signed with MGM, made a good showing with his first featured role in *Madame Curie* and was even more impressive in the title role of his next film, *See Here, Private Hargrove*, but he resented his wife's grander laurels. Jennifer said he was growing more and more sarcastic toward her. He'd started to drink heavily, at times staggering home in the morning with no explanation. Their marriage was disintegrating, and rumors flew around about a romance between Jennifer and her mentor, Selznick. Robert and Jennifer co-starred as lovers in their only film together, *Since You Went Away*, in 1944, the same year that they separated. On the screen they said farewell at a train station, as he went off to war, never to return. It was as touching and memorable a scene as can be found in any World War II movie. Robert turned in another stellar performance that year in *Thirty Seconds Over Tokyo*. He kept on making movies and established himself as a dependable leading man, even as his personal life was falling to pieces. He and Jennifer divorced in 1945, and four years later she married Selznick. Robert made *Till the Clouds Roll By*, in which he played Jerome Kern; *One Touch of Venus*; and *What Next, Corporal Hargrove?* He was cast opposite such leading MGM beauties as Hedy Lamar, Katharine Hepburn, Ava Gardner, and June Allyson.

When he made *The Clock* with Judy Garland, who could have guessed that the two wholesome stars portraying a couple who meet, fall in love, and marry in the course of a 48-hour leave were actually a pair of time bombs ticking away toward self-destruction? Twenty-two-year-old Judy was no problem on the set. She was falling in love with Vincente Minnelli, who was directing the picture, but Walker was bitter and vindictive over his broken-up marriage. Alcohol transformed his charming, good-natured disposition into that of a monster. Judy more than empathized and treated him with great tenderness. On several nights, she, her makeup woman Dottie Ponedel, and publicist Betty Asher rescued Walker from a bar. Sometimes they had to save him before he was beaten to a pulp—he was letting loose with some kind of macho rage and challenging bigger men to brawl. More often, they found him sitting alone in a shroud of depression. Judy, who understood his self-hatred, always coaxed him home and sobered him up so that he'd be able to work the next day.

The "bad boy" got his picture on the front pages, thanks to a series of drunk-driving arrests and public displays of drunkenness. He suffered terrible anxiety attacks and a few total breakdowns. The papers suggested that the loss of Jennifer's affection was the root of his problem, but he vehemently denied that he still carried a torch for her. To prove it, he kept on working, playing clean-cut, sensitive types who reflected none of his own tormented psyche. As further proof, in 1948 he married Barbara Ford, daughter of director John Ford. The "marriage" lasted six weeks. "He fraudulently never intended to be anything more than a husband in form," Barbara told the court. Some nights he didn't come home, and when she questioned him about it he struck her. Several months later, he was again arrested for drunk driving, and shortly thereafter suffered a complete nervous breakdown.

MGM production chief Dore Schary considered Walker his protegé. He urged the desperate young man to get help at the famous Menninger Clinic in Topeka, Kansas.

"I'm not crazy," Walker shouted at him. "I won't go there."

"That is not my diagnosis," Schary pleaded. "You're sick. If you had TB, you'd treat it, wouldn't you? You need help, Bob."

Walker finally decided he was right. He spent nearly a year at the clinic, where doctors diagnosed his ailment as schizophrenia. Though he ran away twice to bars, looking for trouble—and finding it—he was able to come back

The picture of domestic bliss: Walker, wife Jennifer Jones, and sons.

to Hollywood, apparently cured, in 1950. He told interviewers, "I basically felt inadequate, unwanted, and unloved since I was born. Liquor was an outlet, an escape. Now I've been released of my inhibitions, fears and self-doubts that were terrifically painful. I'm happy."

The hardest thing he ever had to do was face his friends and co-workers again. Alfred Hitchcock gave him a chance to re-establish his career and prove his newfound stability, ironically enough, by playing an elegant psychopath in *Strangers on a Train*. The role played beautifully against his boy-next-door image. It was a complex role, with subtle gestures to suggest an underlying homosexuality, and Walker's best performance ever. Hollywood was happy to have him back. He finished Hitchcock's movie, then immediately went to work with Helen Hayes in *My Son John*, Leo McCarey's loathsome Commie condemnation.

"My career has never been more stimulating," he told his friend Ida Lupino while he was filming *My Son John* in 1951. "I think this is going to be my best year."

But by the year's end, closing shots from *Strangers on a Train* would have to be used to complete *My Son John*.

Walker still suffered from bouts of terrible depression. On Sunday, September 28, two weeks short of his thirty-third birthday, he'd been drinking all day, and was getting violent and difficult to control. His sons were staying with him while their mother vacationed with Selznick, but they were visiting a friend that day. The late afternoon sky was black, and a driving rain pounded against the secluded house at 14238 Sunset Boulevard, where the housekeeper struggled in vain to quiet him. His friend Jim "Red" Henaghan, the writer, came over to try to calm him, to no avail. At 6:00 p.m., they called his doctor.

He was in a frenzy by then. "Doc, I feel terrible. Do something quick—please!"

Henaghan and the doctor tried to subdue him, but their efforts only resulted in the panic-stricken Walker flying away from them and out into the downpour. They chased him across the front lawn.

Another doctor arrived. He administered a dose of sodium amytal, a fast-acting hypnotic sedative that was being used experimentally on schizophrenic patients during the early fifties. Walker had been treated often with the drug. Even though it could induce respiratory failure when administered in the presence of another depressant, like alcohol, the doctor saw no alternative. Although 3 grains was the normal dosage, the doctor gave him 7.5 grains, not unusual for such an extreme case, and just half the lethal dose of 15 grains. Sodium amytal, however, is cumulative in the system, and Walker had taken it twenty-five to thirty times. He passed out immediately after the injection. Henaghan covered his exhausted friend with a blanket and turned to leave the room with one of the doctors. The second doctor called them back. Something was wrong . . . very wrong. Walker was semi-comatose and showing signs of respiratory failure.

They took turns giving him artificial respiration but were unable to revive him. One of the physicians told Henaghan, who just couldn't believe what was happening, to call the fire department inhalator squad. He did so and called another specialist, too. The doctors began injections of caffeine and heart stimulants. These too had no effect. Walker was fading fast. "Where the hell is the fire department?" one of the doctors shouted.

Henaghan raced up the secluded cul-de-sac to the main road in search of the ambulance. At last, through the drenching rain, he saw the flashing red light. He jumped and waved his arms and finally flagged them down and guided them to the house. They had passed up the hidden entrance several times. He said a prayer as they burst through the bedroom door.

The medical team labored for 90 minutes. Henaghan's wife joined him in his vigil. The doctors were now huddling in the bathroom.

"How does it look?" Henaghan asked them.

"I'm sorry." The specialist shook his head. "I'm afraid the man is dead. Respiratory failure occurs in one case in ten thousand."

Henaghan screamed and collapsed into a chair by the bed. There lay Bob, hair tousled, his left arm and the sheet caked with blood. Felled by a 1 in 10,000 shot.

So Walker's death was reported by his closest friend—minus the drinking —with the approval of MGM. A certain Hollywood "underground" of people close to him insist that Walker, "Hollywood's Unhappiest Man," was being protected. They believe that he never got over his broken marriage, and that in illness and despair, the idealistic "boy next door" ended his own life.

CARL "ALFALFA" SWITZER
Dogged to Death

It was lunchtime at the busy Hal Roach studio and the commissary rang with the clatter of dishes and the banter of hungry employees. Above the din, Roach could hear singing. Suddenly the talking stopped as people turned to find the source of this impromptu entertainment. In the back of the room sat two young brothers, dressed in coveralls, singing hillbilly songs. They'd taken a big chance sneaking onto the lot, but their guts and ingenuity paid off when Roach, delighted by the younger brother, eight-year-old Carl, added the freckle-faced beanpole to his *Our Gang* series. Roach nicknamed him "Alfalfa," and in 1935, he cast him in his first episode, appropriately titled *Beginner's Luck*. As the love interest of four-year-old Darla Hood, nothing could keep Alfalfa and his cowlick down. Though he was a trained singer, he became known for his screeching, off-key serenades. Tugging at his Adam's apple, he'd start with a squeaking warmup, "Mi Mi Mi Mi." He could sing, emit bubbles, and cross his eyes in amazement, all at once. Little Darla, a prepubescent sweater girl, would listen unflinchingly, even wistfully, as a dreamy-eyed Alfalfa crooned, "I'm in the mood for love, simply because you're near me." In sixty shorts, his clubhouse escapades with Spanky, Buckwheat, and the rest of the gang were a running hit until the series ended, in 1942. After that, Alfalfa was a teenaged has-been—though he refused to fade away from Hollywood.

"He used to haunt the offices of movie producers," said Darla Hood, who retired from the screen at the ripe age of fourteen, "but they would always say, 'Hey Alfalfa, sing off-key for us!' It drove him crazy."

The role dogged Switzer everywhere. He could only land bit parts in a dozen or so films over the next decade, including *The Gas House Kids, Going My*

Way, Pat and Mike (playing a busboy), and *The High and the Mighty* (playing Ensign Kein). To support himself he worked in a variety of odd jobs, most often as a bartender and as a hunting guide. He numbered Roy Rogers and Henry Fonda among his clients.

A starry-eyed Switzer fell in love and eloped with a Kansas heiress in 1954, but the marriage ended after five weeks. His only comment about it came when he told Hedda Hopper, "Bear hunting and marriage don't mix." He was first arrested for drunk and disorderly conduct shortly after that. Frustration was getting the better of him.

Roy Rogers set Carl up in a small role on two episodes of his show in 1956, but hunting remained his prime source of income. He lived in a small apartment in the sprawling San Fernando Valley, in an area that was full of nondescript tract homes that seemed a millennium away from the excitement of Hollywood. Carl was living practically hand to mouth, unhappily anonymous and full of indignation and rage over his stunted career.

"Alfie was always making big talk," a friend said of him. "And when he was drinking, he was always looking for a fight. He went to my house once and threw some punches at me, and I had to order him out with my .22!" The former clown now had a record of barroom brawling. Once, he was even shot and wounded by an unknown sniper outside a bar.

At thirty-two, Alfalfa pinned all his hopes for a comeback on his role of Angus in *The Defiant Ones*. But by the time the film was released, Carl Switzer was dead.

"Open up! Police!" Jack Piott shouted at Bud Stiltz's front door. Flashing a phony badge, the studio photographer and Switzer, his drinking buddy, pushed their way into the house.

"I want that fifty bucks you owe me and I want it now!" the former kid star

"Not so fast," Alfalfa snarled, demonstrating how to disarm a robber. Twenty years later he found himself on the wrong end of a gun once again.

shouted abusively. Alfalfa had borrowed and lost a valuable hunting dog that belonged to Stiltz. He'd paid a $35 reward plus a $15 bar tab to the finder and now insisted that Stiltz repay him. "I'm gonna take fifty dollars worth of damage out of your face!" he'd threatened over the phone. Now he was there to collect.

"I don't owe you any fifty bucks," Stiltz insisted. "You lost the dog, Switzer. You pay."

Stiltz's fiancée, Rita Corrigan (ex-wife of cowboy actor "Crash" Corrigan), and her three children heard the shouting from the next room.

The drunken Switzer picked up a heavy glass-domed clock and brought it crashing down on Stiltz's head, badly cutting his eye. Then he chased Stiltz, who was running for his pistol, into the bedroom. They struggled over the gun as Rita's fourteen-year-old son screamed at the doorway. The gun fired aimlessly, sending the terrified Rita and her children dashing to safety at a neighbor's house.

Switzer disarmed Stiltz and pulled a hunting knife on him. "Stick him! Stick him!" Piott cheered from the sidelines, but Switzer lost his balance and Stiltz sent him hurtling into an open closet, slamming the door after him. Then he grabbed the gun.

Switzer threw open the closet door, his knife drawn. "I'm gonna kill you, you motherfucker." As he charged, Stiltz fired one shot at his stomach and Switzer fell to the floor, mortally wounded.

Stiltz broke down twice during his court testimony. He was convulsed by tears when the jury ruled the shooting "justifiable homicide."

Meanwhile, on after-school television, Alfalfa lived. The *Our Gang* series started appearing as *The Little Rascals* in 1955. To the "television babies" of the fifties, he was then and forever the lovable, freckle-faced Little Rascal.

ALBERT DEKKER
The Distinguished . . .
Extinguished

Albert Dekker, still dapper at sixty-three, and his longtime fiancée, Geraldine Saunders, made a distinguished couple. The cultured actor's marriage to the svelte fashion model was set for less than a month away. On Thursday evening, May 2, 1968, they attended the opening of Zero Mostel's new play, *The Latent Heterosexual*, at Hollywood's Huntington Hartford Theater. "He was in fine spirits," Saunders said in a later interview. "We were going to go out again on Friday, but my numerous phone calls to him that evening went unanswered." Indeed, the next time she would see Dekker he would be neither distinguished nor alive.

When Saturday night passed with still no word from Albert, his fiancée grew increasingly concerned. First thing Sunday morning, she went to his Hollywood apartment at 1731 North Normandie only to find his door covered with notes from friends who were also trying in vain to contact him. She slipped a note of her own under the door. When she returned that evening and found it still in place, she went immediately to the manager.

The manager opened the front door which had been locked but not bolted. Everything seemed to be in order until they tried the bathroom door. It was chained from the inside. They forced it open—and Saunders passed out. "It was so horrible," she said.

The 6 feet 3 inch, 240-pound Dekker was kneeling nude in the bathtub, a dirty hypodermic needle sticking out of each arm. A hangman's noose was around his neck but not tight enough to have strangled him. A scarf was tied over his eyes and something like a horse's bit was in his mouth. Fashioned from a rubber ball and metal wire, the bit had chain "reins" that were tightly tied behind his head. Two leather thongs were stretched between the leather

Albert Dekker, refined and dignified.

belts that girded his neck and chest. A third belt, around his waist, was tied with a rope that stretched to his ankles, where it had been tied in some kind of lumber hitch. The end of the rope, which continued up his side, wrapped around his wrist several times and was held in Dekker's hand. Both wrists were clasped by a set of handcuffs. Written in lipstick, above two hypodermic punctures on his right buttock, was the word "whip" and drawings of the sun. Sun rays had also been drawn around his nipples. "Make me suck" was written on his thorax and "slave" and "cocksucker" on his chest. On his lower abdomen was drawn a vagina. He had apparently been dead since Friday and his awkward position had colored his lower body a deep blood purple. "This one has everything but a vampire bite," remarked a deputy coroner.

During the brief investigation, detectives noted that there were no signs of forced entry or a struggle. They labeled the death "indicated suicide . . . quite an unusual case." Finding no convincing evidence for suicide, the coroner rejected that theory. His final report said "accidental death, not a suicide."

"Suicide? I don't believe it!" cried veteran actor George Sanders.

Another of Dekker's respected colleagues, Paul Lukas, emphatically defended his friend. "Al never would have left the world in such a shambles. He was a man of culture and breeding." Dekker had been a happy man. He was a well-known intellectual and student of classical literature, a poet, and a sculptor. Lukas was sure that he was murdered. It was a complete, grotesque, horrible puzzle to his friends.

As a young graduate of Bowdoin College in Maine, Dekker intended to become a psychologist or psychiatrist. But a persistent alumnus who had seen Dekker in several school productions urged him to pursue a career in the theater. He wrote a letter of introduction for him to take to one of the most formidable actors on the stage, Alfred Lunt. "Al has a fine mind," Lunt later said of the man who became a life-long friend, "and a soul in which unkindness is wholly absent." In 1927, Dekker made his impressive stage debut opposite Lunt, playing four varied character roles. By the time he made his film debut a decade later, he was a well-established Broadway star.

The sandy-haired, blue-eyed Dekker excelled in character roles, especially multidimensional villains. He appeared in more than 100 films, among them *Gentleman's Agreement, Two Years Before the Mast, East of Eden, Suddenly Last Summer, Beau Geste, Strange Cargo,* and *The Man in the Iron Mask.* He played the title role of the bald, mad scientist who reduces five humans to doll size in *Dr. Cyclops.* He often said that he found it much more challenging to play a heavy than a hero. "Who wants to be America's sweetheart?" But in private life, he seemed like the perfect good guy—a family man and a champion of liberal causes. He married New York actress Esther Guernini in 1929, and they had two sons and a daughter. Dekker was long active in Democratic politics, and won a California State Assembly seat by a landslide in 1944. He was known as an ardent supporter of unwed and indigent mothers' rights. He introduced a bill against capital punishment, but it died in committee, with some people opposing it because it would take the excitement out of a murder trial. He served a two-year term, then went back to his first love, acting.

Albert Dekker as an American spy posing as a photographer in Once Upon a Honeymoon *(1942).*

In the early fifties, Dekker was a triumph on British television, and on Broadway in the weighty *Death of a Salesman.* He was so convincing in the role of Willy Loman that his nine-year-old son raced backstage after the suicide scene to make sure his father was still alive. Dekker won a Tony for his portrayal of the Duke of Norfolk in *A Man for All Seasons,* and got rave reviews in New York opposite Spencer Tracy in *Conflict* and in the role of the worn matinee idol in *Grand Hotel.* Dekker loved the theater. "New York is a small town. Everyone on the street stops an actor to say hello when he's in a current show."

Then suddenly, his charmed life came crashing down, victim of the mid-fifties, Senator Joseph McCarthy-inspired maelstrom. Dekker watched the witch hunt for communists, and couldn't remain silent. When he publicly denounced the red-baiting McCarthy, calling him "insane," he began receiving death threats. Though he'd served in the California legislature, his political views were suddenly suspect. He was on the blacklist. He couldn't work as an actor for the next nineteen years. "All I could do was lecture at colleges and women's clubs."

During that bleak time, his sixteen-year-old son, Jan, died of an accidental but self-inflicted gunshot wound. "He had been experimenting for over a year on a rifle silencer," the grieving Dekker said in an attempt to explain.

Dekker was one of Hollywood's blacklist victims who managed to hang in until the nation's political climate about-faced in the late sixties, and yesterday's "reds" became heroes. In April of 1968, just a month before his death, he completed a role in Sam Peckinpah's *The Wild Bunch.* Peckinpah, William Holden, Ernest Borgnine, and Robert Ryan were still on location in Mexico when they got word about Dekker. They all agreed that suicide was out of the question. He was the life of the set, they said. He'd entertained them day and night with "his endless dialects and stories."

Technically, the details of Dekker's horrendous finish began to look more and more like the work of an assassin. "The-most-puzzling-sentence-ever-in-an-obituary"—from UPI—"The police said he had been found bound and handcuffed . . . and they listed the death as a suicide," wrote one New York columnist. Another obvious question was, if Dekker had been alone, how could he have legibly written on his own backside? The police confirmed that he'd been injected with a drug, but after three days it was unidentifiable. Geraldine believed that Albert could have been bound and choked only if he was unconscious; after all, he was a very large, healthy man, quite capable of defending himself against an attacker.

The puzzle had one more potentially significant clue. "Al was very trusting. He flew home from Mexico with his pay, thirty thousand dollars," Geraldine revealed. "We were about to close a deal on a house in the Encino Hills. Al was staying alone at the Normandie Street apartment until our house went through escrow. He'd only lived there a week." Also in the apartment was $40,000 from two television roles. Dekker was using straight cash as a bargaining leverage for the house. "When he died," his fiancée continued, "the whole seventy thousand dollars was missing. I think it was someone he knew and let into the apartment."

Also missing were some expensive camera equipment and his tape recorder, which he'd been using to prepare for a role he'd been offered in *Fiddler on the Roof.* The police toyed with a theory that Dekker was a closet homosexual who practiced his eccentricities very discreetly with anonymous male prostitutes, and that this time, something had gone wrong and the frightened partner had quietly let himself out. They made inquiries, but Dekker had no reputation among male hustlers. Nor did any of his friends consider him the least bit "kinky." However, Los Angeles County Coroner Thomas Noguchi had a theory of his own: autoerotic asphyxia, a surprisingly prevalent sexual practice in which orgasm is achieved by chancing death. Noguchi explained that during the solitary experience, the victim is "almost always handcuffed . . . sometimes blindfolded . . . and some don transvestite clothing." The rope is rigged as a pulley that the participant can control, but things can go wrong —that's the risk. But no one could ever prove Noguchi's theory. It's entirely possible that the murderer "arranged" the whole bizarre tableau. In reflecting on the puzzle and all of its pieces, one detective admitted to Saunders that "Dekker was slickered." But she couldn't get the police to reverse the "accident" decision.

The case is closed to further inquiry. The death of the scholarly Albert Dekker remains a frustrating, confounding mystery.

ALDOUS HUXLEY
No Regrets

"Hopelessly uncivilized," Aldous Huxley pronounced on his first visit to the garish metropolis where one could become immortal by play-acting on celluloid. It was 1926 and Clara Bow was the reigning queen, the Charleston the theme song. Huxley was thirty-two, and already had written three scathing books satirizing England's lost generation. Was it accidental that in the years following his trip to Hollywood he turned his visions to the mystical and the expansion of the mind? At a time when most British intellectuals turned toward politics, he became the cosmic problem solver. "I should like to go on forever learning," he said, and he traveled the world in search of knowledge, but in 1937, the writer and his wife, Maria, returned to the Hollywood Hills —this time to stay. He passed such vacuous faces on escalators and streets, he said, that at first he was appalled, but he quickly came to love the "cheap, fantastic, glimmering lifestyle. . . ."

"Then too," he reflected on his new land, "the events of the place and its people are new, surging, not stifled nor quite yet fixed forever in certainties."

Huxley was a startling figure even in this town of bankable faces and figures. He was tall and reedy, with a head always bent forward in rumination, and eyes cast in a perpetually peculiar gaze, the result of a childhood illness that nearly blinded him. The eye disease also crushed his hopes of becoming a scientist, but he was still fascinated with experimentation. All of Huxley's penchants—automatic writing (writing with eyes closed, guided by forces from beyond), hypnosis, parapsychology, magnetic passes, and miracle potions to make life eternal—intertwined perfectly with the palm trees and movie studios. He didn't "need" success in Hollywood the way F. Scott Fitzgerald did, but he succeeded.

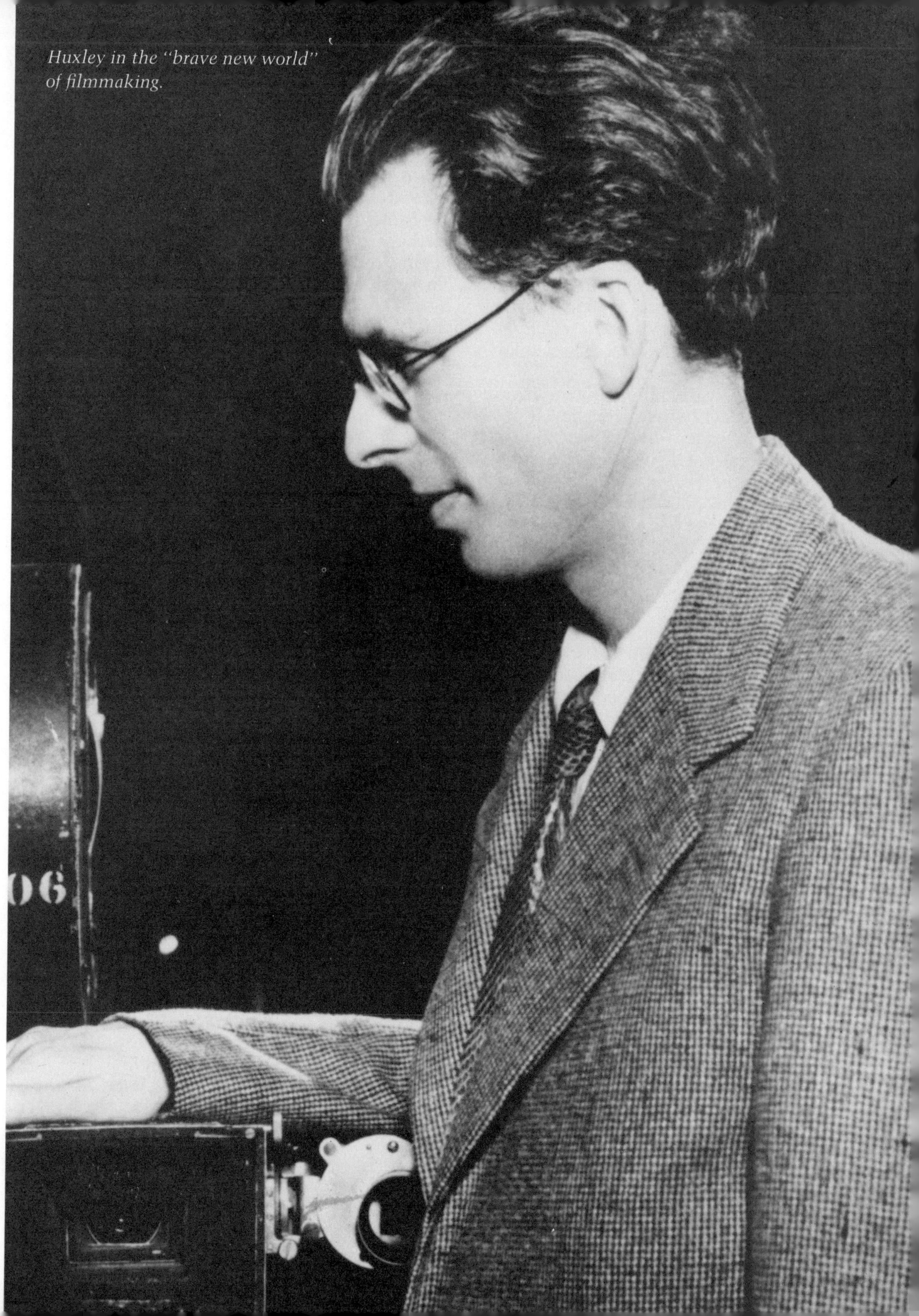

Huxley in the "brave new world" of filmmaking.

The local intelligentsia welcomed him. "His knowledge and memory were awe-inspiring," said Salka Viertel, an eastern European writer who was known as "the Garbo specialist" at MGM. Her Santa Monica home, then a significant distance from "the city," became a gathering place for a coterie of European intellectuals, artists and writers seeking refuge from their turmoil-ridden homelands—or from the studios. These two authors had many friends in common: Igor Stravinsky, Upton Sinclair, Garbo, Bertrand Russell, Anita Loos. Huxley's social circle also included Charlie Chaplin and his wife Paulette Goddard, astronomer Edwin Hubble, and the English psychologist Dr. Humphrey Osmond.

"Nearly all of Huxley's best work was done in the latter, American half of his life," was the appraisal of his friend Christopher Isherwood, a fellow British writer turned Angeleno, an opinion not shared by all critics. Anyway, the local color inspired him. First he produced *After Many a Summer Dies the Swan* (1939), a novel about science and life-prolonging experiments as viewed from a Southern California castle, owned by an aging New World baron whose mistress was a goggling starlet with an ice cream fountain in her boudoir. The characters bore a most unflattering resemblance to William Randolph Hearst and Marion Davies.

That same year, he completed his first screenplay, an adaptation of *Pride and Prejudice* that became the MGM classic starring Laurence Olivier and Greer Garson. Unlike a number of other novelists, he adapted readily to the new medium. He also adapted *Jane Eyre* for the 20th Century–Fox film that starred Orson Welles and Joan Fontaine. However, screenplays remained only a sideline between novels for Huxley, and the bulk of his scripts were never produced. Two originals that he wrote with Isherwood, a Disney adaptation of *Alice in Wonderland*, a drama of the life of Gandhi, and a screen version of *Brave New World* never left the printed page, the last because he couldn't obtain the rights to his own book. (While he was writing the script, he asked Anita Loos, "What will the Hays Office say about babies in bottles?") But Huxley didn't take it personally. He seemed to have an innate understanding of the machinations of Hollywood and its empty promises. Instead he used his experiences as grist for novels. He wrote *Ape and Essence*, his 1948 novel, partially in screenplay form, describing the Hollywood of 2013 through a screenplay rescued on its way to the incinerator. When one of the characters asks for a raise, the boss tells him, "Bob, in this studio, at this time, not even Jesus Christ Himself could get a raise." Huxley swore that he actually overheard that bit of dialogue at Universal Studios during the shooting of *A Woman's Vengeance*, based on his short story "The Giocanda Smile."

Huxley, man of the world, tried a new kind of "trip" in 1953. He wanted "to know and constantly be in a state of love," and to achieve this open state, he began experimenting with LSD, mescalin, and psilocybin. He and Dr. Osmond, who was at the forefront of experimentation with hallucinogens, coined the word "psychedelic" to describe their experiences. Huxley tried psychedelics ten or twelve times in the next 10 years, and always preceded the experience with extensive preparation and wrote a detailed follow-up. A month after his first venture with mescalin, he wrote a small book about it

The futuristic British author made Hollywood his home, where, with a small group of artists and intellectuals, he pursued spiritual fulfillment . . . mystically and chemically.

called *The Doors of Perception*. Jim Morrison abbreviated the title for his rock band, The Doors. Huxley considered psychedelics, along with the splitting of the atom and manipulation of genetic structure, as the three major scientific breakthroughs of the twentieth century. Often, however, he felt that the sheer beauty of nature and life was enough to give him an ecstatic high without psychedelics.

"Live here and now. Do not be a slave of emotional memories of the past that act only as barriers. Be aware of now! Let go! No regrets—no looking back," he whispered tenderly to Maria when all of his transcendental aware-ness could not rid her of cancer. The reflections came from the *Tibetan Book of the Dead*. Maria was dying, and nothing could be done to save her. Huxley, however, believed in "going forward," and he needed a woman's companionship and strength, so a year after Maria's death in 1955, he proposed to Laura Archera, who'd been a close friend of both Huxleys for more than a decade. She was a former concert violinist turned film editor, thirty-five years old to Huxley's fifty-five, and had never been married before. From their first meeting, the soft-spoken giant of a man had appealed to Laura, and she now accepted his proposal without hesitation. They shared a deep and abiding love. "One never loves enough. How can I love you more?" he told her.

Life was good, but Huxley, nearly thirty years after *Brave New World*'s prediction of test tube babies as the supreme triumph of science over nature, now foresaw other ways for science and politics to render the future a living hell. On the one hand, he predicted that in the future there'd be a birth control pill, and he suggested harnessing energy from the sun. On the other, he envisioned a world where two-thirds of the people "would be caught up in a population explosion and extreme poverty and social unrest, with acute danger of Communist control. The other one-third, with highly developed science, technology, and military oriented society, would have citizens descending into steel dungeons of civil defense." And of the bomb, the committed pacifist feared that "Never have so many been at the mercy of so few."

The Huxleys themselves were at the mercy of a devastating disaster in 1961, when a fire raged through the hills of Hollywood. Aldous managed to save his manuscript of *Island*, his novel in progress, and Laura rescued her precious Guarneri violin, but the house and the rest of their possessions were completely destroyed. Huxley's priceless library, which contained many original printings, and out-of-print works as well as all of his original manuscripts, went up in smoke. *Time* magazine painted a poignant picture of the great writer weeping by the roadside as he watched his life go up in flames: "Flames licked through dry grasses and gutted twenty-four luxury homes in Hollywood Hills. Destroyed were author Aldous Huxley's two-story house, his manuscripts, and mementoes of a lifetime. While firemen restrained the nearly blind British author from running into the blaze, Huxley wept like a child."

"As an old hand at fiction," Huxley responded in a letter, "may I congratulate the write-up artist who penned the account of my actions on the night my house was burned down. . . ."

He and Laura were safe. Anything else he could deal with . . . almost anything.

Two years later, a malignancy for which Huxley had previously undergone surgery reappeared. Laura stood by helplessly as her husband grew pale and weak that summer, a ghostly aura overtaking his peaceful demeanor. At sixty-nine, he was in pain, but not aware that he was dying of throat cancer. He intended to overcome this, too. He clung to his motto—he was still learning. Too feeble to write, at times even to speak, he learned to dictate with a tape recorder to finish his now classic essay, "Shakespeare and Religion." It was a long, slow process. Huxley, tiring easily and constantly interrupted by severe coughing fits, told Laura, ". . . but, I can see how one can do this." Through self-hypnosis, he reduced the use of almost all the prescribed pain-killing drugs, training himself to move away from the pain by seeing, in his mind's eye, a white dot on a black background.

Huxley, appalled by his weakness and the length of time it would take to be normal again, worried about being an imposition on those around him. Friends and family read him letters, books, and news reports, and the devoted Laura encouraged him to tape his thoughts, to bring forth everything he was inwardly experiencing. He spent a good deal of time just looking at things, appreciating the beauty of life around him. Two days before he died, Laura held a salmon-pink rose before him for a long, long while.

"Is it enough?" she asked him.

"It is never enough," he sighed.

It was not until the day he died that Huxley realized he would never recover. That day, November 22, 1963, his pain increased. He had needed three injections to sleep during the night and by 9 a.m., he was extremely restless. No position would relieve him. It was the final struggle of a healthy spirit trapped inside a decaying body. To ease his labored breathing, the doctor dilated his bronchial tubes intravenously. A delivery boy brought in oxygen tanks. "Did you hear about the President?" the young emissary asked, but Laura silenced him with a look. She knew she was losing Aldous. Neither she nor Huxley knew that John Kennedy also lay dying in a Dallas hospital. Her only concern now was her husband. He motioned to her to get a dollar from his pants to tip the boy.

At 10 a.m., asking for a large pad of paper, Aldous arduously began to write, "If I go . . ." This was his first outward indication that he knew death hovered near. He regarded dying, when one had to face it, as the great adventure of life, believing the soul's future was influenced by one's feeling at the moment of death. "What are you feeling?" Laura whispered.

"At this point, there is so little to share," he answered with difficulty. He wrote another note. He wanted 100 mms of LSD, intramuscularly. Believing that one should both live and die nobly, he was preparing for a noble departure, just like his characters in *Island*.

Laura went to tell the doctor and his staff what she was about to do. They were all staring at the television, stupefied. The President was dead. Laura, momentarily jolted, pushed it from her mind. There would be time enough later. Only Aldous was important now.

The first injection seemed to quiet the great thinker, to relieve him. She gave him another an hour later. "You are light and free. You let go easily, forward and up. You are going toward the light . . . to a greater love." Placing her mouth just inches from Aldous's ear, Laura held tightly to his hand. Much as he had for Maria 8 years earlier, Laura now guided him, helping him to leave with no regrets. At 3:15, she asked if he could hear her and he squeezed her hand. She asked again at 4:00 and got no response. His breathing grew less and less, and finally, at 5:15, was no more . . . a peaceful and dignified passing, worthy of this great and gentle man.

Shortly before he died, someone asked Huxley what advice he might have to bequeath to the world. "It is a little embarrassing," he replied, "that after forty-five years of research and study, the best advice I can give to people is to be a little kinder to each other."

ERNIE KOVACS
Death in the Fast Lane

Fade in: Camera follows the long handle of an axe that is deeply embedded in a typewriter. Lying around it are several crumpled papers and an empty bottle of booze. Over this, in typewriter face, come the words: "Written and Produced by Ernie Kovacs." Kovacs stood against a wall, facing a firing squad, with the Haydn String Quartet playing in the background. His final request was to smoke a cigar. The aroma seduced the soldiers, who dropped their guns and gathered round to inhale more deeply, as the frustrated Captain looked on.

Then there was the cannibal chief who was lighting a fire underneath a steaming cauldron of stew, with Ernie as the main ingredient. The moustachioed madcap Hungarian signaled and waved until the chief returned to light Ernie's cigar, after which he sat back and puffed contentedly.

Or how about the one where Ernie was walking through a museum, and offered a Dutch Masters to a statue of Napoleon. The Emperor refused it the first time, then accepted when Ernie persisted; however, when he removed his hand from his vest to take it, his royal pants fell down.

Ernie Kovacs loved cigars. Dutch Masters, the original sponsor of his fifties television series, helped make him a rich man. At the height of his career he was spending $13,000 a year on Havana cigars, sleeping about 3 hours a night, and rejuvenating with steam baths and twenty cigars a day. "This is the only life I've got and I want to live it the way I like. If I go, I want it to be my way," he told his friends. And so he did—a cigar was his demise.

In the fifties, Kovacs was the proverbial kid in a candy store who blazed a revolutionary trail through the "Golden Era" of television. He was one of the first in the infant medium to experiment with new camera and sound techniques, working strictly by instinct, and without a live audience to gauge his efforts. He thrived on taking chances. He thought nothing of defying convention by spending so much on props that he couldn't afford a band. Pure Kovacs

"The Moustache."

meant performing the *1812 Overture* slamming drawers and snapping celery stalks as percussion instruments. Or he could do a show with no dialogue at all. What could be more effective when strolling by a statue of *The Thinker*, and hearing it mumble "Hmmm, hmmm," than Kovacs's masterful double take? Or his frozen bewilderment at scratching a spot on a seascape and seeing the water drain out to leave an empty beach? Another classic Kovacs is the young woman comfortably settled in her bubble bath, suddenly startled as a parade of people and animals emerge one by one from the tub.

Kovacs created many equally memorable characters like Percy Dovetonsils, the lisping poet; Pierre Ragout, the French storyteller (whose version of *Snow White* has her telling the wicked queen's guards, "Je wasn't born yesterday."); Wolfgang Sauerbraten, the Bavarian disc jockey; or Irving Wong, the Chinese songwriter. He could be cynical and irreverent as well, with children often being the target of his humor. As Uncle Buddy, he encouraged his two irritating wards to walk on the railing of the Staten Island ferry . . . "Uncle Buddy used to wear a blindfold and then he would turn around three times real quick." Miklos Molman, his drunken Hungarian chef, would torment children in the peanut gallery, cracking his whip and constantly guzzling booze. When upstaged by a loud puppet, Molman cut its strings, sweeping it into the garbage. Nothing was sacred. No one else was doing "black comedy" on television in the early fifties.

Despite his Uncle Buddy impersonation, Ernie loved children, especially his own. He was devastated when his ex-wife, Bette, kidnapped their two daughters from his custody in July 1953. Detectives narrowed the search to Florida and each weekend for two years, Kovacs and his father relentlessly searched the bayous for them. During this time, Ernie developed severe colitis and often would find himself sitting in pools of blood. For two Christmases, he bought his girls gifts, only to be bitterly disappointed. Finally in June of 1955, he found them in a one-room shack behind a restaurant where Bette worked as a waitress. The girls hadn't even been taught how to brush their teeth, let alone sent to school. Kovacs "kidnapped them back" and got no further trouble from Bette, although, at the time of his death, there was still a warrant out in Florida for his "crime." The search had consumed him, and he now found that he owed $400,000 in back taxes to the government and over $50,000 to private detectives. Poker, which he played incessantly and badly, had doubled his debts. The only light during those dark times shone from Edie Adams, the sexy blonde comedienne known as Daisy Mae on Broadway, now a regular on his show. She became his wife in 1955 and was a calming force in his chaotic life. By 1962, with help from a business manager, the Kovacses were making headway into their enormous debts.

About that time, Ernie was negotiating a five-picture deal with Alec Guiness, with whom he'd become good friends while filming *Our Man in Havana*. The picture biz welcomed Ernie. He became very close to Jack Lemmon and director Richard Quine while making his first film, *Operation Mad Ball*. Quine went on to direct Kovacs in three more films, *Bell, Book and Candle*, *It Happened to Jane*, and *Strangers When We Meet*.

He was still in demand in television, as well. Dutch Masters was so contin-

Ernie hard at work at Columbia Studios.

uously overwhelmed with viewer response that in 1962 they obtained permission to rerun the silent commercials Kovacs had made a decade before. He had also won a Cleo, advertising's Oscar, for turning on the firing squads, the Napoleons, et al., to Dutch Masters' product.

The checks were pouring in, as Colgate Palmolive anted up for development of a series of silent commercials for them. Ernie was also headed to Broadway, where he was scheduled to direct a drama in February and a musical comedy in the fall. With offers from every medium, "The Moustache" had cut his debts in half while still living the flamboyant Coldwater Canyon style of Beverly Hills.

January 13, 1962, started as a typical day in his life. He was up at 6:00 a.m. to get to Griffith Park to begin a day's shooting on *A Pony for Chris,* a television pilot in which he played a snake-oil salesman, opposite his silent Indian partner, Buster Keaton. Ernie tooled across town in his vintage white Rolls-Royce, puffing on a beloved Havana, his mind racing ahead to other projects, future meetings, new routines.

At 6:30 p.m., he finally left the set. The next stop was ABC Studios on Prospect Avenue, where he'd just finished writing, directing, and taping his seventh special for Dutch Masters. He was doing the editing at night, despite warnings from his friends to slow down his pace. That night, anxious to complete the musical transitions between the comedy segments, he worked for three hours.

At 10:00 p.m., Ernie stopped in PJ's for a quick drink with a friend. "See you . . . maybe I'll check back later for a nightcap," he said as he left. Then he joined Edie at director Billy Wilder's home in Brentwood, for a shower honoring Ruth and Milton Berle's newly adopted son. Most of Ernie's friends and poker pals were there: Jack Lemmon, Dick Quine, Frank Sinatra, Joey Bishop, Dean and Jeanne Martin, Yves Montand, Lucille Ball and her new husband, Gary Morton, the Kirk Douglases. Kovacs looked fatigued. Edie wasn't the only one to notice it. "Stop worrying . . . I'll live forever," he told Jeanne Martin. He went on laughing, joking, and telling stories.

The gentlemen adjourned to play cards while the ladies opened the shower gifts. The party broke up at about 1:00, but Ernie was still going strong. He planned to stop for one more drink at PJ's before he went home to bed. "Want a ride?" he asked Yves Montand, but Montand was riding back with the Berles.

It was a typically misty Los Angeles winter night. A fine rain had begun to fall, and the winding roads were slippery. Ernie, whose driving was about as bad as his poker game, asked Edie to switch cars with him, so that he could have her more maneuverable compact, a white Corvair station wagon. She left in the Rolls moments before Ernie, steering along the same 10-minute route through the Los Angeles Country Club grounds to Santa Monica Boulevard.

As he headed east on Santa Monica, Kovacs reached into his breast pocket for a Havana. In his other hand, he tried to light a kitchen match by flicking it against his thumbnail. He took his eyes off the road, just momentarily, while doing 50 mph. Suddenly, his tires caught on the raised concrete lane dividers. Instinctively, he jammed on the brakes, but too hard. His car skidded to the right. Still clenching his cigar, Ernie frantically steered left, but the compact smashed broadside into a power pole. Thrown half out of the wreckage, his skull fractured, his ribs crushed, his aorta ruptured, he died within seconds. The fatal distraction, his unlit cigar, lay on the ground just beyond the reach of his outstretched arm.

Edie could not bear to see him at the morgue, so Jack Lemmon identified the body for her. On the morning of the funeral, she asked another favor. She wanted Ernie to be buried with his Havanas but couldn't do it herself.

". . . But when I went down with the bloody cigars," Lemmon explained, "it was so awful and bizarre. There he was, how they had dressed him all up, and this pimply-faced kid is there saying, 'We're terribly proud of the job we've done. . . .' Now I go to put the cigars in, but I can't open the pocket. He's got it pulled in the back and everything else, and I'm trying to get the cigars in the pocket and I'm thinking, Holy Jesus, and now they're flaking all over the place . . . and then I started to laugh because what else can you do?" No one would have laughed harder than Ernie.

DOROTHY DANDRIDGE
Living in Black and White

The midnight show was really cooking. Outside, a gentle rain cooled the Sunset Strip, but inside the Cafe Gala, the seductive singer leaning against the grand piano was raising temperatures. Eyes closed, lips parted, Dorothy Dandridge tantalized the intimate audience in the darkened room with "Moanin' in the Mornin'." Her body shook like sizzling bacon when she sang "I'm Gonna Be a Bad Girl."

This was a comeback of sorts for the twenty-eight-year-old performer, on the heels of the breakup of her marriage to Harold Nicholas, half of the famous dancing Nicholas Brothers. Dorothy had been performing since the age of four, when she toured with her sister Vivian as "The Wonderful Children" in a dance and tumbling act. With their mother, actress Ruby Dandridge, as manager, the girls performed through the 1930s in a trio (with Etta Jones), called The Dandridge Sisters. They sang with big bands, too, frequently with The Jimmy Lunceford Band, at fashionable spots like New York's Cotton Club, where Dorothy met Harold one night when he was sharing the bill. She made her film debut at only fourteen in the Marx Brothers' classic, *A Day at the Races* (1937), and continued appearing in small roles including a bit in *Since You Went Away,* and a song in *Hit Parade of 1943.* She and Harold appeared together in the "Chattanooga Choo Choo" number in *Sun Valley Serenade,* after which she retired to become Mrs. Harold Nicholas.

Dorothy had been held on a tight rein during her blossoming teen years by a strict "nanny" who once physically probed the frightened girl after a date, to make sure her virginity was intact. This gruesome episode, combined with the woman's tales of the evils of sex, made Dorothy frigid. Time and time again she denied Nicholas, who had been quite the ladies' man before his marriage. They agreed that he could resume his old habits discreetly to satisfy

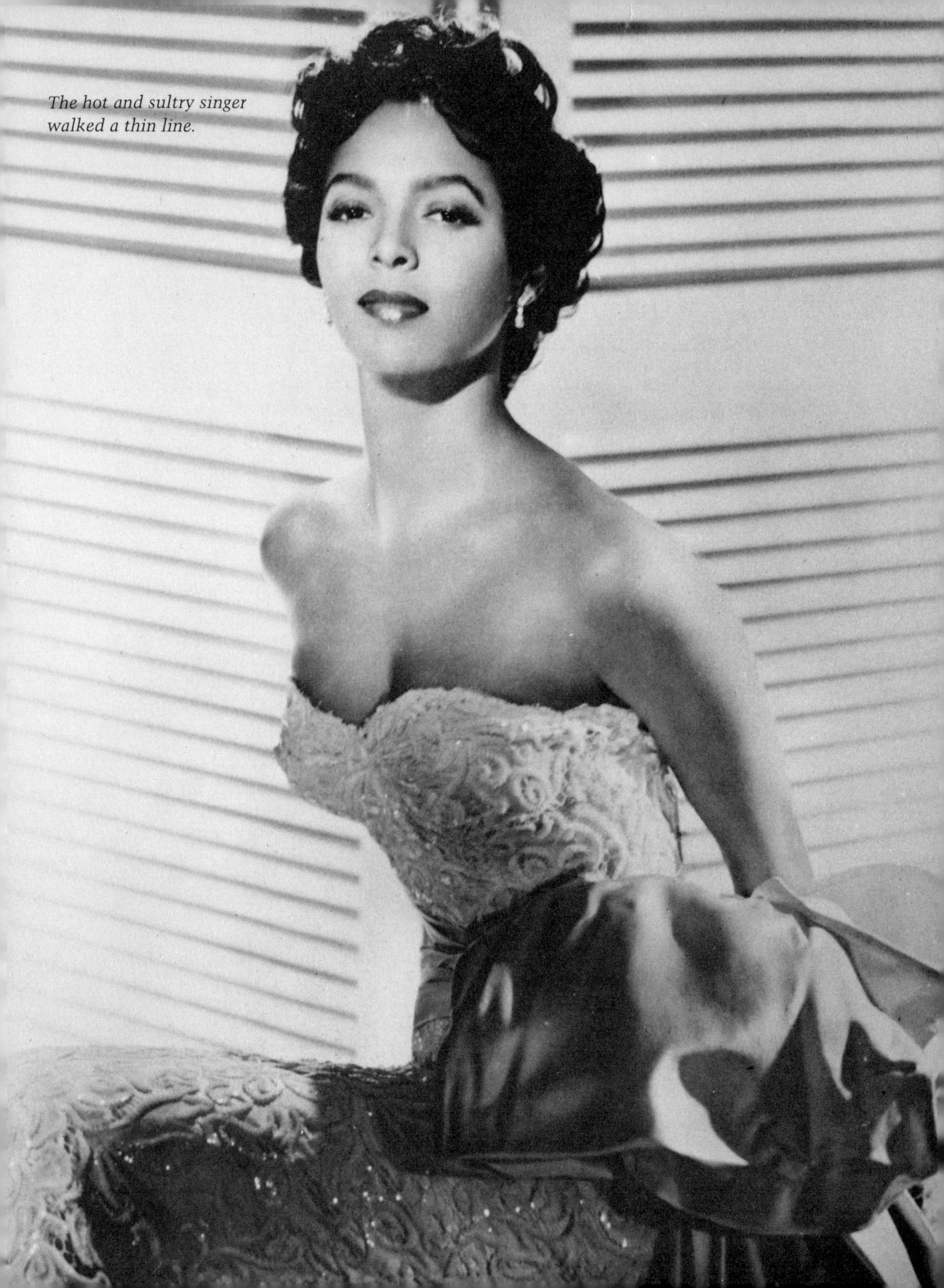

The hot and sultry singer walked a thin line.

his manly needs. When Dorothy became pregnant, she used it as an excuse to avoid sex altogether. Nicholas would sometimes storm out of their Los Angeles apartment, staying away all night. On one such night, alone, Dorothy went into labor. She was so sure her husband would return that she refused to go to the hospital without him. Instead, she delayed the delivery, fighting labor until the pain became overwhelming. When he had not returned by morning, she surrendered and asked a neighbor to drive her to the hospital, where she gave birth to a daughter, Harolyn.

As her marriage disintegrated, Dorothy threw herself into the rearing of her child, a child her husband would not even hold. She stubbornly refused to listen to her mother and friends when they noticed the first signs of abnormal development. Eventually, it became too obvious for even Dorothy to ignore. She took Harolyn to the finest specialists, the best hospitals, the most prestigious clinics, but the diagnosis was always the same—irreparable brain damage. An anguished Dandridge would punish herself for the rest of her life, convinced that by delaying delivery she had caused the damage.*

Harold realized that life with Dorothy and a retarded child was not for him. He wrote her from Paris to say that he would not be coming back.

With her private life in a shambles, Dorothy decided to revitalize her career. She enrolled in a drama school, sharing a class with another struggling but soon to be realized actress, Marilyn Monroe. Marilyn left the class when Columbia dropped her option and shortly thereafter posed nude for a calendar for a much-needed $50 in cash.

Dorothy hooked up with Earl Mills, a sharp manager who recognized her talent and beauty and understood her physical inhibitions. He introduced her to Phil Moore, or rather, reintroduced her. Moore had worked with Dorothy years earlier, when she was still part of The Dandridge Sisters, and had gone on to win fame as Lena Horne's coach. He began working closely with her, encouraging her to let go, building her confidence. "I was afraid to give strangers sexy looks," Dorothy said later in a personal interview, but it was more than that. She was afraid of her sexuality, afraid to be a woman; Moore changed all that. As her coach, accompanist, and her gentle lover, Moore lit the fires of sensuality in her. Packed into a tight gold lamé or befringed strapless gown, Dorothy was 112 pounds of dynamite. Divorced from Nicholas in 1951, Dorothy Dandridge made it back, alone.

Desi Arnaz hired Dorothy to sing with his band at the plush Mocambo, where within a year, she was the headliner. Although in two of the three films she made that year she played a tawny-skinned, scantily clad, jungle princess, MGM was still paying close attention to her real talents. They noted her club successes in New York, San Francisco, Las Vegas, and South America and watched as she crossed a very difficult line—the color line. She was the first Negro to play the Waldorf-Astoria's Empire Room, and her appearances in other segregated clubs helped open the door to desegregation across the country. Only Nat "King" Cole and Lena Horne achieved such popularity with white audiences. MGM, in an enlightened move, cast her in a straight story

*Though this is a possibility, it is not necessarily the reason her daughter was retarded.

about Negroes called *Bright Road* (1953), her second film opposite handsome Harry Belafonte, an equally light Negro. Her biggest success, however, came when they were paired for a third time.

When Dorothy heard that the part of Carmen Jones was up for grabs, she went after it with a vengeance. Director Otto Preminger doubted her believability as the heartless temptress from Bizet's opera *Carmen*, and wanted her instead for the "goody role" of Cindy Lou. She devised a plan to change his mind. Dressed in a messy black wig, an off-the-shoulder blouse, black satin skirt slit thigh high, and high-heeled pumps, Dorothy marched into Preminger's office. Slinking across the room toward him, she put her foot on the edge of his chair and proceeded to stare down the dome-headed Preminger, himself known for outspoken, outrageous behavior. Dorothy got the role.

Before filming started, Dandridge flew to Brazil to fill a contractual engagement. While there, she fell in love with a handsome millionaire. The mixed couple was able to move among high society with greater ease than Dorothy had ever experienced in the United States. She was willing to give up her career, forget *Carmen Jones*, and remain in Brazil as his wife. Her lover did make a proposal, but it was not what Dorothy had dreamed of. It seems he was already married, but he wanted her to be his mistress. Devastated, Dandridge, for the first time in her life, turned to pills to alleviate her pain. She returned to Los Angeles drained and depressed, but Earl Mills helped her pick up the pieces and advised her to see a therapist.

When shooting began, Dorothy became terrified of the responsibility of carrying the picture. The usually brusque Preminger used a gentle hand to guide her over the difficulties. As was her pattern, she willingly placed herself at his command, as her director and her lover.

Since she had no opera training, her singing was dubbed by Marilyn Horne, but the fiery, seductive performance was pure Dorothy. As Carmen, Dandridge commanded attention. She became the first black woman to grace the cover of *Life* magazine which called her "the most beautiful singer since Lena Horne," and featured a story on her role in the all-Negro version of the opera. More important to Dorothy was the story *Ebony*, the "black *Life*," did, naming her as "a credit to her race." The accolades poured in, and even greater triumph awaited, when, in the spring, Dorothy became the first Negro nominated for the "Best Actress" Oscar. Rapidly becoming an international celebrity, Dorothy had a hectic, nonstop career worthy of her full-fledged stardom, but the film offers she'd hoped would come did not materialize. Hollywood didn't know what to do with a black love-goddess, even though the Association of Hollywood Photographers voted her one of the five most beautiful women in the world. Producers wanted her for the lead in *Lady Sings the Blues*, the story of blues queen Billie Holiday, but they were unable to find financial backing. (The project did not come to life for 15 years, until 1971, with Diana Ross in the title role.) In *Island in the Sun* (1957), she set another precedent—the first interracial romance ever filmed by a major studio. However, because miscegenation was still taboo on the Hollywood screen, producers were forced to compromise the dialogue, to the extent that rather than having John Justin say "I love you" to Dorothy, he could only say, "You know how I feel." Although she felt she was making progress for her race, Dorothy was disappointed at its flagging pace. Between films, she continued to wow audiences of all races with her sexy, sassy style. Oxford University declared her their 1956 May Queen, while her infectious good humor made her the toast of London's cafe society. Her next starring role came from an old friend and lover.

One week before shooting was to begin on Otto Preminger's *Porgy and Bess* (1959), his second all-Negro production, most of the sets were destroyed in a mysterious fire, sparked, no doubt, by the increasing racial tensions brewing in the country. The start was delayed eight weeks, but Dorothy and Sidney Poitier scored critical success in the title roles, and Dandridge, who described Bess as "kind of a loose woman . . . in tight clothes," was awarded a Golden Globe for Best Actress. That same year, she starred in *Tamango*, in which her intimate scenes with Caucasian Kurt Jurgens were filmed twice, the more modified version for release in the States.

Between the national premiere of *Porgy and Bess* in New York and the world premiere in London, Dandridge married for a second time. Jack Dennison was a white businessman in search of capital. His first move as Dorothy's husband was to fire the ever-faithful Earl Mills. He then proceeded to misman age Dorothy's career while making terrible investments with her money, in cluding an unsuccessful restaurant on the Sunset Strip with Sammy Davis, Jr. as his partner. As the fortune she had amassed dwindled in her husband's greedy, incompetent hands, Dandridge began drinking heavily in private and again turned to pills. Despite warnings from family and friends, her obstinacy was her downfall once more, when she invested all that was left in an oil well deal. She and several other celebrities lost almost everything in the swindle. Dorothy awoke one morning to find Dennison gone and Harolyn delivered to her doorstep by the private institution where Dandridge could no longer pay the bills. Broke and alone, forced to place her often violent daughter in Ca marillo State Hospital, she declared bankruptcy. She had lost $150,000 in the oil scam and, with Dennison's help, had racked up debts of $125,000. Desper ate, she called the one man who had always been there to lean on, and Earl Mills came running back to his "Angelface."

Mills was shocked when he saw the quantity of pills her doctors were prescribing. He sent the downtrodden beauty to Mexico to get well, and lifted her spirits with occasional television appearances, like *Cain's Hundred* and *The Perry Como Show*, but there were precious few roles for Negroes in the early sixties, even those as beige as she, and Dorothy was forced to live on neutral ground between black and white. "Why do I always have to be a passionate woman of easy virtue because I'm Negro?" she lamented.

She and Nat Cole sought a sponsor with the courage to back them in a TV sit-com about a Negro couple in show business. "We Negroes finally con vinced the entertainment world not to stereotype us as just maids, porters, and so on," Dandridge campaigned to the press. "But now too many producers are afraid to use us at all. Rather than do wrong, they do nothing." As for her series idea, they did nothing. It was no longer a question of climbing to the top—Dorothy Dandridge was struggling just to stay on the mountain.

Dorothy's first dramatic television role was in the short-lived Cain's Hundred.

Champagne and pills were a source of solace, but Dorothy was by now overwhelmed by the obstacles, and falling ever faster. A thin ray of hope in the form of another idea offered a way out—a reason to go on living. She decided she would write her autobiography.

"You'll set Negro womanhood back a hundred years," her friends told her. Perhaps they saw only a black woman who slept with white men, who was addicted to pills, who had run her life into a dead end. Perhaps out of jealousy, shortsightedness, or fear that such a book by a black woman would be considered "uppity," they attacked the idea unmercifully. The overwhelming disapproval from good friends made her so physically ill that for several days she lay totally incapacitated, quite literally near death. Once she got past being hurt, Dorothy got angry. Her inspiration, combined with a $10,000 advance Mills had negotiated, gave her the confidence to follow through. Together with Mills, her sometime-lover and best friend, she wrote *Everything and Nothing*, a sensitive and emotional account of her life. Her successes, her racial advancements, her struggles, her love affairs with Preminger and Peter Lawford, the awards, the divorces, her daughter, her guilt, her bankruptcy, both financial and emotional . . . it was all there. Weary, she asked what a person who is still young and attractive was supposed to do when life had lost its meaning. For Dorothy Dandridge at forty-two, it had become just a matter of carrying on. So, carry on she did.

On September 7, 1965, Dorothy and Mills flew to Mexico to finalize a two-picture deal for $100,000. She was also set for singing engagements in South America, Japan, and the famed Basin Street East, in New York. She talked excitedly about her comeback and felt sure that she could be bigger than before. On the flight home, she complained so much about a twisted ankle that on the way home from the airport, Mills took her to a doctor, who

Peter Lawford, onetime lover of Dorothy Dandridge, soberly carries her to her rest.

discovered a slight fracture and advised her to have it set in a cast. She made an appointment for the following day, her last day in L.A. before her New York club date. She spent part of the evening talking with a friend in her small but elegant West Hollywood apartment, then was on the phone with her mother until the wee hours of the morning. She packed until 7:15 a.m., when she called Mills to ask if he could make the doctor's appointment later in the day. He called back to say that he had changed it to noon. "Thanks, Earl . . . I'll sleep for awhile and I'll be fine." Those were the last words he or anyone heard her say.

Mills called at 11:00 and again at noon. When Dorothy didn't answer, he thought she'd just decided to sleep in, but when she still didn't answer at 1:30, Mills became concerned. His thoughts jumped to the envelope Dorothy had given him a year earlier containing instructions to be followed upon her death. "I know you'll be the one to find me, Earl," she had told him. As he rushed to her apartment, he prayed that she was wrong.

He opened the front door with his key, but it was chained. "Angelface?" There was no answer. Nothing but the sound of his own heart, pounding in panic. Running to his car, he grabbed a tire iron from the trunk and used it to break in. Almost immediately, he found Dorothy lying on the bathroom floor, nude, except for a scarf around her beautiful head. She had bathed, powdered, and applied deodorant. With her face cradled in her hands, she appeared to be sleeping. "Angelface?" Mills whispered, reaching for her. Dorothy was cold, dead for nearly two hours. "No . . . no . . ." he sobbed. "What happened, Angelface? . . . What happened?"

Exactly what killed Dorothy Dandridge is as much a puzzle as the pieces of her confused life. At first the coroner believed that the cause of death had been a bone marrow embolism resulting from the fracture, although it is a rare occurrence with such a small break. He also discovered Tofranil, a drug used in treating psychiatric disorders, in her system. Practically impossible to overdose, it does not induce drowsiness or sleep. Though the amount in her system was not enough to suggest a suicide attempt, there is at least the possibility she may have accidentally overdosed. Stumped himself, the coroner released both theories to the press.

Though she had reached the heights of fame and fortune during her lifetime, Dorothy Dandridge had only $2 in her bank account when she died. She had fought prejudice, pills, and liquor, faced desertion by family, friends, and lovers, had long borne the cross of blame for her child, and never forgiven herself for her financial ruin. At last, she had lost the battle to a fall on a flight of stairs.

GEORGE REEVES
Whose Speeding Bullet?

The Beverly Hills Police called it "indicated suicide," but the friends and family of television's Superman, George Reeves, disagreed. "My God!" said his mother, Mrs. Bessolo. "I had just spoken to him; he was in a splendid frame of mind."

Alan Ladd called the police theory "a lot of bullplop . . . he was never happier."

He certainly appeared to be happy on the last night of his life. He was making merry, looking forward to his exhibition boxing match with the light-heavyweight champion, Archie Moore. In three days, right after the match, he was to be married to ex-New York showgirl Lenore Lemmon, a flashy brunette who had the distinction of being barred from both New York's Stork Club and El Morocco for fighting. After a brief spell in the dumps, his career was soaring again.

"George was ambitious, an achiever," protested another close friend, Gig Young. "He was a clean guy, in no way capable of bumping himself off."

On that night, June 16, 1959, Reeves, Lenore, and a houseguest, writer Robert Condon, were exuberantly toasting the future until 12:30, when the intoxicated trio went to bed. Two carousing friends, knocking persistently, woke them up half an hour later.

"I'm in no mood for a party," an irate George snapped at his visitors. His Colonial style home in posh Benedict Canyon was nicknamed "The Grand Central Station of Hollywood" by his many friends who were welcome at any hour. But the usually gregarious Reeves was in an uncharacteristic mood tonight. He threatened to throw them out but apologized almost immediately.

"I didn't mean any of it. I'm sorry, of course you can come in."

Lenore and Condon poured drinks all around and George returned to bed.

"He's sulking now," his fiancée teased. "He'll probably shoot himself."

They heard a noise from the upstairs bedroom. "See? He's opening a drawer to get a gun."

A single shot rang out; the four stood frozen. One of the men rushed upstairs and found Reeves, nude, sprawled face up on the bed. There was a bullet hole above his right ear and a luger on the floor nearby.

Police had difficulty getting a coherent account of what happened from any of Reeves's four highly inebriated friends, but Lenore swore that she had only been joking after he left the room. "I'm not clairvoyant. I'd have stopped him . . . I'd have stopped him," she sobbed.

Exactly what happened that night may never be known. Did a despondent Reeves commit suicide? An examination of the scene and his career raises as many questions as it answers.

Years earlier, the possessive Mrs. Bessolo discouraged her son from a life as a professional athlete. "He was a great ring prospect in 1932 and entered the Golden Gloves," noted sportswriter Mannie Pineda. "But at the last minute, his mother wouldn't let him fight. She was afraid he'd get banged up and ruin his acting career."

So, after seven broken noses, Reeves willingly ended one career and began another. In 1940, he married Eleanora Needles whom he had met while studying dramatics at the Pasadena Playhouse. They were divorced nine years later, shortly before his biggest success, as the "Man of Steel." Reeves had minor, though strong, roles in *So Proudly We Hail, From Here to Eternity, Blood and Sand, Samson and Delilah*, and *Gone with the Wind* (as Brent Tarleton, one of the red-headed twins enamored of Miss Scarlet), but it was the small screen that made him a star. For over 35 million viewers, the strapping 6 feet 3 inch Reeves would "leap tall buildings in a single bound" in *Superman*, one of television's first color shows, running from 1953 to 1957. As the caped hero, Reeves flew into thirty countries and was translated into fifteen languages. Fully 48 percent of his audience were adults, and the numbers included Emperor Hirohito of Japan, who once sent him a fan letter.

Offscreen, Reeves was known as Mr. Nice Guy. "Anyone in trouble could count on George," said Jack Larson, *Superman*'s Jimmy Olsen. Not only was the door to his home always open, but "Honest George—the people's friend" had been known to stick $100 bills in the pockets of out-of-work actor friends, cracking, "Now go out and make a million."

Reeves' portrayal of Superman was so successful that when the series ended, no one in Hollywood could, or would, picture him as anyone else. Though residuals from the show allowed him to live comfortably, he was not a man to rest on his laurels. He wanted to keep working, but, hopelessly typecast, he was unemployed for a year and a half.

He continued to make public appearances, usually in his cape and tights. Things began to look up. He still couldn't play a mortal man, but Superman was winning once again. Reeves and Lenore made plans for a honeymoon in Spain, after which he was to begin a six-week tour of Australia that was to have netted him $20,000. He'd formed his own production company and was planning to direct and star in a science fiction film. His personal manager had put together the best deal—*Superman* was to resume production in 1960 with new scripts and a larger salary. The résumé that lay on a desk a few feet from where Reeves's body was found read, "George Reeves looks at life today as a challenge any actor should welcome." Alan Ladd was right; George Reeves was never happier.

Lenore didn't agree. "It was the Hollywood system which drove him to kill himself. He wanted to bring me the moon and diamonds and moonbeams and he just couldn't do it because he just couldn't get a job. He didn't even say good-bye. We didn't have any beef. He just went upstairs and shot himself. It was that simple. His heart was broken because . . . he couldn't bring me the things he really wanted."

*The mortal Reeves,
not as fast as a bullet.*

Imagine Lenore's surprise when she discovered that Reeves had left not only moonbeams but the bulk of his $71,000 estate to Toni Mannix, wife of Loew's vice-president, Eddie Mannix. "Mr. Mannix and I have been friends of George Reeves for a number of years," she told the press. They were good enough friends that she had given George a luxury car as a birthday present.

At about the time Reeves made his wedding plans public, he began receiving round-the-clock nuisance calls—hang-ups—sometimes twenty a day. Convinced that it was Toni, he filed a complaint with the police. When they questioned her, police found out that Mrs. Mannix was receiving the same calls. "Then who the hell is after me?" Reeves demanded to know. He became worried enough to set up a virtual arsenal in his house. The week before his death he added two knives, a club, and a .22 pistol to his collection.

Mrs. Bessolo wanted to know who was after her son, too, and spent $50,000 of her own money in a futile search. "My son was not a man driven to desperation," she insisted. Until her death in 1964, not a day passed that Mrs. Bessolo didn't mention her rejection of the suicide theory.

Gig Young had some hunches of his own. "Women went wild for George. He did a lot of loving in places maybe he shouldn't have." Young believed that a murderer surprised Reeves in the bedroom. The unusual death scene seemed to support that opinion.

Reeves was found lying on his back on top of the empty cartridge, whereas most self-inflicted gunshots propel the victim forward, away from the shell. Stranger still for a suicide was the absence of powder burns on his skin. The pistol would have to have been held at least sixteen inches away; not impossible, but highly unlikely considering that the bullet was lodged high in the wall. Would a person trying to kill himself awkwardly hold a gun sixteen inches below an oddly tilted head? The private detective Mrs. Bessolo hired didn't think so. He did, however, believe that Reeves could have been shot in that position if he were wrestling the gun from an intruder, someone who could have easily climbed in the bedroom window. Besides murder, there was another possibility. Several times that week, George and Lenore had been playing with the new luger, even firing it indoors. It was never officially considered that the drunken actor may have been fooling around with it when it accidentally discharged. Whatever happened in the bedroom, Reeves was found with an astonished look on his face.

The world was astonished, too. Children old enough to read told little brothers and sisters that Superman had shot himself. Thousands of confused children turned to their parents for an explanation. "What Do We Tell Our Kids About Superman's Death?" the headlines declared. Psychologists were consulted to help deal with the shock and disbelief. "Tell them that Superman is not dead . . . that Reeves was only 'play acting' " was the advice they gave. "He wasn't really Superman, he was an actor." It was what Reeves had been trying to tell Hollywood for years.

Nine people have bought and sold his home since 1959. Many of them claim it is haunted. On more than one occasion, the owners returned home to find the image of George Reeves waiting for them, pointing a luger at their heads . . . as if they were intruders who again surprised him.

SAL MINEO
Victim Without a Cause

At seven, Salvatore Mineo, Jr. was already a member of a street gang in his tough Bronx neighborhood. When his troublemaking got him thrown out of parochial school, his mother hoped dancing school might provide an outlet for her son's excess energy. It did—Sal beat up every kid in the neighborhood who called him a sissy. He stayed in dance class and became a local hero. All the kids on the block looked up to Sal even when he was nine years old. In a few years, Mrs. Mineo's son would be the idol of millions of teenagers, worldwide.

Sal found a sudden motivation to attend acting school. Apprehended after he masterminded a $5,000 theft, he was given two choices, reform school or theatrical high school. He gladly chose the latter, and advanced with remarkable speed. There was no more trouble out of Sal. A year later he made his Broadway debut in *The Rose Tatoo,* starring Maureen Stapleton and Eli Wallach. He rose from the ranks of understudy to play crown prince as Yul Brynner's son, in *The King and I,* staying with the show for two years, until 1954, when Hollywood "discovered" Sal Mineo.

Auteur* director Nicholas Ray picked Mineo out of a lineup of boys who wanted to portray gang members in *Rebel Without a Cause* (1955). "I saw this kid in the back who looked like my son except he was prettier. I called him over and asked him what he'd done. He said he'd just played Tony Curtis as a young boy in *Seven Bridges to Cross.* I asked Sal to take off his jacket and start sizing up those big guys . . . and because of the improvisation they did, decided Sal would be great for the part of Plato."

---

* Studio control often hampered individual expression. The auteur theory sprang from a group of dynamic, socially conscious directors of which Ray was a member. They conclude that the director is the "author," and that each film is a work of art stamped with the author's personal creativity.

A teenaged Mineo prepares for the title role in The Gene Krupa Story.

The next step was to see how Sal would click with James Dean, fast rising symbol of restless youth. "I was sick, I wanted the part so badly," Mineo recalled. "We went through a scene and nothing happened between us. Nick finally walked over and suggested we sit and talk for a while. When Jimmy found out I was from the Bronx, we started gabbing about New York, and then progressed to cars, and before we knew it, we were buddies. Then we went back to the script and this time it went off like clockwork." The improv not only got Mineo the part, but his portrayal of the sensitive, confused Plato also won him his first Academy Award nomination. Sal was deeply affected by Dean's death in a car accident a year later. "The very last time I saw him I had a feeling—I was sad and yet vibrant. I mean, those are the feelings I can understand, but I just knew that I was feeling something that I didn't feel with anything or anybody else."

There were rumors that the adventuresome Dean and the worshipful Mineo had been lovers. "We could have been . . . just like that," Mineo told a friend years later, "but we never were."

Mineo's image was in perfect synch with the troubled youths of the fifties, as kids the world over identified with the desperation behind his street punk characters whose lives and deaths were dictated by the switchblade. It was an image that would come to haunt Mineo for the rest of his short life. In 1955, however, it brought him luck, plus an Emmy for his television movie portrayal of *Dino*. When the powerful teleplay about a misunderstood New York delinquent was released as a theatrical feature in 1957, Sal became "the baby-faced hero of the popcorn set." Mobs of girls ambushed him in public, and though he dated many, he was rarely serious with one girl. Teen magazines devoted issue after issue to him. He was receiving 5,000 letters a week, prompting Bob Hope to joke, "All the schools in the Bronx will be closed tomorrow because it's Sal Mineo's birthday." Because of his great popularity with teens, he "let myself be talked into singing . . . Everyone's entitled to one mistake." Though Mineo thought he lacked talent in this area, he scored a gold record for his recording of "Start Moving."

His tough image at times worked against him, making him a tempting target for belligerent strangers on the street or in restaurants, but Mineo became adept at handling success and all its trappings. He had plenty of success to handle when he purchased a $200,000 home for his parents in New York—garnering critical acclaim in the title role in *The Gene Krupa Story*, and for the role of Dov Landau in *Exodus*, his second Oscar nomination. The role in *Exodus* ironically prevented Mineo from getting a part he very much wanted, the young Arab in *Lawrence of Arabia*. Because he'd played a Jew who shot four Arabs, the Jordanian government refused to allow Mineo into their country to make the movie. It was the first in a series of career disappointments.

It was fashion, not the Jordanians, that really did him in. With his nomination for *Exodus*, Mineo's career peaked. His well-cultivated, juvenile-delinquent image was suddenly as much a liability as his olive complexion. The progressive sixties had arrived, ushering in a new generation that couldn't relate to the Mineo image of switchblade street-culture. He tried in vain to shake the typecasting, but the blade became his "Sword of Damocles." He was offered fewer and fewer roles. At twenty-six, he was the perpetual teen-ager who never had a childhood. In 1965, he tried to cash in on the new direction. He formed a production company whose first project was a record-ing for Bobby Sherman. That same year, an article in a teen magazine reported the breakup of Sal's latest romance over, of all things, The Beatles. He couldn't understand his girlfriend's exuberance for the mop-headed quartet and found the entire "Beatlemania" outbreak "silly." It was a natural reaction, for to Mineo, the Four Lads from Liverpool and their clean, scrubbed image repre-sented the enemy.

Mineo's cultivated, juvenile delinquent image made him a teen idol of the fifties but proved his greatest liability in the progressive sixties.

As his savings dwindled, Mineo turned first to television, and then to the stage, both Broadway and his West Coast stage debut, but failed to stir much attention. His name hit the headlines in 1967 when a girlfriend, despondent over their failed romance, attempted suicide. She recovered, but his career was not as lucky. His 1969 productions of *Fortune and Men's Eyes*, both in Los Angeles and on Broadway, were innovative and controversial, even compelling, but both met with only moderate success. He returned to films that year in *Krakatoa, East of Java*, and in 1971 made *Escape From the Planet of the*

The senseless murder of the two-time Academy Award nominee sent a shudder through the Hollywood community.

Apes. Though his agent promised it would expand his career, it would be Mineo's last film.

Still trying to make a comeback, Sal, now thirty-seven, returned to the theater in *P.S. Your Cat Is Dead.* His favorable reviews in San Francisco produced the advertising switch, "P.S. Sal Mineo Is Alive." The Los Angeles show with Keir Dullea was due to open in a week and Sal's hopes were riding high on it to bring him back to Hollywood's attention.

Returning from rehearsal on Thursday, February 12, 1976, Sal had pulled into the garage of his apartment, just below the Sunset Strip, in a quiet, well-kept area of West Hollywood. The building was owned in part by his attorney, Marvin Mitchelson, the palimony lawyer, and Mitchelson's mother was also a resident there. At 10:00 p.m., while preparing for bed, she heard terrified screams from outside. "No! My God! No!" Neighbor Raymond Evans heard them, too, and ran for his door. "My God! Help me!" the voice wailed. There was one more horrible scream and then, silence.

Evans found Mineo lying on the concrete near the entrance to his garage. He had been stabbed repeatedly during a fierce struggle. His chest was covered with blood. Evans immediately applied mouth-to-mouth resuscitation, but Mineo was mortally wounded, stabbed through the heart. He died as the paramedics were arriving, a victim of real-life switchblade sensibilities.

During the investigation, three witnesses stepped forward to describe the man they saw running away through an alley. Mineo still had his wallet and, at first, police thought he resisted during a holdup, but they finally eliminated robbery as a motive altogether. They eventually developed a working theory that Mineo, a bisexual, was murdered during a lover's quarrel. Although the massive manhunt continued for two years, authorities were unable to uncover a suspect.

Two years later, in a Michigan jail, a prisoner bragged to his cellmate, "I killed Sal Mineo." Lionel Ray Williams, twenty-one, was serving a term for forgery when he decided to share his secret. He described stabbing Mineo with a hunting knife, laughing about how easily he had gotten away with it. The cellmate told authorities who, after taping subsequent conversations in the cell, formally charged Williams with the murder. The former pizza delivery boy already had a long record of arrests by the time he was fourteen. His crimes became progressively more vicious, not just street robberies, but one incident after another where he cruelly inflicted pain and enjoyed it. He liked brutalizing people. No wonder police couldn't find a motive in Mineo's slaying —there wasn't one.

Three years and a day after the murder, Williams was found guilty and received the maximum sentence of fifty-one years to life. He casually un-wrapped a stick of gum as the judge also read convictions for ten armed robberies and the recommendation that there be no chance for parole. Pro-nouncing Williams to be a "sadistic killer" and a "midnight marauder," the judge was convinced that, "if released, he will no doubt kill again."

Here was a different breed of young hoodlum—one who really lived by the switchblade, a weapon Sal Mineo had been trying to escape for years. It jinxed his career and his life—a life snuffed out for the sheer pleasure of the crime.

MARILYN MONROE
Reluctant Death of a Love Goddess

Walking down Hollywood Boulevard today makes it difficult to believe that Marilyn Monroe has been dead for more than twenty years. Her beautiful image beckons from t-shirts, posters, greeting cards, coffee mugs, pillow cases, book jackets, even key chains. The Boulevard is like one continuous shrine to the twentieth century's own Venus. She's much more than just a goddess for an era; she has an even stronger hold over people today than she had at the peak of her legendary career. Her crypt is continually adorned with flowers, candles, and notes from loving fans, many of whom have never even seen her movies.

The Cinderella story of the deprived, abused waif who soared to the heights of international fame can still weave a magic spell. In her unrealized quest for love, she married and divorced Yankee slugger Joe DiMaggio and Broadway playwright Arthur Miller. Though she had affairs with many others, even, it's claimed, a President of the United States, true happiness always eluded her. When her nude, lifeless body was discovered in her bedroom during the pre-dawn hours of Sunday, August 5, 1962, every major paper in the world carried the headlines: "Marilyn Monroe Dead!" "Marilyn Commits Suicide!" Her death came as a terrible shock, but the cause was not surprising to the millions of fans who believed that she was as vulnerable and weak as her breathless image.

Images, however, are the creation of press agents. While Marilyn Monroe had her vulnerabilities, she was also a fighter and there are those who believe that's just how she went out—fighting.

"I don't feel that Marilyn Monroe committed suicide . . . somebody murdered her. It was an out and out case of murder. You can quote me on that,"

Glorious Marilyn.

states Jack Clemmons unequivocally. The ex-Los Angeles police officer was the first official to arrive at Monroe's home at 12305 Fifth Helena Drive after her death. He had received a call at 4:25 a.m. saying Marilyn Monroe was dead and checked it out personally to make sure it was not a crank. From the moment he arrived at her home in the fashionable West Los Angeles neighborhood of Brentwood, he felt the scene "was not kosher."

Already present in the house were Monroe's psychiatrist, Dr. Ralph Greenson; her physician, Dr. Hyman Engelberg; and her housekeeper and companion, Mrs. Eunice Murray, who told Clemmons she saw a light under Marilyn's door at about 10 p.m., but had thought nothing of it. When she awoke at midnight to find the light still on, she decided to look in on Marilyn. Mrs. Murray became alarmed when she found that the door was locked. She called Dr. Greenson, who arrived fifteen minutes later, followed shortly by Dr. Engelberg. Clemmons figured this meant that the doctors had waited almost 4 hours before calling the police.

"I asked them about it, but one of the doctors gave me an answer that didn't make any sense. . . . I felt it should have been explained. There was no real excuse for their delay and I didn't like their attitude. They were secretive. It left a very bad impression on me. . . . There was something—other than the obvious."

Clemmons found other disturbing indications regarding the physical evidence at the scene. "I saw at once that her body had been moved from somewhere else and positioned on the bed. I think I asked one of the doctors if anyone had moved her and he said, 'No,' but I don't believe it. She would not have been found in that position . . . stretched out, face down, legs completely parallel."

The phone was lying near her hand, on the floor. Rigor mortis and postmortem lividity (the settling of blood after death) had already set in to such a degree that Clemmons felt she'd been dead even hours longer than the doctors let on. There was more. Clemmons saw no glass by the bed or in the vicinity, nothing to wash down the forty-seven Nembutals she supposedly swallowed. Also, there was no note. After making the supreme decision to take her own life, Monroe, a star of the greatest magnitude, acutely aware of her public, almost certainly would have left her final words.

"I had a distinct feeling that they [the doctors] were hiding something. I wasn't sure what at the time, but I had an uneasy feeling about the whole thing." That was only the beginning of the discrepancies Clemmons noted. "They told me one story when I got to the house and later on they told the investigating detectives a different story." The police report deviates from both of these stories and the follow-up report varies even further.

Mrs. Murray, who believes that Monroe's death was an accident, later told the investigating team that she saw the light under Marilyn's door at 3:30 a.m. and then called Dr. Greenson. At his instructions, she looked in through the bedroom window, and reported back to him on the phone that Marilyn was lying on her bed with the phone in her hand. She said she looked "strange." Greenson said he would be right over and told her to call Engelberg. Greenson arrived at 3:40, broke open the window, and approached the bed.

A vivacious Marilyn keeps the reporters laughing at a 1956 press conference.

After removing the phone from her hand, he examined Marilyn and found her to be "possibly dead." "We've lost her," he said to Mrs. Murray, who was waiting outside the bedroom door. She did not enter the room, but from the doorway, even she could see the rigor mortis.

Though Greenson could have pronounced her dead at that time, he waited to let Engelberg, who arrived at 3:50, make the official pronouncement. The two doctors then considered what they should do next. Greenson wanted to call the mortuary. "I strongly insisted," said Engelberg, "that because of who she was and [because] it might be suicide, we should call the police. Dr. Greenson and I discussed this back and forth." Hence, the delay in calling the authorities. The second story allows only a 25-minute lapse between the doctors' arrivals and the call to police. Sgt. Clemmons' story sets that interval at 3 hours and 55 minutes.

At 5:25 a.m., Guy Hockett received a call from the coroner's office. Hockett worked for Westwood Memorial Park Cemetery, where Monroe was to be buried. Acting as the coroner's representative, Hockett and his son, Don, arrived at Fifth Helena Drive to remove the body of Marilyn Monroe. Rigor mortis was now so advanced that they had trouble getting the body on the gurney. Hockett felt certain that she'd been dead at least eight hours, estimating the time of death at somewhere between 10:00 p.m. and midnight. "I was astonished," he later said, "to read in the paper that she'd been dead less than three hours when her body was found." He told police on the scene (Sgt. Clemmons had, by then, returned to the station) that he was annoyed by the number of people in the room—three men and three women, one of whom was Pat Newcomb, Marilyn's press agent, whom Marilyn's lawyer had called at 4:00 a.m., fully 25 minutes before the police. As the coroner's representative, Hockett was to make a preliminary search for valuables and medication bottles, but by this time, the bedroom was a mess. Evidence had been disturbed. The Hocketts removed the body, outsmarting the swarm of waiting press who had already descended on the scene. They took her body to the city morgue where, after an autopsy, it lay unclaimed until Joe DiMaggio hurried to Los Angeles from his home in San Francisco.

Deputy Medical Examiner Dr. Thomas Noguchi painstakingly led his team of assistants through the autopsy. Their all-important report, however, raises more questions than it answers.

Marilyn's final statistics, though every bit as cold as a morgue, are the basis for a heated controversy. A blood sample revealed the presence of 4.5 milligrams of barbiturates, the equivalent of between forty and fifty pills swallowed within a 2- to 3-second period. Yet, her small intestine, where the undissolved pills would have gone, was never tested due to "lack of facilities." In addition, no pill residue was found on any internal organs or in her stomach.

Along with 13 milligrams of the fast-acting sedative pentobarbital in her liver was 8 milligrams of chloral hydrate in her bloodstream, Marilyn's usual dose of sleeping medication. Because of its unpleasant taste and irritating characteristics, she always took it with milk, but there was no milk coating her stomach. The large quantity of drugs still in her system suggests that death occurred soon after they were introduced. Although all these drugs are

At a Friar's Roast for Milton Berle, Marilyn laughs at the antics of Jerry Lewis and Dean Martin.

ingestible in capsule form, none were found in her digestive tract or stomach, nor was there any trace of dye stains from the capsules. If this is true, the lethal dose of barbiturates in her bloodstream was not taken orally, but possibly came from an injection. A bruise was noted on the left hip. The post-mortem discoloration of her colon, and on the back of her arms and legs, suggests that she was lying on her back for a while after her death . . . but she was found lying face down. It seems that someone may have moved the body.

Marilyn had been to Dr. Engelberg the Wednesday and Friday before her death on Saturday, and had received shots on both visits. Because there was no pill residue in her system, many believe Monroe was injected with the deadly drugs in a place where the needle marks wouldn't be obvious; the armpits, for example. The bruise on her hip could also have been an injection area. Any more than the two fresh Engelberg needle marks would have been a very serious indication of foul play. Noguchi however, in a highly significant oversight, did not make note of any fresh needle marks on the body. There is the additional possibility that a lethal suppository was inserted, causing the inflammation of the colon. Because the autopsy never mentioned such vital observations, it is now impossible to be certain if Monroe was given a lethal injection.

"She didn't swallow that stuff," Clemmons said. "It was put into her by a suppository or a needle, both of which, in my opinion, would have required someone she trusted and had confidence in. That narrows it down pretty well, doesn't it?"

There were few people whom Marilyn trusted. Robert Slatzer claims to have been one of them. He was a close personal friend, and he also claims to have been married to her before DiMaggio. The union was annulled after three days. Both he and Clemmons have their suspicions.

"It was common knowledge that Bobby Kennedy and Marilyn Monroe were having an affair. Everybody knew that," Clemmons stated. Slatzer said Marilyn had confided to him that she'd been seeing Kennedy, but that recently, he'd been avoiding her. He had his private number changed and was not returning the messages she left for him at the Justice Department. She was hurt and upset by the rejection, and something new . . . she was angry. Marilyn had reached a plateau. Always insecure about her education and background, she was drawn to educated, powerful men, and intimidated by them at the same time. For them, she was an amusement, not someone with whom to become seriously involved. RFK's unceremonious termination of their relationship was the last straw. Marilyn gathered up her sagging self-esteem and got rightfully angry. This was not only a healthy move, it was a potentially dangerous one.

It is commonly thought that Monroe was depressed that last summer because she was fired from the production of *Something's Gotta Give*, the only time in her career she'd been fired. It was not widely publicized, however, that 20th Century–Fox had reinstated her for $100,000, and the film was to be completed when co-star Dean Martin finished a prior commitment. Besides that, she'd had offers for plays, including one from Anita Loos, dozens of films, a Las Vegas show, and she was considering a layout for *Playboy*.

On a personal level, Marilyn was taking big strides, the first of which was to purchase a house, the first real home she'd ever had. She was excitedly fixing it up, remodeling, buying furniture, even puttering in the garden. She was also reevaluating the people in her life, weeding out the users and the phonies. The Monday following her death, she had an appointment with her lawyer to change her will. Mrs. Murray describes her as full of life, standing on her own two feet. Dr. Greenson said, "She was getting better; she was on the road to what looked like some sort of stability. And she died—unexpectedly and suddenly."

"I'll never believe that Marilyn took her own life," columnist Dorothy Kilgallen stated. The two women knew each other socially, and at first Kilgallen believed that Marilyn committed suicide, dying as she tried to reach RFK. Years later she came to believe otherwise. "There are too many conflicting stories from the people who were there that night. The whole thing stinks."

(Kilgallen was, herself, found dead in her New York apartment from a lethal combination of liquor and pills the night before she was to disclose new evidence in the JFK assassination.) When another columnist, Walter Winchell, printed some of the discrepancies noted by Clemmons, Clemmons lost his job.

Robert Kennedy checked into San Francisco's St. Francis Hotel with his wife and several of their children on August 3rd. Clemmons swears that RFK was in Los Angeles on the 4th, possibly under an assumed name, at the Beverly Hills Hotel. As an officer of the Los Angeles Police Department, he had been informed of his presence, a standard procedure for such a prominent visitor. He believes that Kennedy took a flight back to San Francisco late Saturday.

On the last day of her life, Marilyn was home all day. A nightstand she picked out the day before was delivered, and around 5 p.m. Dr. Greenson arrived for a session. Shortly after he left, young Joe DiMaggio, Jr., called. Both he and his father had remained close friends of Marilyn's. He wanted to tell her that he had broken off with a girl Marilyn didn't like, and they spoke excitedly about it for 15 minutes. She felt so happy after the conversation, she telephoned Greenson to tell him the news. "She was in a very up mood," remembers Mrs. Murray. That was the last time she saw Marilyn alive. Peter Lawford called just a half-hour later and said she sounded drugged, slurring her speech as she asked him to "tell Pat [Lawford] goodbye . . . and the President . . . and yourself."

On the Monday morning following her death, L.A. Police Chief William H. Parker, who was hoping to replace J. Edgar Hoover as head of the FBI in an RFK administration, legally impounded Monroe's telephone records for July and August. They contained $209 worth of long distance calls—to the White House perhaps? . . . the Justice Department? . . . Hyannis Port? The impounded files disappeared completely after Parker's death, in 1966.

The public so readily accepted the idea of poor, unhappy Marilyn taking her own life that the possibility of murder received no support until 1974, when Slatzer demanded a reopening of the case. "I have made a long study," said Slatzer, who has written two books on the subject, "and have come to the unalterable conclusion that Marilyn Monroe did not commit suicide."

In response to the questions raised by the autopsy, Dr. Noguchi stated in his book, *Coroner,* that after examining the body with a hand-held magnifying glass, he saw no needle marks whatsoever. He also firmly states that the yellow dye from Nembutal capsules does not rub off. The reason that none of the massive quantity of pills she swallowed was in her stomach was also simply explained. A "pill addict's" system is so used to digesting them, the pills are literally "dumped" into the small intestine, which admittedly, he regrets, was never tested. By the time the case was reopened, the evidence had been destroyed. Noguchi goes on to say that an accidental overdose in this situation is highly unlikely and that he leans heavily toward suicide. However, he cites that another examiner who shared the same opinion was allowed to listen to several taped sessions between Marilyn and Dr. Greenson, after which he changed his theory to murder.

Milo Spiriglio, director of Nick Harris Detectives, has worked on the case

The incomparable Marilyn Monroe.

for ten years and has put out a book of his own. In it, he says that he inter-viewed Dr. Ronald Kornblaum, Chief Medical Examiner of the L.A. County Coroner's Office and a spokesman for Abbott Laboratories, manufacturers of Nembutal, both of whom assert that the yellow dye *does* stain the intestines.

There's money in being the last person to have seen Marilyn alive, as well as in writing books claiming she was murdered. The stories keep coming. There stands, however, one compelling piece of evidence; this woman who supposedly died from swallowing forty-seven yellow pills had no pills, no residue, no tiny crystals, not one trace of them in her system, only their equivalent in her bloodstream. The conclusion reached by a growing number of inquirers is that thirty-six-year-old Marilyn Monroe, the world's reigning sex goddess, was murdered because she posed a threat. Any evidence that she was intimate with the Kennedys was removed. Her body and bedroom were carefully arranged to appear as though her death were a suicide.

Says Clemmons, "What we have here is truly the unsolved crime of the century."

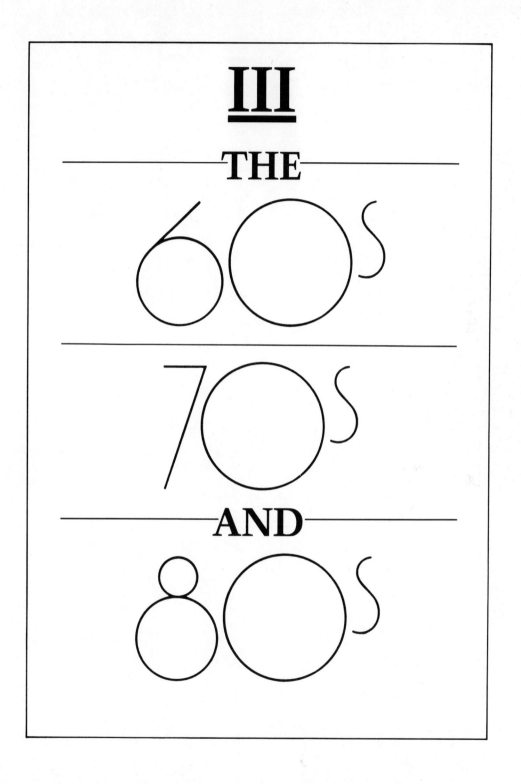

III

THE

60s

70s

AND

80s

LENNY BRUCE
. . . and nothing but the truth.

Lenny Bruce was a "sick comic." Many things made him sick: racism, hypocrisy, poverty, starvation, war, discrimination, bigotry, the bomb, and all things that violate human dignity. "All my humor is based on destruction and despair," he said. "If the whole world were tranquil, without disease and violence, I'd be standing in the bread line . . . right back of J. Edgar Hoover."

He spoke in public, in burlesque houses and jazz clubs, as if he were in his own living room, spouting off whatever was on his mind with a naked honesty that was a threat to convention in the fifties. It was Lenny who established the stand-up comic as a legitimate social commentator. Today it's hard to believe that his satire was so shocking, but he founded his comedic "school of hard knocks" at a time when Hollywood still showed the world as being a chaste domicile where married couples reposed in twin beds.

"The way I speak, the words with which I relate are more correct in effect than those of a previous pedantic generation," he said. "Dig—if I talk about a chick on stage and say she was a 'hooker,' an uncontemporary person would say, 'Lenny Bruce, you are crude and coarse. If you must be specific, you should have said prostitute.' But wait a minute. Shouldn't the purpose of a word be to get close to the object the user is describing? The word has become too general. He prostituted his art. Can he write anymore? Not like he used to—he prostituted his work. So the word 'prostitute' doesn't mean anymore what the word 'hooker' does. If a man were to send out for a $100 prostitute, a writer with a beard might show up."

The first time he was arrested for obscenity was in San Francisco, for using, "just in passing," he said, the "crude and coarse" word "cocksucker." "[The police] said it's against the law to say it and to do it. They said it was a favorite homosexual practice. Now I found that strange. I don't relate the word to a

Lenny Bruce—A comic with nothing to hide.

homosexual practice. It relates to any contemporary chick I know or would know, or would love, or would marry."

Lenny married a contemporary chick named Honey Harlowe, aka Harriet Lloyd, a gorgeous, curvaceous shiksa, with red hair long enough to sit on, who had a class striptease act. They met in Baltimore in 1951. Lenny and Honey were nuts about each other from the start. He realized it was true love while he was on a three-month stint in the merchant marine. He used all the money he had saved to call her from Spain, tracking Honey through a chain of clubs so that he could propose.

Their first home was with Lenny's mother, Sally Marr, in her one-bedroom Brooklyn apartment. Small, buxom, brunette Sally began *her* show business career in a 1922 dance contest. Her pretty face and well-turned ankle had turned the head of the judge, Rudolph Valentino. Mickey Schneider, a shoe store clerk from a good family, noticed her too. They married the following year but shortly after their baby, Lenny, was born in 1925, Mickey moved out. (As a young comic, their son chose the name Bruce for himself "because Leonard Alfred Schneider sounded too Hollywood.") To support her son, Sally worked mostly as a domestic until the early forties, when friends finally convinced her to use her comedic talents professionally and she began to pursue a stage career.

"The first time Lenny was ever on stage was as a part of my act," says Sally, the first woman comic-satirist. Both onstage and off, she was a profound influence on her young son, instilling him with a deep respect for love, honesty, and fair play, and providing him with the foundation upon which he built his controversial career.

Lenny made his first big score in October of 1948 on the radio version of *Arthur Godfrey's Talent Scouts*, with a 3-minute bit he called "The Bavarian Mimic." He did the voices of Cagney, Bogart, and Edward G. Robinson as Germans. Instead of Bogie saying, "All right Louie, drop the gun," "Herr" Bogart said, "All right Schmeagah, drop the Yeagah." The routine got him his first decent club bookings.

Honey got some better club bookings, too, as a singer, but when times got rough she'd go back to stripping while Lenny worked as a gardener. They got high together, too, those first few years, just a little and just on pot. After Kitty was born in 1955, it was much more often and on much stronger stuff. Lenny could walk away from dope when he had to; Honey could not. Their marriage couldn't stand the strain. When they divorced in 1956, Lenny got custody of Kitty. Sally put her career on hold to be manager to Lenny and full-time mother to Kitty, who would remember her father as being sick a lot and in trouble most of the time. For Lenny, it was the time when he really hit his stride, and it became, simultaneously, the best and worst years of his life.

"Nineteen sixty and '61 is when all the trouble started," Sally remembered. That's when Lenny released a recording of his routine "Religions, Inc." It began, "The Dodge-Plymouth dealers had a convention, and they raffled off a 1958 Catholic Church. . . ." "Lenny made fun of all religions in it. He never had any trouble before that. He would say to me, 'You know why they're picking on me? Because I'm a Jew.' And nothing could convince Lenny that

Lenny with the maitre d' and the manager of the Sunset Strip's Crescendo Club,
1959.

he wasn't being picked on because he was a Jew. . . . I felt that way, too."

There were many in the early sixties who picked on Bruce because they felt he was nothing more than "foul-mouthed." *Time* magazine labeled him "the sickest comic of them all." Yet, plenty of people wanted to hear what Lenny had to say. He was able to pack a midnight concert at Carnegie Hall despite a crippling snowstorm that had brought New York City to a virtual standstill. He was a smash in London, wrote his autobiography, *How to Talk Dirty and Influence People,* and made numerous records, including "Lenny Bruce and the Law," produced by his dear friend, rock pioneer Phil Spector. Nevertheless,

Bruce was continually harassed and arrested on obscenity and narcotics charges. (He used heroin on and off all his adult years.) As many police saw his show as anyone else, standing in the back of clubs, just waiting for the one word, the one gesture . . . for an excuse to bust him. When Bruce got cagey and delivered "the words" in Yiddish, the cops countered by sending in Jewish policemen. "My ex-wife was the type of person who would get upset when I opened the bathroom door while she was 'fressing' the maid." That obscure Yiddish word, along with schtup, schmuck, tits and ass, and cocksucker, got him busted for obscenity at LA's Troubador. "If you get arrested in Town A," Bruce explained, "and then Town B, with lots of publicity—then when you get to Town C, they *have* to arrest you or what kind of a shithouse town are they running?"

Bruce contended that such harassment violated his constitutional rights to free speech. It was bullshit. Who were the police to determine what was obscene? It went against his sense of justice and he took it upon himself to change things. Deciding their arrests should be on less dubious grounds, the police would simply plant dope on him. He was even busted for pills for which he had legal prescriptions. Yet, Bruce did not really consider the police his enemy. "He knew most of them," his mother laughed heartily. "He used to say 'They have a job to do, and I'm their job!' No, Lenny's enemy was the system."

Though he loved the challenge, Lenny's legal defense was devouring his money. His problems multiplied as fearful club owners hesitated to book him, or flatly refused to. The owner of the Sunset Strip's Renaissance Club, and close friend of Lenny's, refused to be intimidated. Lenny opened there, but found himself closed down the second night in a most unique way. Someone, Bruce always suspected the LAPD, yanked out the club's toilets, intentionally violating the Alcohol Beverage Control law regarding restroom facilities. England had its own solution. After being hailed there in 1962, he was refused entry the following year. By now, Bruce had become obsessed with his legal battles, constantly reading, studying, making tapes. During his final performances, he would read transcripts from his trials rather than his usual routine. Audiences couldn't relate. He wasn't funny anymore, just possessed by an obsession that was eating him alive.

In 1963, Bruce was legally declared a drug addict. "He wasn't an addict," Sally Marr insists, a position supported by a doctor's statement. "He was a user . . . that's what made him dangerous. How do you think he won five trials? Junkies don't win trials. He won with no lawyer and he only finished the eighth grade! Junkies don't work. He was never late for work."

So consumed by his court cases that he made only $2,000 in 1965, Bruce declared bankruptcy. He was about to lose his three-story "House on the Hill," high atop Hollywood Boulevard, where he lived with Sally, Kitty, and a few friends. Though by summer of that year he had beaten all but one of the obscenity raps (which he refused to appeal in the proper form), and the penalty for his last narcotics bust had been reduced to simple probation, Lenny's obsession would not let up. He could have performed again with less harassment, but at thirty-nine, suffering from emphysema, and grossly overweight, up to almost 200 pounds, he barely moved from his typewriter, where he toiled day after day trying to clear his name. His last performance was on June 25, at Bill Graham's Fillmore West, in San Francisco, opposite Frank Zappa's band, The Mothers of Invention.

Lenny spent the last night of his life, August 2, 1966, trying to teach Kitty to stand on her head, yoga style. It was a happy evening. The following afternoon, Sally dropped Kitty off at her sewing class, and was on her way to pick her up when she passed the house and noticed reporters and several news trucks. This wasn't an unusual sight when your son was Lenny Bruce, and Sally's first thought was that if she stopped in as she'd planned to, she'd get trapped there and would be late to get Kitty. She drove on.

While Sally was waiting for her granddaughter to come out of class, a close friend appeared. "What are you doing here?" she asked, surprised.

"Something terrible has happened to Lenny."

"Oh my God! He's been busted again."

"It's worse . . . he's dead." Sally's face went gray. Her purse fell to the floor.

Kitty came out of class about that time. "Grandma! What's the matter?" she gasped. Later, after the shock wore off, her grandma told her that her daddy wasn't going to be feeling sick anymore.

Sally learned that a friend of Lenny's, a photographer from San Francisco who was staying at the house, had returned there a little after 6 p.m. He found things oddly quiet. "Lenny?" he'd called out nervously. Then he found his host crumpled on the bathroom floor, with a needle in his arm. Lenny had wanted just a little taste that day, but had turned on to a bad batch. Sally believes that the friends staying in the house at the time panicked, and rather than get involved with the authorities, left. Lenny was sitting on the toilet, with his pants around his knees, when he OD'd and fell to the cold tile floor. Paramedics turned him on his back. The police, who had continually arrested Bruce for bad taste, indulged in a bit of their own when they allowed the press into the bathroom, two at a time, to photograph Lenny's body on the floor. "It was a terrible thing for the cops to do," his friend Dick Schaap wrote later. "Lenny hated to pose for pictures."

"I didn't have any money to pay for the funeral," Sally recalled sorrowfully. "Phil Spector buried Lenny. He loved Lenny. That's the thing . . . in all the books and stories about Lenny, nobody interviewed his close friends—people like Buddy Hackett, who brought Lenny out to Universal and got him his first job as a writer, and Shecky Greene, Jackie Gayle, Frankie Ray Perelli, Russell Bledsoe, Jo Jo D'Amore, Seymour Fried. They never went near these people because they loved Lenny and they would've said good things about him. . . ."

". . . and they didn't want to hear that!" piped in Benita Carmen, a friend from Baltimore.

Bruce tried all his life to prove that people hear only what they want to hear. The dizzying heights of his resurrection got him seen and heard—in posters, books, a play, a movie, and record albums—and turned him into a martyr, something he always dreaded. He just wanted to bare the pain of truth in his soul to anyone who'd listen. "I am influenced by every second of my waking hour," he said. "Dig, there is only what is."

SAM COOKE
One Sour Note

Sam Cooke, the son of a Baptist minister, was singing gospel in his father's church before he could walk. He grew up to be one of the country's most popular singers. At twenty-nine, he owned a $14,000 Ferrari, a $20,000 Rolls-Royce, his own publishing company and his own record company, but the young man with everything met a grisly end in a cheap motel in a South Los Angeles ghetto. To friends and fans who knew Sam as a well-groomed, intelligent charmer, his death was a baffling shock that has never been fully explained.

When he was a teenager, Sam was the lead singer with a popular gospel group called The Soul Stirrers. His soulful renditions and sexy good looks caught the eye of a talent manager who figured Sam's "black magic" could excite white audiences too. With his father's permission, young Cooke left the gospel circuit. He became a star at the age of twenty-two, with his recording of his brother L.C.'s composition "You Send Me." Released in 1957, it sold 2.5 million copies and rocketed to #1 in the charts. His next song made it to #31 and his self-penned, third hit, "Wonderful World," climbed to #12. He was a sensation and RCA realized his manager was right. In 1960, Sam Cooke became the first major black artist to sign with the prestigious label, paving the way for the soul artists who would dominate the pop charts through the mid-sixties.

Cooke's second marriage, in 1959, was to his high school sweetheart Barbara Campbell. They brought three children into their "wonderful world," which included their $100,000 home in the exclusive Los Feliz Hills, near Hollywood. He continued to write most of his own hits: "Cupid," "Chain Gang," "Another Saturday Night," "Bring It On Home to Me," "Ain't That Good News," "Twistin' the Night Away," and "Havin' a Party," all of which

The dynamic Sam Cooke altered the course of pop/soul music, achieving international success that most black performers only dreamed of in the early sixties.

sold more than 10 million copies worldwide. Sam Cooke had everything going his way in 1963, when tragedy suddenly struck. The Cookes' only son, Vincent, age two, drowned in the family swimming pool. It was months before Sam could work again. But when he was ready to revive his career, he found himself hotter than ever.

In June of 1964, Sam opened at the Copacabana in New York. A 12-foot portrait reading "Sam—The Biggest Cooke in Town" was hung in Times Square at a cost of $10,000 a month. He could easily afford such publicity. Besides his possessions and his companies, he had a golden ear for talent. As head of SAR/Derby Records, he discovered and worked with Lou Rawls, Billy Preston, Little Richard, and the Womack Brothers. His brother, L.C., also had a brief solo career under Sam's SAR label, and continued composing, but he never again achieved the heights of his first hit. Sam's close friends described him as a generous and much loved man. His international eminence, only a dream to most black performers, emerged as a beacon of hope and achievement in the midst of the growing racial tensions of the early sixties.

Was there another side of Sam Cooke that got him in trouble? A number of his friends still think that he was set up on the night of December 10, 1964, the night Cooke sang "Ain't That Good News" for some pals in an Italian restaurant in Hollywood, not knowing that this would be his final performance.

In the booth next to Sam's were three men and a twenty-two-year-old Eurasian woman named Lisa Boyer. One of the men introduced the singer to her, and they seemed to hit it off. When Lisa got up to leave, about 1:00 a.m., Cooke offered her a ride, suggesting that they could continue their conversation in a quieter spot. She agreed and they left together for PJ's. A crowd besieged Cooke as they entered, so his companion waited at a lonely table in the rear. When Cooke finally looked for her later, he saw her talking with another man. He lunged furiously at the stranger, but friends caught him and cooled him down. He and Lisa left immediately but did not go to her Hollywood Boulevard hotel. Instead, she later testified, he sped along the freeway toward the Polaris Motel, a shabby place whose residents often rented by the hour.

"Slow down! I'm frightened!" she claims to have pleaded with him. "Please, Mr. Cooke, take me home!"

"You're such a lovely girl, such pretty long hair. I just want to talk to you," he cajoled. "Don't worry, I'll take you home." Pulling into the motel parking lot, he walked quickly to the manager's office. Miss Boyer testified that she resisted entering, but if she did, the stocky, fifty-five-year-old Bertha Lee Franklin didn't notice. Franklin looked at Cooke's signature in the register, without recognizing her famous guest.

"You'll have to put 'Mr. and Mrs.,' " she said, handing him a key.

"He dragged me to the room, locked the door, and threw me on the bed, pinning me there," Boyer told a packed courtroom at the coroner's inquest. "He kept saying, 'We're just going to talk,' but he pulled my sweater off and ripped my dress." She asked to go to the bathroom, but finding its door lock broken and window painted shut, she knew she was trapped.

No one could touch Sam Cooke's smooth, soulful tones.

When Boyer came out, still in her bra and slip, Cooke was naked. He went to use the bathroom. When he did, she bolted for the door, grabbing her clothing as she ran. She stopped at the manager's office, pounding on the door. By the time Mrs. Franklin, who was on the phone with the motel owner, Evelyn Carr, could get to the door, the terrified Boyer had fled into the night.

She ran beyond the parking lot before stopping to put on her clothes. Boyer now realized she had also taken most of Cooke's clothes. She left them there, found a phone booth a block from the motel, and called the police. "Help me! I've been kidnapped! I don't know where I am. Please come get me!" She gave them the number in the booth, and waited.

Meanwhile, Mrs. Franklin heard another knock at her door, and again put down the phone to answer it. There was Cooke, in a rage, demanding to see his sweetie. He wore only a sport coat and shoes, though Mrs. Franklin could not see this through the office window. "There's no one here," she told him. He took off for his Ferrari, pulling it up to Franklin's apartment. Leaving the motor running, he jumped out to again pound on her door.

"You've got my girl in there! I know you do!" he shouted. "Now let me in there."

"If you want to search this place, get the police," Franklin shouted back. "There's no one in here. Go away!"

"Damn the police!" Cooke screamed. Slamming his shoulder to the door, he broke it down. Evelyn Carr listened anxiously over the phone as the incensed Cooke tore through the apartment looking for Boyer. When he did not find her, he turned his anger on Mrs. Franklin, grabbing at the woman's arms, twisting and turning her around. She fell to the floor, the half-naked Cooke falling on top of her.

"I was scratching, kicking, biting, everything," Mrs. Franklin said at the inquest. Barbara Cooke wept silently.

"I got up. He came to me. I pushed him back again, then I grabbed the pistol and started shooting." She fired three shots at close range, penetrating his chest, heart, and both lungs.

"Lady! You shot me!" Cooke screamed in disbelief. He clung to her, his blood spilling everywhere. Evelyn Carr called the police.

"I started fighting again," Mrs. Franklin continued. "I grabbed a stick. The first time I hit him, it broke. . . ." She hit him over and over until he released his grip and fell to the floor. He died within minutes.

It was assumed that when Cooke emerged from the bathroom and found Boyer gone, he ran to the window and saw her knocking on Mrs. Franklin's door. This is why he refused to believe the girl was not there. Franklin, who kept the pistol around because of numerous robberies in the area, was in fear for her life. "If he had nerve enough to run into my apartment and jump me," she told the coroner's jury, "how did I know what he was going to do?" They agreed.

The death was ruled justifiable homicide, causing a flurry of protests from Sam's friends. They claimed that Lisa Boyer, an "unemployed receptionist," was a prostitute who had "escaped" from Cooke with most of his clothing, including his wallet. Barbara said he had left the house with $150 and police discovered $108 in a money clip in the jacket he was wearing. Lisa had no previous police record, and both she and Mrs. Franklin voluntarily took lie detector tests which cleared them of any further suspicion.

Friends shook their heads in wonder when barely two months later Bobby Womack, one of Cook's protegés, married Barbara Cooke . . . and her inheritance. The union did not last.

"We knew [Cooke] well . . . he sang at our son's birthday party," an old friend later confided. "He didn't cheat on his wife and I could never picture him running half-naked anywhere. He was a refined man . . . and a nice man."

Singer/preacher Little Richard worked with Sam Cooke and loved him. Of that bizarre night, he says, "It wasn't talked about. Everyone kept quiet . . . It was just one of those things."

INGER STEVENS
Looking for Love

The world came apart for 5-year-old Inger Stevens—and her seven brothers and sisters—when their parents got a divorce. At thirteen, Inger sailed from her native Stockholm to join her father, who was a Fulbright scholar at Harvard. The Salvation Army met the frightened young immigrant who spoke no English, because her father was too busy to go to the dock that day.

"I think I matured earlier," she said in retrospect. "It's a question of having to assume responsibility. A child can sense unhappiness in a home. I learned quite early that life is not a finishing school."

Her father remarried three years later and dragged her off to Manhattan, Kansas. Inger felt alienated from her father and stepmother, and she kept completely to herself. She finally ran away for her first taste of show business. She performed, under the name of Kay Palmer, in a Kansas City burlesque house for $60 a week. Weeks later, wearing a skimpy Santa suit, she was belting out "Santa Claus Is Coming to Town" when she made eye contact with a customer in the front row . . . her father. Though he dragged her home, he couldn't stop his determined daughter. She packed up for New York two years later, in 1952, one week after she graduated from high school.

To pay for classes at the Actors Studio, Inger worked in the garment district by day and as a chorus girl in the Latin Quarter by night. In between, she pounded the streets in search of stage work. With her classic blonde, blue-eyed, Swedish beauty, and teeny 20-inch waist, luck smiled down upon her. Her first roles were in commercials. She began to build a reputation with roles in several television plays for the premiere season of Playhouse 90, and at last, in 1956, came the Broadway debut that she'd awaited for so long. During the unmemorable show's brief run, Inger married her agent, Tony Soglio. He was an older man who turned into a tyrant almost immediately after the "I do's."

Her innocent beauty belied her troubled nature.

He was given to fits of jealousy and uncontrollable temper, and wouldn't allow her to even have friends. She divorced him only six months later, charitably explaining that she had been "too young." While she was in Los Angeles filming her first movie, *Man on Fire*, the bedimpled actress told reporters, "Since I've come to America, I'd rather sleep with air conditioning than with my husband."

The young starlet soon found herself deeply involved with another older man, 52-year-old Bing Crosby, who was her co-star in *Man on Fire*. When his ardor turned to another woman (Kathy, whom he eventually married), Stevens was devastated. She threw herself into her career to forget. She remained in Hollywood and played leading lady to Yul Brynner in *The Buccaneer* and to Harry Belafonte in *The World, The Flesh, and The Devil*. Certain close confreres were aware that offscreen, she played leading lady to a very prominent, but very married star, in a very clandestine romance. Inger never revealed her lover's identity to anyone; it was typical of the way she could keep her emotional life bottled up inside, intensely secret from her friends. When the affair ended, there was no one to whom she could turn. Instead, she drank enough cleaning fluid to put an end to her distraught life—almost. During the three days that she lay unconscious, phlebitis set in, swelling her legs to four times their normal size. Her life was saved, but Stevens's ordeal left her with an agonizing affliction . . . complete blindness. She remained in darkness for two weeks, then her vision miraculously returned. She went right back to work.

In 1961, Stevens was in Portugal when she narrowly escaped death again, as one of a few to survive a plane crash that killed eighty. "I still hate to talk about it," she shuddered during an interview two years later. "The plane started burning and I thought I would be burned alive. I put on my coat, of all things, and curled up on the floor. Somehow I escaped and now I feel as if I were on borrowed time . . . that the worst is over and it's clear sailing." Then she added, "But it is reassuring to know you can continue to function under pressure and not give in to hysteria." Functioning under pressure was what she was good at. Handling the pressure and hysteria from within was another story.

Later that year, Inger seemed to find happiness in romance at last, but strangely enough, she again chose a romance she was forced to keep secret. She was married in Tijuana to Ike Jones, a businessman, musician, producer, and one-time star end with the UCLA football team. She kept the marriage a secret because Jones was black. The American public probably could never have accepted the Nordic, wholesome-as-buttermilk Stevens they'd come to know, if they knew too much. Even several years later, a member of the President's cabinet, Dean Rusk, would feel compelled to offer his resignation when his daughter entered a similar mixed marriage. (President Johnson did not accept it.) Thus, the couple signed a contract, agreeing to keep the marriage a secret for the sake of her career, which had, like Inger herself, made a strong recovery through her "Scandinavian determination."

Stevens was now seen frequently on popular shows like *The Twilight Zone*, *DuPont Show of the Week*, and *Dick Powell Theater*, and turned in a critically acclaimed performance on film in *The New Interns*. Back on Broadway in

1963, she replaced Barbara Bel Geddes in the smash hit *Mary, Mary.* But for Inger, it wouldn't be a long run. She had struggled a long time, but she finally had it . . . the lead in a TV series of her own. As Katy Holstrum, *The Farmer's Daughter*, her refreshing style and sensational beauty lit up America's hearts and living rooms for three years, in one of the most successful shows of the decade. Inger portrayed the live-in housekeeper for a widowed congressman, played by William Windom, and his two children. Her first season, she won the Golden Globe and was nominated for an Emmy for "Best Female TV Star." (She lost the latter to Mary Tyler Moore.) When fans pleaded to see the TV couple marry, ABC scored a publicity coup aided by an unwitting cast of international dignitaries. Enlisting the help of Washington, D.C.'s renowned "social director," Perle Mesta, the network threw a gala party in the capital to announce the "congressman's marriage." Bewildered ambassadors from all nations shook hands with an official couple they had never met—Congressman Windom and his wife, a farmer's daughter—or as Windom referred to her, "a lady of secrets."

Stevens, still suffering from the extreme mood swings that had always plagued her, sought psychiatric treatment while she was serving on the advisory board of the Neuropsychiatric Institute of the UCLA Medical Center. The benevolent star also chaired the California Council for Mentally Retarded Children and, for a short time, considered devoting all her time to this cause. Few people knew that she had two mentally retarded cousins back in Sweden. She was also a weekend painter, and organized a celebrity art exhibition at a fashionable gallery to raise funds for her causes.

At all these public appearances, Inger was escorted by her agent or a close friend, while Ike remained tucked away at their Malibu home. Only in the seclusion of their celebrity beach colony could the couple drop their mask and behave normally. Meanwhile, Inger's career was soaring. She made her song-and-dance debut on *The Danny Kaye Show*, in 1966, and her acclaim in films like *A Guide for the Married Man, Madigan, 5 Card Stud*, and *Hang 'Em High* gained her the distinction of being the first female TV star to make it big in movies, à la Steve McQueen, whose popular TV series, *Wanted—Dead or Alive*, made his name a household word. The last two years of her life, she had seven starring roles, with her final film, *Dream of Kings*, sparking talk of an Academy Award nomination. "Farmer's Daughter New Sex Symbol," declared the press, while Paramount Studios anointed her successor to Grace Kelly. Yet she still had not found happiness. Her nine years of marriage to Jones were tumultuous, but she had borne up well and they had stuck together . . . until March 1970.

Inger came home from a two-week vacation with an announcement. She was in love with someone else, an actor named Burt Reynolds, with whom she had just completed *Run Simon, Run* for TV. She intended to marry him in three months. With that, she packed her things and moved to her second home, on Woodrow Wilson Drive, high in the Hollywood Hills. She had previously asked Lola McNally, her studio hairdresser and friend, to stay in the house while it was empty. Now that they were roommates, Inger confided to her how anxious she was to end her stormy relationship with Jones. During

Inger in **A Dream of Kings**, *1969, National General Pictures—"The Farmer's Daughter" turned sex symbol.*

the five weeks the women lived together, Lola noticed Inger's mood acceler-
ating. She was excited about her new romance and about her new television
series, forebodingly entitled *The Most Deadly Game,* co-starring Ralph Bel-
lamy and George Maharis.* She had returned from production meetings full
of enthusiasm. Lola thought nothing about spending the night of April 29th
at a friend's. She even telephoned Inger at 11:15 that night and "there was no
hint of trouble." But Inger was just hiding her emotions again. Sometime in
those early morning hours, the demons that had haunted her all her life, fed
by the broken marriage, took control. Helpless against them, she swallowed a
bottleful of barbiturates.

Lola returned to the house that last morning in April at 10:30. Walking into
the kitchen, she screamed when she found Inger lying facedown on the floor.
"Inger! Inger!" she cried, shaking her, but the actress, too far gone, could only
mumble unintelligibly. She died on the way to the hospital. The extremely
high dosage of Tedral in her system left the coroner with no doubt that the
thirty-six-year-old's death was a suicide, though he speculated that Stevens
was trying to call for help when she passed out. For fans of the vibrant Katy
Holstrum, Inger Stevens's suicide was a shocking incongruity. The beautiful
woman who had talked of taking responsibility, of functioning under pressure,
had died alone, afraid, and out of control.

Though Jones claimed her body and paid for the funeral, he could not prove
to the courts' satisfaction that they had been legally married. Stevens had long
since lost the Tijuana marriage certificate and their contract of secrecy was
not enough. Her brother and sister testified that Stevens and Jones had lived
together as man and wife, producing many papers on which she'd signed her
name Inger Jones, but the court would not accept it. Instead, they turned her
$162,000 estate over to her parents, whom she seldom spoke to, and who had
not cared enough to see their daughter in more than eighteen years.

* Yvette Mimieux became her replacement.

JANIS JOPLIN
Tell Me I'm Good

Seth and Dorothy Joplin knew that Janis always needed more attention than their other children. "She was unhappy and unsatisfied without it," explained Dorothy. "The normal rapport wasn't adequate." From a very early age, Janis just had to have approval. She'd do anything anyone asked her, just to please them. In the act of pushing herself to be the best at everything, she made excellent grades, even skipping a year in elementary school. Her early childhood in the oil refining town of Port Arthur, deep in southeast Texas, was near-perfect. "Then the whole world . . . just turned on me."

"I was a misfit. I read, I painted, I didn't hate niggers. Man, those people back home hurt me." Once she let her position on integration be known, two boys followed Janis everywhere, calling her "nigger lover." The more the kids taunted her, the more she rebelled and the more she withdrew.

"It was almost like she drew the hatred to her," a high school friend recalled. As a teenager, Janis went through ravaging changes. Her pretty blonde hair turned mousey and limp. She grew to a hefty size, and her skin broke out so badly she was left with deep scars that required sanding. She was tough and loud as a defense against her loneliness. When groups of children gathered to throw things at her while shouting their favorite names for her—"pig," and "freak," or "creep"—little pieces of her fragile spirit were shattered. The wounds never healed. Most people saw only the rough, jagged edges Janis thrust outward. She was determined to seem in command in public, but alone in her room, when she sang in the style of her idol, Bessie Smith, all the pain and frustration poured out. In art school Janis made friends with the "beatnik" crowd, who encouraged her to sing before an audience. In 1963, at the age of twenty, she moved with them to the North Beach area of San Francisco.

Singing for small groups in smoke-filled coffeehouses, Janis quickly became

The sixties Rock Carnival Queen—an insecure little girl cried out from behind the hardboiled image.

a part of the loose, communal lifestyle of the early sixties with all of its trappings. Her singing seemed headed nowhere, and she began drinking heavily—but that wasn't enough of an escape. She learned to shoot methadrine and heroin, too. After a year of abuse, she retreated to Port Arthur hoping to pick up the pieces.

The irresistible lure of a good, solid band called her back to San Francisco. In early 1966, the earliest days of the Haight-Ashbury "district," there was only a small group of rock bands. Big Brother and the Holding Company was at the forefront, along with The Grateful Dead, Quicksilver Messenger Service, Country Joe and the Fish, Jefferson Airplane (before Grace Slick, who was in another S.F. band, The Great Society). Most of the members of Big Brother—Dave Getz, James Gurley, Peter Albin, and Sam Andrew—knew Janis's bluesy style and wanted her to front their group. At last Janis was accepted! The adventure of it all thrilled her, and she burst onto this new, hip, free-loving scene with gusto. Night after night at Bill Graham's Fillmore Auditorium, she stood mesmerized by Otis Redding and Tina Turner. She used what she learned from those soulful greats and she and her band grew in reputation. They began to attract the usual following of groupies, and on many a night "Big Brother" kicked Janis out of the back of the van, telling her to find her own way home while they partied with their female fans. Seemingly undaunted Janis talked coarsely over breakfast about her own conquests, in an effort to fit in, to be "one of the guys." Even with local fame nothing had changed. She was still a misfit. She returned to drugs and enjoyed bisexual liaisons that offered the affection she so sorely needed. And she drank—a lot. Even though they came to epitomize an electric generation turned on by LSD and hallucinogens, Janis and an L.A. local hero, soon-to-be legend, Jim Morrison, found most of their freedom in the bottle. She lived for a time with Country Joe MacDonald. When that ended she reverted to being loud and drunk, shooting pool with The Dead or another local group, the nonmusical Hell's Angels. She soon became lost behind her own mask. Those around her thought she was as tough as she appeared to be—a misconception that would prove fatal.

Her biggest break of all came at the Monterey International Pop Festival in 1967. Janis tore the audience apart, belting the blues in a ballsy, full-throated style like nothing the flower children had heard before—and they screamed for more. When she repeated this phenomenon three months later at the Monterey Jazz Festival, the media went wild. There had been no hype, no advance publicity. It was all Janis. She was an instant success and Columbia Records hurriedly got her under contract. Her first album, "Cheap Thrills," was released within a year and sold in the millions. Janis throbbed with the hurt, rejection, and loneliness from which the hopeful sixties had sprung. She put herself through an emotional wringer for her audience and they clasped her to their hearts. The girl from Port Arthur had found love among the multitudes.

Time magazine called her "probably the most powerful singer to emerge from the white rock movement." Richard Goldstein, in *Vogue*, raved about "the most staggering leading woman in rock . . . she slinks like tar, scowls like war . . . clutching the knees of a final stanza, begging it not to leave . . . Janis Joplin can sing the chic off any listener." Though she gloried in it, the overnight success frightened poor Janis, insecure to the core. She didn't believe she deserved it and had no idea what was expected of her. Running at full throttle—like she felt a rock star was expected to do—her anthem became "Sex, Dope, and Cheap Thrills," washed down with a stiff belt of Southern Comfort bourbon. If the public liked her outrageous, then that's what she would give 'em. Hitting Jim Morrison over the head with a bottle of scotch not only secured the drunken battle for her, it made great copy. She wanted to be considered scandalous, especially by men, but she intimidated most of them because the bewildered creatures could see no further than the hard-boiled exterior that was, by now, second nature to her. "It's not easy living up to Janis Joplin, you know," she once confided to a friend. ". . . That stuff made me famous!"

By the time Joplin appeared at the Woodstock festival in 1969, her onstage persona, nicknamed "Pearl," was a reflection of her offstage existence. Loose, sloppy, usually drunk, and occasionally foul mouthed, she carried on like a debauched carnival queen. The bottle of Southern Comfort sat on top of an

Janis letting loose at the San Jose Pop Festival.

amplifier, always within reach. "Tell me I'm good!" she begged, and the crowds would always cry for more. It was never enough for them or for her. "On stage," she told an interviewer, "I make love to twenty-five thousand people. Then I go home alone." When offstage she continued to use dope. It made her lazy and irritable. The pain in her voice was real. Outwardly, she could incite a crowd to riot, which was starting to make booking her a difficult job. Intelligent and defiant, she fooled most of those around her into believing she wasn't dependent on anything—not drugs, or people, or love. The title of her second album said it. "I Got Dem Ol' Kozmic Blues Again, Mama."

The following summer brought what should have been an auspicious occasion—Janis's tenth high school reunion. She could have returned to many towns in triumph, the rock queen of a generation . . . but not Port Arthur. Here nothing had changed, except now she was more of an outcast than ever before. Sitting behind granny glasses in a local bar, feathers in her hair, her arms wrapped by dozens of bracelets, she granted a painfully revealing interview to the local media.

"Did you entertain in high school?" the reporter asked.

"Only when I walked down the aisles." She laughed but under that laugh was the echo of "pig" and "freak." Always the tough broad, Joplin laughed her way through a "hometown girl makes good" scene, except it wasn't good. There was no red carpet, no welcoming committee . . . nothing. Janis felt mortally wounded. All she really wanted was for the town of Port Arthur to approve, to tell her she was good. With no such plaudits, she flew to Los Angeles to complete "Pearl," her third and most successful album. It would also be her last.

Janis, plagued by her usual lack of confidence, put herself under the gun to make "Pearl" a success. She needed, and got, a great deal of support, as friends helped her remain dope-free for five full months, but, "The only people who love me," she quipped, "are on my payroll."

Yet, she did have love, as well as plenty of money. She was building a "dream house," her first home, in Northern California. Janis planned to live there with Seth Morgan, a bright, twenty-one-year-old Berkeley student. He and Janis, now twenty-seven, were engaged to be married. "I love to go to parties and like to have a good time," she sang, "but if it gets too pale after awhile, I started looking to find one good man . . . it ain't much, it's only everything." *

Janis, and her life, had suddenly become a paradox—a happy blues singer. What kind of an album could come of that? It ate through her tough facade, straight to the tight ball of fear in the pit of her stomach. Everything was so right, so good; she couldn't possibly deserve it. Something would screw it all up, she knew that—it was the waiting that was unbearable. Perhaps she didn't realize the wait was over. When several friends from the "old days," including a female ex-lover, arrived at the Landmark, the seedy Hollywood hotel where she liked to stay, the delicate balance she'd maintained for five months top-

---

* "One Good Man." Words and music by J. Joplin, copyright 1969 Ascap/Columbia Records/ CBS Inc. 51 W. 52nd St. N.Y., N.Y.

pled under their influence. Somewhere around September 11th, Janis started using drugs again. Only a few friends found out. She'd promised to quit as soon as the album was finished. She pushed Seth to come down on her about it, but no one was really worried. Everyone thought Janis knew what she was doing, she always seemed in control.

About that time, Jimi Hendrix was found dead in his London flat. Janis was shaken up but not shocked. "It just decreases my chances," she told a friend. "Two rock stars can't die in the same year." Whether or not she believed that, she expressed the desire to quit dope again, just as soon as she used up what she had left.

The recording session broke early for dinner on Saturday evening, October 3, 1970. Janis and the band went out for Chinese food in Hollywood, then returned to the studio to hear the instrumental track to Nick Gravenites's "Buried Alive in the Blues." If ever a song had her name on it, this was the one. Janis was enthused about doing the vocal track the following night, the night Seth was to arrive from New York. He had planned to fly in earlier, but they'd had a quarrel over the phone, and in a fateful move, he postponed his arrival by one day.

After the session, Janis and Ken Pearson, the organist from her Full Tilt Boogie Band, went for drinks at Barney's Beanery. In the old days this glorified pool hall and hamburger joint was a favorite hangout of John Barrymore, Jean Harlow, and Clara Bow. The fifties and sixties drew a rougher crowd—James Dean, the Hell's Angels, and Janis Joplin. This night she was drinking a screwdriver in the darkened bar, talking excitedly about the album and her future. A fan punched up one of her songs on the jukebox. Janis threw back another drink. Pearson said she was in good spirits. He dropped her off at the Landmark about 12:30, Sunday morning.

Her room was neatly arranged for Seth's arrival. Janis washed up and slipped into a short nightgown. This was her last night alone, her last night to get high, so she figured she'd shoot up one final time and throw away the rest. She'd purchased some stuff that afternoon—very high-quality stuff. No doubt she knew that after using heroin again for only three weeks, her tolerance was not what it had been. But she wasn't aware that the new batch was ten times more powerful than what she was used to. She filled her veins with the usual amount, dropping the rest into the wastebasket. She slipped her works back into their Chinese box and put the box in a drawer, under some clothes. With $5, she walked to the lobby for cigarettes, stopping momentarily to chat with the clerk. Everything was cool—Janis was high. She wasn't afraid of anything now—or ever again.

The clerk watched Janis stroll the short distance to her room. There she bolted the door behind her. Once again Janis had put a wall between herself and the world. Only a step from the door her muscles constricted, her fists clenched, and her body contorted with a jolt that threw her to the floor so violently it almost broke her nose. She landed between the bed and the nightstand, still clutching her cigarette. It was about 1:40 a.m. Almost two days passed before anyone broke down the door and discovered her body.

Janis had made two provisions in her will. First, she wanted $2,500 set aside for a funeral party. The invitations read, "Drinks are on Pearl." Two hundred guests were entertained by The Grateful Dead and other Northern California bands from the old days. By the wee hours, practically all of the Bay Area had crashed the scene, helping themselves to anything that wasn't nailed down. Her second request was to be cremated and to have her ashes scattered from an airplane over Stinson Beach in Marin County, California. It was her favorite spot, a place where, for a few scattered moments of her life, she'd felt loved.

The rock-and-roll world was already reeling from Hendrix's death sixteen days earlier. Now it had happened to Janis. In nine months, Jim Morrison would complete the Rock-and-Roll Heaven trilogy. Even The Rolling Stones' Altamont concert had been marred by violence and death. The times they were a'changin' . . . the flower-power of the sixties had OD'd.

SHARON TATE
Night of Horror

August 8, 1969, was a sweltering summer night, the third day of a heat wave that had seared Los Angeles. The Sunset Strip was crowded with the long-haired, barefoot children of the "drug culture." Some of them were hippies, whose generation of love and peace would culminate in a few weeks at Woodstock. However, there were other beings out there, presumably human, who did not have love or peace on their minds. High above the perpetual party on The Strip, four people prowled the quiet canyons of Beverly Hills in an old Ford, looking for a house. When they found that house the sweltering silence of Benedict Canyon would be shattered by the screams of five defenseless people, victims of one of the most horrifying, savage slayings in American history—a crime few want to remember but nobody has ever been able to forget. The night was so hot . . . that in the morning America would be a different place, forced to question the very direction of its civilization.

By the next afternoon everyone knew—the headlines screamed, "Mass Murder in Beverly Hills—Sharon Tate and 4 Others Dead in Blood Orgy of Ritual Murder." The people of Los Angeles, shaken the previous year by Robert Kennedy's assassination, were now incapacitated with shock. The savagery was unthinkable, the victims so prominent. Everywhere doors were bolted and security guards hired, especially in the affluent entertainment community, whose residents now lived in stark fear for their own safety. After all, the mutilated victims were among Hollywood's best and brightest: twenty-six-year-old Abigail Folger, heiress to the coffee fortune; her thirty-two-year-old lover, Wojtek Frykowski, a Polish producer and savant; Jay Sebring, thirty-five-year-old internationally known hair stylist; Steven Parent, an eighteen-year-old student; and the most well known, Sharon Tate, twenty-six, actress

Sharon "loafing."

and wife of acclaimed Polish director Roman Polanski. Murdered too was the Polanskis' unborn child. Sharon Tate had been 8½ months pregnant.

Tate had met Polanski in London in 1966. They fell in love while he was directing her in his parody *The Fearless Vampire Killers*. From the beginning they were an unlikely couple. He, the diminutive Pole, child of war-torn Europe, the genius behind *Rosemary's Baby*, and she, the doe-eyed, honey blonde. "She was so sweet and lovely," he said of Sharon, ". . . I didn't believe people like that existed. She was beautiful, without phoniness . . . fantastic . . . an angel who I'll never meet again in my life."

The daughter of an Army Intelligence officer who lived in dozens of towns in the United States and abroad, Sharon spoke Italian fluently and possessed what many called a European flavor. Just six months old when she won her first beauty contest—Miss Tiny Tot of Dallas—she went on to win several more titles as a teenager and, against the wishes of her father, decided to pursue a movie career.

While making the rounds of agents' offices in Hollywood, the stunning twenty-year-old was quickly spotted by producer Martin Ransohoff, who signed her to a multipicture contract and plunged her into classes of all kinds. "Bodybuilding, speech, voice, singing, dancing, dramatics . . . you name it, I took it," Sharon told an interviewer. "A pretty face will open doors and that's it. You have to have the talent to back up what you have going in front." Except for two *Beverly Hillbillies* episodes, Sharon's television appearances were in a black wig and under a false name—Ransohoff's idea, until he was sure Sharon could handle herself. Once he felt confident of her ability, he cast her in *Thirteen,* later retitled *Eye of the Devil,* starring David Niven and Deborah Kerr. Then Ransohoff set about convincing Polanski to use Sharon instead of Jill St. John in *The Fearless Vampire Killers.*

After a two-year love affair, Sharon and Roman were married in London in 1968. His influence changed her career outlook. "Roman has helped me grow tremendously. . . . He's a very strong man mentally. That's what I need—

Roman Polanski is about to receive a kiss from Sharon Tate in this scene from The Fearless Vampire Killers, *which Roman also directed. They fell in love during the shooting and married two years later.*

someone who leads, but doesn't dominate . . . a man is sexiest to me when he's vital and creative." She had just completed a part in *Don't Make Waves*, opposite Tony Curtis, when she was offered her first important role. Though she didn't care much for either the book or the film, *Valley of the Dolls* was a big career break. The role, a starlet who knew that her only talents were packed into her bra, capitalized on Sharon's classic beauty and wide-eyed sex appeal, but her real acting ability still lay virtually unexplored. A disappointed Tate went right into *The Wrecking Crew* with Dean Martin, cast as a kung fu expert. As her coach the studio hired Hollywood's foremost martial-arts instructor, the legendary Bruce Lee, who had not yet begun his brief but celebrated career in front of the cameras. He and the Polanskis became close friends. Though Sharon was getting much needed exposure, she hoped to show what she could really do in a film she and Roman planned, based on *Tess of the D'Urbervilles*, a novel she insisted he read. They were making plans to do the film when the lowest of mankind shattered her lofty ambitions.

On August 8 Sharon was anxiously awaiting Polanski's return from London, where he was working on a film. They spoke earlier in the day and she told him the heat was making her edgy; she wished he'd hurry home. He had promised to be home for his birthday on the fifteenth and she had already enrolled him in a class for expectant fathers. Keeping her company in their rented home on Cielo Drive were their close friends "Gibby" Folger and Wojtek Frykowski. Frykowski was something of a legend among the sophisticates who ridiculed the Communist regime in his native Poland, where he and Polanski were so well known. Twice married and considered a bit of a playboy, he had been described as a "Polish Hemingway hero." "He had style," a friend commented. "He was more than an intellectual. He was the kind of guy intellectuals love to have around. Women loved him." Eventually, both Polanski and Frykowski left Poland to escape repression and censorship. Frykowski and Gibby, who were introduced by a fellow artist and Pole, Jerzy Kosinski (the author of *Being There* who now claims he narrowly escaped being there that night), had lived in the house while the Polanskis were away and were staying on until Roman returned. At 12:30 a.m. on that hot night, Gibby was reading in the bedroom, while Wojtek had fallen asleep on the couch in the living room.

Sharon, wearing a bra and bikini bottoms to beat the heat, was talking with Sebring in the master bedroom. Sebring was the premier men's hair stylist about town. He'd been featured in *Time* and *Newsweek* and boasted a client list that included Paul Newman, Henry Fonda, Frank Sinatra, Steve McQueen, Sammy Davis, Jr., and George Peppard. At one time, he'd been engaged to Sharon, but she ended their three-year affair when she met Polanski. Sebring was not bitter and, in fact, looked upon Roman and Sharon as his only real family. He lived a short distance up the canyon in a "jinxed" house; it had once been the unhappy home of Jean Harlow and Paul Bern, the scene of restless domesticity where Bern had shot himself. But Sebring didn't believe in jinxes.

Meanwhile, Tex Watson, Patricia Krenwinkel, Susan Atkins, and Linda Kasabian had been driving frantically for hours, searching for the secluded home on Cielo Drive. The four young runaways were messengers of death, sent on their mission by Charles Manson, a small, psychotic man with icy, penetrating eyes. "He was aware of your deepest fears and anxieties just by looking at you," said Watson, who lived with other members of the "family" at the abandoned Spahn Movie Ranch out in the desert. Far away from curious eyes they indulged in group sex, lots of LSD, and daily sermons from the man they believed to be Jesus Christ, returned as Charlie "Man's Son." He believed that the Beatles were speaking to him on their White Album, urging him to

The angelic Mrs. Roman Polanski was 8½ months pregnant with their first child when she became a victim of one of Hollywood's most savage murders.

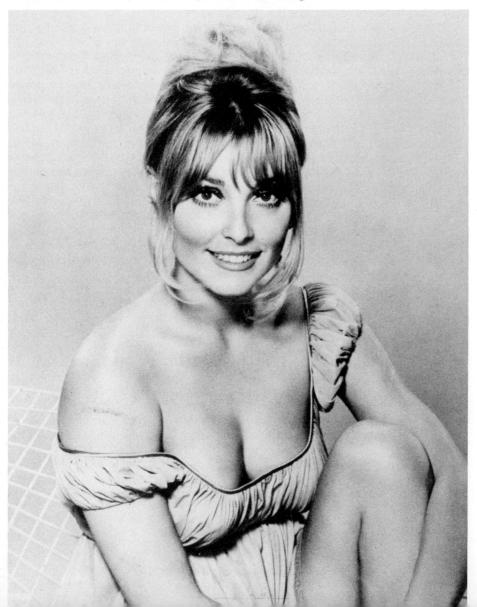

begin "Helter Skelter," his name for the imminent black/white race war. To begin his war Manson had chosen a house on Cielo Drive where he had once played his songs for an unimpressed music producer. He was aware that the man had moved but was sure some new "piggies," on whom he could seek revenge, had taken over the house.

"I don't know how many people are there," he instructed the chosen four, "but destroy everyone in the house. Make it as gruesome as possible. Use knives. Mutilate them. Write something on the wall that will shock the world." Before leaving the ranch, Tex snorted a large amount of speed. When they finally found the secluded house, he cut the phone wires and led Krenwinkel and Atkins over a hill that came down right inside the front gate. Kasabian, new to the "family," remained at the car. At that moment the headlights from Steve Parent's Rambler lit up the gate.

Parent, a recent high school graduate working two summer jobs to afford college in the fall, was just on his way out. He had dropped by to visit William Garretson, the nineteen-year-old grounds keeper who lived in the guest cottage behind the main house. The cottage was remote enough so that Garretson would not be found during the ensuing slaughter. Listening to music through headphones while the others were being butchered, he didn't see or hear anything.

"Halt!" Watson yelled when Steve stopped to push the gate control button. He emerged from the shadowy bushes, a gun in one hand and a knife in the other. "Please don't hurt me; I'm your friend . . . I won't tell!" Steve held up his left arm as a shield. Through the open window Watson slashed the upheld arm with the knife, severing all the tendons. Then, point-blank, he shot the boy four times, killing him instantly. Though exhilarated by the murder, the three waited to see whether anyone had heard the shots. Apparently no one had. Walking past the Christmas lights that twinkled from a split-rail fence, the death-dealing trio, each armed with a knife, entered the house.

"What time is it?" mumbled Frykowski, not yet half-awake. Watson kicked him in the head. "What? Who are you? What do you want?"

"I am the devil and I'm here to do the devil's business . . . another word and you're dead," answered Watson. Frykowski stood frozen in silence when Gibby appeared, followed by Krenwinkel with a knife pointed at her back. Gibby looked at Frykowski helplessly. He could only shake his head. Sharon had thrown a negligee over her shoulders as she and Sebring were being led to the living room. She hesitated at the door and Watson jerked her into the room.

"Hey, watch it," Sebring protested. "Can't you see she's pregnant?"

"One more word and you're dead," Tex repeated ominously.

"He means it," Frykowski urged, as they tied his hands behind his back. Watson, his veins flowing with speed, looped the rope around the necks of the other three, stretching it tight over a rafter. Sebring protested again.

"I told you," Watson screamed. He fired at Sebring, who crumpled to the floor. Sharon and Gibby screamed. "Give me all your money," Tex demanded. Atkins followed a terrified Folger to the bedroom, returning with $70. "That's all?"

"How much do you want?" Sharon pleaded.

"Thousands."

"We don't have it in the house but we can get it for you."

"I'm not kidding," Tex warned.

"I know." Sharon whimpered. Sebring, in agony, groaned at her feet. Watson lunged at him like a mad dog, stabbing him five, six, seven times.

"No! Stop! What are you going to do with us?" Sharon cried.

"You're all going to die."

Frykowski fought back. Attacking Atkins he kicked and dragged her to the floor. "Kill him!" Watson commanded, but the rope around Frykowski's wrists had slipped and he had the upper hand. Fighting for his life he tore at her hair. She stabbed his leg several times before finally dropping the knife on the couch. Watson couldn't get a clean shot at him. He jumped on top of the pair, smashing Frykowski's head again and again with his pistol until the butt shattered into three pieces. The incredibly strong Frykowski dragged his two attackers out of the living room onto the front porch, leaving a trail of blood behind him. Outside, he looked up to see the horror-stricken face of Linda Kasabian.

"Help me! Oh, God, help me!" he cried.

"I'm sorry . . . I'm so sorry," she sobbed. He screamed and pleaded for more than ten minutes as Watson mercilessly stabbed him over and over. His blood was everywhere. From deep within him, Frykowski let go one terrible scream. Watson shot him twice, watching with frenzied satisfaction as his target collapsed in a heap on the red-stained flagstone.

"Make it stop!" Kasabian screamed, frantically racing back to the car.

"It's too late," Atkins yelled after her. Then she saw Folger fleeing into the night. "She's getting away!" Atkins screamed to Tex. Abigail Folger, her white nightgown streaked with blood, ran for her life across the lawn. Krenwinkel, in ruthless pursuit, tackled her to the ground. Folger, rolling onto her back, ceased her struggle.

"I give up," she moaned. "You've got me." Krenwinkel and Watson stabbed her twenty-eight times. Her nightgown, drenched, turned completely red. Watson stopped when he saw Frykowski struggling to drag himself away. He ran to finish him off. In all, he had stabbed Frykowski fifty-one times, shot him twice, and bashed his head and face thirteen times. Kicking the motionless body, he went back to the living room where Atkins was holding Sharon.

She was the last to die. Crying, she pleaded with them to take her with them so that she could have her baby before they killed her. "Please, just let me have my baby." She sobbed and called for her mother. Tex reached forward with his knife, cutting her cheek. He later remembered how beautiful she was as she pleaded for her life. Then he savagely stabbed her sixteen times.

"Are they all dead?" Atkins asked.

"Yeah, write something." Tex parroted Manson's orders. Atkins thought for a moment. She dipped her hand in Sharon's blood and tasted it. Pleased, she soaked a towel in the blood and smeared "pig" on the front door.

When they got back to the ranch, they saw Manson dancing naked in the moonlight with a girl. They told their master about their brutal night of debauchery. Manson especially loved the "devil's business" line. "Do you have any remorse?"

"No," they answered.

"Okay. Go to sleep . . . Hey, Tex . . . was it really Helter Skelter?"

"Yeah, it sure was Helter Skelter, Charlie."

The next night Watson, Krenwinkel, and another family member, Leslie Van Houten, killed Leno and Rosemary LaBianca in their Los Feliz home. Manson had tied up the victims, assuring them they would not be hurt.

Three days after her death, Sharon Tate's movies were released nationwide. For the first time in her career she received star billing.

Within days of the LaBianca murders Linda Kasabian escaped from the ranch with her daughter. A year later she became the star witness in two sensational trials. Watson, arrested in Texas, was tried separately after extradition. It was revealed that the "family" had a "death list." Frank Sinatra was on it; so were Elizabeth Taylor and Richard Burton, Steve McQueen, and Tom Jones. A new shock wave rumbled through the wealthier neighborhoods as once more, Los Angeles' "Beautiful People" barricaded themselves behind a wall of fear and panic. Hundreds of others lined the streets in hopes of gaining admission to the courtroom, as if they had to see for themselves that people like this really existed. The trial, a virtual circus of Manson theatrics and media publicity, riveted national attention, even drawing President Nixon into pronouncing his verdict before the jury rendered theirs. All five were sentenced to death, commuted to life in prison when the death penalty was repealed before they could be executed. Their paroles have been consistently denied.

Manson, who had already spent more than half his life in prison before the murders, sings his songs in solitary and, to this day, claims to control family members on the outside.

Nine years later, Polanski found in nineteen-year-old Nastassia Kinski a beauty comparable to his wife's to star in his award-winning *Tess*. The film was dedicated, simply, "To Sharon."

Polanski has never been relieved of the guilt he suffers for not having been home that terrible night. To this day he believes that together, he and Frykowski could have driven off the attackers. Trouble has followed him; in 1977 he was accused of rape by a teenaged "model." After serving forty-two days in Chino, he fled to Paris rather than face more jail time meted out by a biased, prejudicial judge who later disqualified himself for those very reasons. Polanski has never been able to return to the United States.

Nor has he forgotten Sharon. "Before she died," Polanski wrote in his 1984 autobiography, "I sailed a boundless sea of expectation and optimism . . . Since her death, my enjoyment of life has been incomplete. . . . Even after so many years I find myself unable to watch a spectacular sunset, or visit a lovely old house, or experience visual pleasure of any kind without telling myself how she would have loved it all. . . . In these ways, I shall remain faithful to her till the day I die."

FREDDIE PRINZE
Catch a Falling Star

Freddie Prinze was only nineteen when he first appeared on *The Tonight Show*, on December 6, 1973. That one performance got him in a television pilot called *Chico and the Man*, and by April, he was a star. "He was absolutely lovable," said producer Jimmie Komack. It seemed Freddie was lovable to everybody . . . except Freddie.

He was graceful, though 6 feet 2 inches and 200 pounds, shy and vulnerable, but streetwise. Always with a sly grin belying his puppy dog eyes, Freddie charmed everyone, especially the women. "He had too many women," explained fellow comedian and close friend Jimmie Walker. "I don't know how he found the time to sleep with all of them. It seemed like half the female population of California hung around him."

Freddie quickly became as well-known in Hollywood circles for his problems as for his amours and groupies. "He was dropping pills when I first met him in 1971," said comedian David Brenner, one of Prinze's closest friends. "I know he used coke quite a bit . . . I told him this town would be his someday `. . . but Freddie didn't love himself and I don't even think that he liked himself very much. He used to ask me, 'Do I deserve it, the stardom, the applause?' He used to call a lot around 4:00 p.m. crying, 'I can't take it.' He just didn't believe he deserved all that had come to him so quickly."

Prinze himself tried to explain, "Because I'm tall and big, people expect me to act as though I know it all when most of the time I am searching for the answers myself."

There was never a transition in Freddie's young life. He went right from a young kid trying out material in the 2 a.m. slot at New York's Catch a Rising Star to a young kid hosting *The Tonight Show*. Before the Golden Boy's rise from subways to chauffeurs, he'd never even lived away from home. Son of a

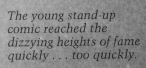

The young stand-up comic reached the dizzying heights of fame quickly . . . too quickly.

Puerto Rican mother and a Hungarian-Jewish father, Freddie, the "Hunga Rican," grew up in the poor Washington Heights area of New York. "I used to wonder how my parents met," he'd tell audiences, "you know, a Puerto Rican and a Gypsy? They were on a bus trying to pick each other's pockets."

He was a fat little boy with few friends. His mother sent young Freddie to dancing school to slim down. After he was mugged, he switched to karate, but his best self-defense remained his agile humor. He joked about the Puerto Rican hospital in his neighborhood—Pablo's Hospital and Body and Fender Repair, and about his apartment, "Our cockroaches are so big, they eat at the table with us." He imitated his friends, Nat and all the guys, and his building's super, Mr. 'Ees not my job, man' Rivera. Within a month of the first airing of *Chico and the Man*, Prinze's face saying, "Ees not my job" was plastered across tee shirts, lunch boxes, and magazines nationwide. As Chico would say, Freddie was "looking good."

With success nabbing him so soon, Prinze believed that he was destined to live fast and die young. Early on, he became obsessed and fascinated with the idea that he'd go before he hit thirty. Wouldn't it be great, he mused to his friends, to die young, become a legend, and have everybody playing your routines twenty-five years from now, like his idol Lenny Bruce. Only a few took him seriously. One was Brenner, who told him, "There once was a Lenny Bruce and the world needed him. But you're Freddie Prinze and maybe the world needs a Freddie Prinze now." Another was Kitty Bruce, who was his girlfriend for a while.

"I knew he loved me because I was Lenny Bruce's child," Kitty told the press later, "but I didn't care; I was in love with him. Comedians aren't men or women; they're melancholy children."

Success kept right on coming, faster than Prinze could prepare himself. He dropped his New York agent, David Jonas, opting for hot Hollywood manager Ron DeBlasio, who, seemingly overnight, booked him into Caesars Palace in Las Vegas at a whopping $25,000 a week. He also got him an engagement at Mr. Kelly's in Chicago, where Freddie recorded a live album, his only album. Though he was rehearsing Chico every day, he still insisted on making nightly appearances in Vegas, on Carson, or in local L.A. clubs. It was exciting being recognized, being a big shot, but the pace was faster than anything he had known before. Cocaine helped him cope. So did Quaaludes . . . and Valium . . . and Ritalin.

On one of his trips to Vegas, Freddie met Kathy Cochrane, a travel agent, cocktail waitress, and co-owner of a beauty supply store—a tall, thin brunette who was five years his senior and twice divorced. They were two lonely, vulnerable, unsophisticated people. Several days later, he called her from Los Angeles to say he was lonesome, that he needed her. Freddie routinely made calls like this to his friends when he was high. On drugs he became a frightened, insecure kid in need of constant reassurance. Kathy needed to be needed. She dropped her life and flew to him. Seven months later, with a baby on the way, they were married.

Kathy's best friend, Carol Novack, became Freddie's secretary and increasingly a lifeboat in his rapidly growing sea of troubles. David Jonas was suing

Chico co-star, Jack Albertson, kisses Freddie's new bride, Kathy, after the ceremony in a suite at Caesars Palace, Las Vegas, October 13, 1975.

him for breach of contract. He and Kathy constantly argued, mostly about his drug problem which was now out of control. Since the first time he received deaths threats from Chicanos, angered that a Puerto Rican was portraying the Mexican Chico, Prinze had been carrying a gun, a .357 Magnum. Desperately depressed, he began to toy with it, to place the barrel against his temple. "It's so easy, Carol," he'd demonstrate, "no pain . . . bliss. You just go home."

With the birth of Freddie, Jr., in March 1976, Prinze made a concerted effort to straighten up. He began karate lessons again and, for a short time, a healthy glow returned to Freddie's dimpled cheeks. Yet, by June he had slipped back into his old habits and the bickering had started all over again. In November he moved out. That same month, under the direction of his psychiatrist, Dr. Kroger, he took the Minnesota Multiphasic Personality Inventory, a psychological exam. The results were frightening. "This person feels unable to deal with the environmental pressures facing him or to utilize his skills or abilities to full advantage . . . He feels unable to cope with life as he sees it. He is cynical and distrustful of people in authority. Diagnostically, there is some probability that this patient is schizophrenic and may require hospitalization or intensive psychiatric outpatient treatment . . . He has problems centering around the control and expression of hostile feelings. He tends to be resentful and irritable. He is restless and tense with rapid mood shifts and a tendency to get involved with more activities than he can handle. He is a lively, high-strung and unpredictable person whose excess energy and high activity level may be confusing or disturbing to those around him. The test results are strongly suggestive of a major emotional disorder."

DeBlasio summed it up, "There were two Freddies." The one on drugs was depressed, fatalistic, hated Chico, and hoped the show wouldn't be renewed. He thought his nightclub act was a bore, that he wasn't funny anymore. The straight Freddie was happy and talked of the future, of his son, and his career. He had recently signed to do both a remake of the movie *It Happened One Night* and a Freddie Prinze "Special" for television. DeBlasio was negotiating a $1 million contract with Caesars Palace and a five-year, $6 million deal with NBC that would give Freddie the right to produce. But Freddie, high most of the time, concentrated on the down side of his life. The Jonas lawsuit had gone to an expensive arbitration hearing where Jonas was awarded 15 percent of Prinze's earnings for the next four years. He began to worry about a costly divorce, and, on top of all this, he was arrested for driving under the influence of "ludes." His death fixation increased. He was hypnotized by the Zapruder film of John Kennedy's assassination, playing his copy over and over. DeBlasio tried to reason with him, pointing out that divorces and fights with managers often happen early on in young careers, "but he was impatient with his own immaturity." He just wouldn't listen. Though he knew his world was falling apart, he was unwilling to pick up the pieces.

By December Freddie was taking six or seven Quaaludes a day and was still unable to sleep. He had been using such huge quantities of coke, five grams a week, that he had burned a hole in his nose, so he resorted to pushing it up his rectum. Girls still followed him home, but as often as not, the twenty-two-year-old Prinze was impotent from all the dope. His weight had dropped 40 pounds and he was bleeding internally. He continued "looking good" for *Chico* rehearsals every day, including the weekly live tapings, and on the fifteenth, he opened for Shirley MacLaine in Vegas. It was the same day that Kathy filed for divorce.

Freddie's distraught spirits were boosted on January 19th, with the biggest thrill yet in his young life. When he was invited to perform at President Jimmy Carter's Inaugural Ball at the Kennedy Center in Washington, he went through the roof. He just couldn't believe it. "I never saw him happier," DeBlasio said later, in retrospect. When Freddie packed to go home, he took Shoreham Americana Hotel stationery as a souvenir of the proudest day of his life.

When he returned home, to reality, he was greeted with a restraining order from Kathy, preventing any visits to either her or the baby. It tore her apart to take this drastic step, but she couldn't trust Freddie's dangerous drug-induced behavior. She hoped the court order would wake him up, and she let her attorney throw in a statement that he wasn't paying her enough support, standard legalese in any Hollywood divorce. It was all too much for Freddie; instead of forcing him to realize the gravity of his situation, the document made him livid. He refused to listen to explanations. He began calling his lawyer around-the-clock. His pistol became his favorite plaything. He spent hours loading it, unloading it, putting it to his mouth and his head. "Life isn't worth living," he would say as he squeezed the trigger, always with the safety catch on. Most people who saw him do this thought he was just trying to be the center of attention, the proverbial spoiled child. How could Freddie Prinze believe he had nothing to live for?

Carol, who worked out of Freddie's high-rise apartment on Wilshire Boulevard, did her best to hold the pieces of his life together, but Freddie often pushed her to the limit. One day shortly after the inauguration, he played a morbid trick on her. He went into his bedroom, fired his pistol, and fell to the floor with a loud thud. She screamed and ran into the room where she found him laughing. "Fooled you, didn't I?" he taunted. Carol burst into tears.

An exasperated Dr. Kroger took away Freddie's gun and cut off his supply of Quaaludes. Losing the drugs wasn't a problem; he could get them anywhere. A few days later, however, Carol witnessed a desperate phone call to Dr. Kroger. "I gotta have my gun and my ludes . . . I just gotta have them . . . no, I won't mess with them," he pleaded. As he hung up the receiver, he laughed, "Fool!"

That day's rehearsal was a disaster. Freddie was high and couldn't remember his lines. At 5:00, he went to Jimmie Komack's office, where they talked over a game of backgammon. Before he left, Freddie took one-and-a-half Quaaludes with some wine, making a total of five for the day. Komack couldn't stop him—nobody could.

"I just drove home on five ludes," he announced triumphantly to Carol as he walked in the front door. He changed into his karate clothes, returned to the living room, and placed his gun on the coffee table. Carol eyed it apprehensively.

"Carol, I love you and I don't want to hurt you for the world, but if you touch that gun, I'll break your arm," said high-flying Freddie. He picked up the phone and called his lawyer, this time to discuss changes in his will. Kathy was out—everything was to go to his mother and his son. The lawyer, dismayed by Freddie's condition, asked to speak to Carol. Freddie nodded off to sleep but was awakened by Dr. Kroger's call. After they spoke, he took two more Quaaludes. Carol also spoke to the doctor, and asked him to come over. Around midnight, Freddie and Carol began packing his bag for the next day's taping of *Chico.* Sitting beside him on the couch, stroking his hair, she tried to get him to fall asleep. He played the guitar for a while and sang Carol a song that he'd written, but he couldn't calm down.

Dr. Kroger arrived at 1:30 a.m. "Doc, in a nutshell, what am I?" Freddie asked him. "Am I psychotic? Am I schizophrenic? What am I?"

Dr. Kroger let out a long sigh. "You're none of those things, Freddie. You're just an immature little boy." Prinze burned. Carol, exhausted, left Freddie in the doctor's care, promising to call when she got home, as Freddie always asked her to do. When she did, she couldn't believe her ears.

"I'm lonely, the doctor's gone," Freddie said, whimpering like an abandoned child. Carol was shocked that the doctor would leave him in such a depressed condition. She knew he probably shouldn't be alone but begged him to try to get some sleep. He called her back in a few minutes. "I can't take it, Carol.

I'm going to do it, now." Carol was already half dressed when the phone rang again. It was Dusty Snyder, Prinze's business manager. Freddie had just called him and Snyder was frightened by the strangeness of his voice. He was going over there. Carol gratefully fell back into bed.

Snyder arrived at 3 a.m. to find Freddie sitting in almost total darkness. "Is it legible?" asked Freddie, indicating a scrawled message on the table. Dusty picked up the piece of Shoreham Americana Hotel stationery carefully dated January 28, 1977. "I must end it," it read. "There's no hope left. I'll be at peace. No one had anything to do with this. My decision totally. Freddie Prinze." Snyder called Dr. Kroger.

"He's been behaving this way all week . . . he's just crying out for attention. Don't worry about him harming himself." But Snyder had reason to worry. He tried to convince Freddie that his mountain of problems was only temporary. He was being too hard on himself. If only he'd be patient . . .

"I know . . . I know," Freddie mumbled. Holding the gun in one hand, he began making phone calls with the other—first to his attorney, then to his mother. He was saying good-bye. "Mom, I love you very much, but I can't go on. I need to find peace." Frantic, she called Carol, who in turn called Freddie. "I can't take it, Carol. I want you and Dusty to clean out my apartment." He added to his suicide note, "P.S. I'm sorry. Forgive me. Dusty's here. He's innocent. He cared." Snyder pleaded with Freddie to give him the gun but Freddie wouldn't listen. He had to make one final call to Kathy—it was her birthday. "I love you, Kathy. I love the baby, but I need to find peace. I can't go on. The attorneys are taking it all." He slipped the receiver back in place.

Prinze jerked suddenly and Snyder made a move for the gun. "Give me that!" he demanded, but as he shouted Freddie pulled away. "Think about your mother, and your son," Snyder pleaded with him. The next few minutes were a blur. Freddie was on the couch. In one fluid movement, the gun was at his head. Snyder heard a muffled noise but didn't realize what had happened until seconds later when Freddie slumped sideways, with blood spilling from his head.

Police rushed Freddie to the UCLA Medical Center where for 33 hours, family, friends, and fans crowded into the waiting room to cry and pray. National news broadcasts updated his condition every few hours, but there was never any chance for survival. The announcement finally came out: on January 29, 1977, Freddie Prinze was dead, due to massive brain damage from a self-inflicted gunshot wound.

"He was so incredibly different from the rest of us," sighed Komack. "At nineteen, to do what he did with *Chico*, at twenty-two to host *The Tonight Show* and not sweat. To stand up in front of the President of the United States at his inauguration and be funny. Half Puerto Rican, half Jewish, a grown-up, charming, troubled, brilliant little boy—he was just different."

NATALIE WOOD
Death of a Survivor

From the age of four, Natalie Wood was surrounded—by people telling her what to think, what to wear, what film to do, when to get up, when to go to bed. She was never alone. Wherever her entourage went, photographers followed, snapping her picture with Elvis Presley, James Dean, Warren Beatty, or Nicky Hilton, the hotel billionaire. With so many people managing her life for her, Natalie lost the fix on her own identity. For years she fought an intense battle to find herself and triumphed at last when she found herself a very happy woman, surrounded by friends, success, and love. Then Natalie met disaster, all alone.

Born Natasha Gurdin to Russian immigrant parents in Northern California, four-year-old Natalie landed a bit part in *Happy Land*, a movie shot in her town with many local residents as extras and bit players. She was such an endearing child that director Irving Pichel remembered her three years later and signed her for a featured role in *Tomorrow Is Forever*, opposite Claudette Colbert and Orson Welles. Welles was enchanted with her, too. "I was just a little in love with Natalie from the very first time we met. I never stopped loving her . . . I never will," he said.

When she was seven, Natalie was earning $1,000 a week. At the age of nine, she was already a full-fledged star with her role in *Miracle on 34th Street*.

Her passage into adulthood was Nicholas Ray's *Rebel Without a Cause* (1955), in which James Dean gave her her first screen kiss. Though she was a seasoned performer by then, her fresh-scrubbed beauty got in the way when Natalie tried to convince Ray that she could play a troubled teen. She got the chance to prove it, however, when she and co-star Dennis Hopper were slightly hurt in a car accident and police held them at the station. They called

*The face that captured
the heart of Orson Welles.*

Ray to bail them out. When he arrived, nearly out of breath from rushing, Natalie pulled him aside. "You see that son-of-a-bitch over there?" said the seventeen-year-old, pointing to the precinct doctor. "He called me a juvenile delinquent. *Now* do I get the part?" She not only got the part of Judy but also received her first Academy Award nomination for "Best Supporting Actress."

With *Rebel* and *Marjorie Morningstar*, Natalie became every youth's romantic ideal of the girl next door. At nineteen she herself married the boy-next-door, Robert Wagner. "I was ten and he was eighteen when I first saw him walking down a hall at 20th Century–Fox," she "confided" to the press. "I turned to my mother and said, 'I'm going to marry him.'" It was the Hollywood fairy tale come true, but not without its problems. During their first year of marriage they were practically inseparable, particularly because Warner Brothers had placed Natalie on suspension. The studio claimed that shortly after her marriage to Wagner, Natalie started a dispute over her weekly salary of $750. "I wanted the right to do outside pictures and to have more freedom," she replied. "Money wasn't an issue." According to Wood, she refused to do another picture until they met her request. Meanwhile, the new bride took full advantage of her time off. The Wagners bought a new home in Beverly Hills, which Natalie delighted in furnishing. They also formed their own company and invested in a yacht. "I have always felt drawn to the sea," she said years later in an interview for *Preview* magazine. "I always feel very serene when I'm near the water or on the water. The only thing I don't like is being *in* the water."

After Natalie went back to work (Warner met her demands) things started to go wrong for the Wagners. Their schedules clashed and the couple saw less and less of one another, each complaining that the other had no time. Natalie wasn't used to being left alone; her psyche wasn't prepared to handle these marital problems. The result was that when she portrayed a tormented teen-ager in the throes of a nervous collapse, in Elia Kazan's *Splendor in the Grass* (1961), it wasn't far removed from reality. The film earned her an Oscar nomination for "Best Actress." It also offered her a new hand to hold when her husband wasn't around; she became romantically involved with her co-star, newcomer Warren Beatty. Her "perfect" marriage ended in traumatic divorce.

"Obviously my career was part of the break-up. We weren't communicating and we were living in a fishbowl. There was tons of publicity about everything we did. I couldn't handle it," she readily confessed. Pills held no answers for her but therapy did—an intensive five days a week for eight years. "I didn't know who or what I was or what I was supposed to do. I was whoever I was playing at any moment. I was whoever they told me to be." She played another role that called for her to have a nervous breakdown, in *Inside Daisy Clover* (1966), and this time her real life was even more similar to her character's. Daisy Clover was a child star, too. "It's a bore to be sorry you were a child actor. So many people feel sorry for you automatically. . . . Everybody missed something or other [in their childhood]." But she did admit that her therapy bills were "at least the equal of the annual defense budget of most Central American nations!"

Yet, the words Natalie Wood and professional were interchangeable, so

Robert Wagner and Natalie Wood, "Hollywood's Happiest Couple," voted "Parents of the Year."

while her personal life came unglued, her professional life marched on without missing a step: *West Side Story, Gypsy,* another nomination for "Best Actress" in *Love with the Proper Stranger* (1963), *Sex and the Single Girl, The Great Race, This Property Is Condemned, Bob and Carol and Ted and Alice.* In 1970, however, after twenty-four years in show business, Natalie Wood announced her retirement. "Hell, I've been a movie star longer than Joan Crawford," the thirty-year-old veteran pointed out. "Let's face it, acting is not really important. Einstein is important. Salk is important. I know they're not going to send my latest movie up in a time capsule."

In 1969 she had married Richard Gregson, a British screenwriter and agent, and gave birth to their daughter, Natasha. Their marriage quickly soured, however, and Natalie was strong enough to walk away from a bad situation. She paused long enough for some serious soul-searching, then continued on into the waiting arms of Robert Wagner. The fairy tale had a happy ending after all, as Hollywood's happiest couple were remarried aboard a yacht in the Pacific in 1972. "It never really ended," she said of their relationship. "It was just interrupted." Three years later they had a daughter, Courtney.

"I am a woman, a wife, a mother, and a working actress, in that order," she said in an interview a few years later, after she had returned to acting. The Wagners appeared opposite Sir Laurence Olivier in a television production of *Cat on a Hot Tin Roof*, for which Natalie's "Maggie" received an Emmy nomination. She followed this with tour-de-force performances in the telefilm *The Cracker Factory* and the miniseries *From Here to Eternity*.

"She knew exactly what she was doing all the time," said co-star William Devane. "She'd been acting for thirty-five years!" —and was still winning awards. In 1981 it was a Golden Globe for "Best Actress." At forty-two, Natalie just got better—a rose in full bloom. After the birth of their two children, she grew 1½ inches in both height and bust measurement while her voice dropped nearly an octave. As the naive girl grew into a mature, sensual woman, she accomplished the nearly impossible: she had kept her career thriving from child star, through adolescence, and into adulthood. Natalie Wood had emerged a sane and stable woman.

"My life is a miracle," she admitted. "I'm happy with my life. I'm amazed sometimes that I'm as happy as I am."

In November 1981 Natalie was working on *Brainstorm*, and was scheduled to start rehearsals for her theatrical debut in *Anastasia*, at the Los Angeles Music Center. Wagner, busy with the second season of his television series *Hart to Hart*, had just returned to work after the startling death of co-star Stephanie Powers's longtime companion William Holden. The Wagners invited Christopher Walken, Natalie's co-star in *Brainstorm*, to spend Thanksgiving weekend with them on their 55-foot cabin cruiser, *The Splendour*, where they'd spent every weekend for the last several years.

Friday, November 17—anchored off Catalina Island, 22 miles from the Southern California coast, the trio plus skipper Dennis Davern went ashore in their motorized dinghy, *The Valiant*. The water was very rough that evening, and after drinks and dinner, Wagner decided the yacht should be moved to a safer bastion. The other three chose to remain ashore rather than brave the choppy waters. Unseaworthy Walken was already queasy and even Natalie, a veteran of the waves, took a seasickness pill. They stayed in two rooms in the Pavillion Lodge, both in Natalie Wagner's name. Saturday, November 18—Natalie and her companions rejoined Wagner on board *The Splendour*, now anchored in Isthmus Cover. At 4 p.m. they took the dinghy ashore to Doug's Harbor Reef and Saloon, where the Wagners were regulars, well known to everyone. Later, they sent back to the yacht for several bottles of wine. The dinner mood and conversation were festive. When a group of local residents arrived for a celebration the Wagners joined in, clapping their hands in time to the music. Two little girls shyly approached them for autographs and Natalie seated the smaller of her fans next to her, talking with the girls while she braided the ecstatic child's hair. Her family reciprocated the kindness by sending two bottles of champagne to the Wagners' table.

Back on the yacht Davern retired to his quarters while Walken, Wagner, and Wood continued the party in the boat's main cabin. Close to midnight Natalie adjourned to her bedroom and changed into night clothes.

At 12:20 Davern, making his final check, discovered that *The Valiant* was gone and reported to Wagner who assumed that Natalie had taken it. No one worried; she was an adept sailor who often took the dinghy out alone on similarly clear and beautiful nights. When she didn't return within fifteen minutes, however, a worried Wagner took a small cruiser to look for her.

At 1:00 Wagner called the restaurant to ask for Doug Bombard, also in charge of the harbor patrol service. Night manager Don Whiting received the call and dispatched three patrol boats, one of which reported first to *The Splendour* to pick up Wagner. Whiting began a search on land.

At 3:25 the Coast Guard was called to join the search.

At 5:15 on-shore lifeguards were alerted and, with dawn's light, a sheriff's helicopter began flying passes over the cove. Wagner returned to *The Splendour*, exhausted and hoping against hope that Natalie would be found safe.

At 7:44 Bombard, at the controls of one of the patrol boats, saw the helicopter circling over a small cave at Blue Cavern's Point, a mile-and-a-half from *The Splendour*. Realizing that they must have found Natalie he raced full throttle to the scene, heart pounding, clinging to hope. His hopes were dashed when he saw her body floating face down just below water's surface. *The Valiant*, 200 yards away, gears in neutral, key in the "off" position, contained four life jackets, but it appeared that she had never even boarded it. Four men pulled her sodden body from the Pacific. Scratches on her wrists and hands lead rescuers to believe that she tried clinging to the rocks in the cove before succumbing to the water.

Bombard broke the terrible news to Wagner. "The search has not ended the way we had all hoped," he said. Wagner fell back into a deck chair, burying his face in his hands. He made a positive identification and then flew home in the helicopter to tell Natasha, Courtney, and Kate, his daughter from a previous marriage, before they heard it on the news.

Crowds of fans, the press, and curiosity seekers had already begun lining the sidewalks around the Wagners' Beverly Hills home. Stephanie Powers, Robert Conrad, Natalie's lifelong friend Elizabeth Taylor, Kate Jackson, Barbara Rush, and others hurried to be with R.J., but he didn't want to see anyone.

Police investigators tried to piece together what had happened and concluded that Natalie, dressed in a blue flannel nightgown, red down jacket, and heavy wool socks, had decided to take the dinghy out alone. She untied it but then slipped while boarding, striking her cheek, which possibly rendered her unconscious. Then she fell into the cold water, a considerable shock, especially after a blow to the head, and drowned. The public wanted to know why Natalie, a poor swimmer with an admitted fear of dark water, would take the dinghy out alone.

"All you landlubbers think alike," said Don Whiting. "For us it's like taking a walk or hopping in a car to go to the store." Whiting, who spent Sunday night aboard *The Splendour*, had come up with his own theory. He guessed that *The Valiant*, continually slapping up against the side of the boat, must

have been disturbing her, and Natalie was just trying to move it when she tumbled over the side. "You can't see anything," Whiting explained. "There's no street lights, no headlights, no nothing. If she banged her head under those circumstances, I can understand it. Cold sober, I wouldn't want to fall into that ocean at night. With a drift, you could be fifteen yards downstream and no one could hear you."

Someone did hear Natalie's cries for help. Marilyn Wayne, a Los Angeles commodities broker, heard a woman calling for help around midnight, about twenty yards from her boat which was anchored some 300 feet from *The Splendour*. "I could hear someone saying, 'Help me, somebody help me.' It went on about forty minutes. I didn't help because I heard another voice answer, 'Take it easy. We'll be over to get you.' It was laid back. There was no urgency or immediacy in their shouts," Ms. Wayne told the press. Later she added, "In retrospect, of course, I realize that hypothermia and exhaustion had set in and that's why she never said anything that sounded alarming. There just wasn't much credibility in that droning repetition. I've run through it in my mind a million times because afterward, there was obviously a great deal of guilt in me." Not one of the other dozen or so nearby boats heard any shouts, though many said that because it was cold, their cabins were shut and it would have been difficult to hear anything.

Coroner Thomas Noguchi reported to the media that an argument had taken place on board *The Splendour* between Walken and Wagner, insinuating that Natalie took the dinghy to get away from the commotion. After questioning witnesses the Sheriff's Department refuted that report, adding that Noguchi was just "juicing it up." The controversy over Noguchi's candor in this case and in the recent death of William Holden led to his suspension and demotion from office. While the press and public wildly speculated about the "argument," one bitter fact remained immutable: Natalie Wood, forty-three, a Hollywood survivor, a strength in the community and the industry, was gone.

Four months after Natalie Wood's death, Filmex, the prestigious annual Los Angeles Film Exposition, dedicated the festival to Natalie "for her enduring career in Hollywood as a star, a beauty and a lady of integrity." Two years later, her last film, Brainstorm, *was finally completed and released.*

JOHN BELUSHI
The Dangers of Smith and Jones

Years before John Belushi's manic energy made him a star, it drove his teachers in Wheaton, Illinois, to the brink of insanity. In one attempt to curb the high-spirited sixth grader, they demoted him to the second grade. It apparently didn't work because that was the same year Belushi's gym teacher declared him the worst student she ever had, and then kicked him in the groin—at least that's the way he remembered it. He was happier after school, when he could channel his unflagging pep into school plays, the class council, drumming in rock bands, and being captain and star linebacker of the football team. "He didn't like to practice or do the drills, but as soon as you turned the lights on, he was super," said his old high school coach, Howard Barnes.

Not all of his teachers kicked him in the groin; some sensed his potential and sent him to a special summer acting program for gifted students at Michigan State. There was no question where Belushi, Homecoming King of '67, was headed after high school. He was born to command attention. In his senior year, he met the great love of his life, Judith Jacklin, then a sophomore. "The first time I saw him was at a party," she remembers. "He was singing 'Louie, Louie' without slurring the dirty words."

After a brief attempt at college, Belushi moved to Chicago where he and two friends "founded" the Universal Life Church Coffee House, a comedy teahouse. His imaginative work there led to two years with Chicago's famed Second City improvisational comedy troupe. Impressed with his perpetual creativity, the National Lampoon people invited him to New York to audition for their show, *Lemmings*, a musical parody of the Woodstock generation. It was *Lemmings* where Belushi first performed his famous Joe Cocker imitation, and where he was seen by Lorne Michaels who, two years later, would cast John in the most vital and controversial television comedy in years.

The mischievous comedian dove headfirst into a fast-paced life.

The television debut of *Saturday Night Live* in 1975 was heralded as a comedy phenomenon, and The Not-Ready-For-Prime-Time Players—Gilda Radner, Laraine Newman, Jane Curtin, Chevy Chase, Garrett Morris, Dan Aykroyd, and Belushi—were the humor of a new generation—the sixties grown up—never predictable, usually irreverent, sometimes gross, always fresh and unique.

Belushi created a menagerie of brilliant characters: the excitable news commentator who tried to remain calm, but "Noo-ooo-ooo!", the Killer Bees, his Kissinger, Roy Orbison, Joe Cocker, Pete, "cheeseburger, cheeseburger" the Greek restaurant owner, and perhaps the favorite, his slashing Samurai.

During his four hectic years with *SNL*, Belushi finally married Judith, after years of living together. He also formed a deep friendship with Dan Aykroyd. "He's Mr. Careful and I'm Mr. Fuck It," Belushi said of their relationship. "I can't figure him out, but whenever I'm with him, I feel safe." Already aware of his need for security, John relied on Judith and Dan as constants in his rapidly changing life. Both were fiercely loyal to him, but neither could be with him all the time.

From their mutual love of music, especially rhythm and blues, Dan and John formed The Blues Brothers as a warm-up band for *SNL* audiences. When Elwood and Jake Blues debuted on the show, their success filled their "briefcase," already full of blues, with a contract from Atlantic Records and a movie *The Blues Brothers*. Both the album and the film resurrected the fading careers of several forgotten black blues artists like Sam and Dave, and James Brown. ". . . They opened the door for me and for so many other performers by getting us rediscovered and appreciated again," Brown told the press. "He knew I was having problems with my career and he said, 'How can I help?' He was *there* for me, understand?"

Belushi jumped into films in 1978 with his typically boundless style, getting involved with several projects at once, while maintaining an almost ridiculous pace. Leaving New York on Sundays, after *SNL*, he'd fly to Durango, Mexico, for *Goin' South*, with Jack Nicholson, then to Eugene, Oregon, for National Lampoon's *Animal House*, then to Los Angeles for *Old Boyfriends*, and back to New York by Thursday for *SNL* rehearsals. There was no time in his schedule for mistakes or even accidents. There was barely time for Judith, who was beginning to work as a writer and book designer. Nevertheless, Judy was devoted, always ready with support and tenderness. "Anyone who knows what they were like together," confided a friend of the couple, "could see how much they loved each other." She took care of him, but neither rain, nor hail, nor explosives could slow him down . . . even when, on the set of *Goin' South*, a squib, a special effects simulator of bullet hits, blew up in his hand.

"We were in Mexico," he recounted, "so they just picked out the splinters, shot me up with morphine, and we went on with the scene. . . . Those were very hard times . . . very tough dealing with fame and success while trying to fulfill your responsibility to your audience. The trick is knowing what you want to do and then resolving everything you have to do to get there. . . . It was so much pressure, so many things going on, so many parties, so many people paying attention to you. I was a madman!

The Blues Brothers—John Belushi and Dan Aykroyd.

"I don't know if [my self-destructive tendencies] are under control. It comes along with a certain kind of lifestyle which you don't change after becoming well known. Everything becomes more heightened, takes on more urgency, and the tendency to self-destruct heightens, too. I'm learning to cope and not deny my own success . . . but . . . I get nervous and I am capable of doing something to blow it on purpose. A lot of actors have that problem." Within the year, he would have a lot more "problems" to cope with, the #1 album, the #1 movie, as well as the #1 television show. He was also filming Steven Spielberg's *1941*. To maintain the pace and help him cope, it was not unusual for John to go nonstop on drugs for several days.

The "Black Rhino," as Aykroyd called him, also applied his extremism to his social life—he ate faster than anyone else, drank more, stayed out later, chain-smoked, and demonstrated great curiosity about all the ways to get high.

Belushi completed two more films in 1980–81, the Kafkaesque *Neighbors*, with Aykroyd, and *Continental Divide*, a deliberate departure from his usual broad characterizations to a more romantic role, where critics could see the makings of a fine dramatic actor in him. "Nobody thought I could do it," he said. "I'm a comic actor, but I'm an actor, too." He said in an interview that his pace had changed, that he was maturing.

"You change. In your twenties, you feel like you're indestructible, that nothing can kill you and you laugh at death. You go on and stay up for days and do as many things as you can; and then in your thirties, you think, Well, maybe I'll be around here a little longer, so I'm going to maybe take better care of myself.

"It was a hectic pace and I really couldn't enjoy my life with my wife. . . . Either I had to straighten out or else I would find out I'd have no friends and no wife and no job and noo-ooo-ooo anything." Asked about his cocaine use during that period, Belushi answered, "I didn't do any more than I did when I was eighteen. I did just as much. I was just noticed more. And I did it because I liked doing it. I'm just noticed more than anyone else. I don't do more drugs than any other schmuck out there in public."

But it wasn't just any schmuck who turned up dead March 5, 1982, in Hollywood. It was the brilliant, beloved funnyman, John Belushi, and everyone wanted to know what happened—his relatives, his friends, his fans, and the Los Angeles Police, who had been well aware of the star's activities during the last five days of his life.

Belushi arrived in L.A. early Monday, March 1, 1982. He checked into bungalow 3 at the elegant Chateau Marmont, and went to visit a friend. It was only 5 a.m. "It's a little early, don't you think?" asked a sleepy April Millstead, but she invited him in. Her boyfriend was asleep, so they talked quietly for a while in the living room. The struggling actress lent Belushi $5 so he could grab some breakfast.

At the door, he turned and asked her one more favor. "Do you think you could score some heroin for me?" The question took April by surprise. People knew John enjoyed cocaine, but heroin? She wanted to say no, but he'd just get it somewhere else without her help . . . who wouldn't do a favor for John Belushi? She told him to come back later in the day.

John returned at 4:30. He had not even been to bed. A few minutes after he arrived, the doorbell rang again and in walked Cathy Evelyn Smith.

Smith, thirty-four, later said she had known John for five years, though April insists that they first met that afternoon in her apartment. After her affair with singer Gordon Lightfoot broke up in 1978, Smith moved to Los Angeles from Toronto with aspirations for a career of her own. With only an occasional gig as back-up singer, she was determined to stay in the music world—if not performing on stage, then performing services backstage, from sex to drugs. She fell in with the Rolling Stones, working for a time for Keith Richards. That was apparently when she was introduced to harder drugs.

"Cathy was a bright, intelligent girl who took a wrong turn," said one friend who had known her for several years. "I'm sure she was not intimate with him [Belushi]. She was just looking to get high with a friend." Variously described as a dealer, a user, a groupie, a "desperate person," and one "who had been abused by a lot of people," Smith was well known on the L.A. entertainment scene . . . and by the LAPD. At the time of Belushi's death, Smith was on probation. To keep the cops off her back, she cooperated with them. Most others found her highly uncooperative, like several fashionable restaurants and clubs that barred her for her loud, obnoxious behavior.

"She just seemed to be on something whenever she came in," said the maitre d' of Dan Tana's, a popular Italian eatery in West Hollywood. Many of the regulars there described her as "an accident waiting to happen"—but the accident happened to John Belushi.

John, Cathy, and April returned to bungalow 3, where Cathy immediately shot up. Watching with great interest, Belushi said he wanted to try it. Smith was only too happy to oblige. Their relationship would continue this way through the week. John had an expert to shoot him up, mostly with coke, and she was able to score all the heroin she needed for her habit—a perfect reciprocal agreement. For the next five days, they would be practically inseparable.

While Belushi had always been a partier, this was not quite his style. Something was different. He rarely slept, subsisting on coke and heroin during the week-long binge apparently triggered by Paramount Studio's rejection of the draft of his screenplay, *Noble Rot.* He was seen carousing at clubs all over town—The Improvisation, The Rainbow, The Roxy, The Comedy Store, and The Central—with the likes of Robert De Niro, Robin Williams, Richard Belzer, and *SNL* writer Nelson Lyon. Later, undercover narcotics officers told reporters some of the celebrities were part of an ongoing investigation. Movie stars, however, don't get busted on their home turf, where powerful studios can protect them. It seems that Belushi's death was not only tragic, but for the police investigators, it was inconvenient, too.

In the predawn hours of March 4, Belushi was depressed and upset. He told a cab driver/musician he met at the Beverly Hills Cafe at 4 a.m. that he felt "screwed over by the business," and taken advantage of by the people he was hanging around with—the wrong people. John turned his new friend on to some coke and when it ran out, he returned alone to his hotel. The Chateau's graceful towers could just be seen above the Sunset Strip. The hotel had always maintained its reputation of privacy and quiet, but in bungalow 3 the phone was ringing . . . it was always ringing. John split for a friend's apartment to get some badly needed sleep.

Bill Wallace had been trying to find John for two days. A karate-kick champion, he'd been instructor and bodyguard to Elvis Presley and was now in charge of working Belushi into shape for his next film. He wasn't at all happy with the shape of things now. "John is going to die soon," Wallace flatly predicted. He knew John did coke and he felt it was out of control. It was.

Belushi's last supper was with De Niro, Harry Dean Stanton, Robin Williams, and Smith at On The Rox, a private club above the Roxy, on the Strip, not far from his hotel. The 5 feet 8 inches Belushi promised De Niro he would lose 40 of his 222 pounds for a role in *Once Upon a Time in America.* The wine flowed generously and Belushi excused himself from the table several times, probably to do drugs. Later in the evening, he was introduced to Johnny Rivers, and the two sang several songs together. Rivers said that Belushi was into the music, but seemed tired. Tired or not, John bought more drugs in the parking lot before Cathy drove him back to the hotel in his rented Mercedes, at 1:45. Except for Stanton, the party moved to bungalow 3.

People came and went all night, and the wine and coke supply seemed endless. After a while, Belushi went to the back and threw up. He thought something he'd eaten had made him ill. The last guests left at 3:30, except for

Smith, who said John asked her to stay. In a sensational interview in *The National Enquirer* that got her indicted for second-degree murder, Smith said she then injected the comedian with the *coup de gras*—the dose that accidentally killed him. For the next three hours, Smith's account is unclear. A hotel employee said that Belushi took the car out at that time, but Smith said they merely continued to get high until 6:30, when John began having hot and cold flashes. He showered and climbed naked into bed, where he fell into a superficial sleep, racked by spasmodic shivering and difficult breathing.

The police report states that at 9:30, Smith, sitting in the front room, heard John's irregular breathing and became "quite alarmed." She shook him awake and gave him a glass of water. "You don't sound too well. Is there anything I can do?" she asked. He told her no, except he didn't want to be alone. She agreed to stay and ordered room service. A little after 10:00, she looked in on Belushi, and found him asleep. When asked later, in an interview, if he might have been unconscious or even dead, Smith said she "really didn't know . . . I had business of my own to attend to." She removed a bent, scorched, spoon and a syringe, and left in his Mercedes. The breakfast maid at the Chateau Marmont, however, remembers Smith calling for service at 7:00 a.m. and receiving breakfast just before 8:00. In addition, a girlfriend of Smith's said that Cathy was already at her house by 10:00 on that cool spring morning and is certain that she had no idea Belushi was in trouble or dead. "She never would have acted the way she did, and she never would have gone back."

When she did go back at 2 p.m., the police stopped her as she was driving in the wrong direction up a one-way street. "This is the way John always goes," she told them.

"John who?"

"John Belushi."

"Step out of the car, please." The police handcuffed Smith and took her in for questioning. Three or four hours passed before they told her.

April Millstead thinks something strange was going on that morning. She called the bungalow at 10 a.m. "Are you a member of the family?" the hotel operator asked her. April said no, but she knew he would take the call. "I have instructions not to let any calls through," she was told, so April left her name. An hour later, two detectives were at her front door asking questions. She is sure they had also been at the hotel at 10:00 when she called. So are several other individuals at the hotel, some of whom confirm that shortly after April's call, the phone in Belushi's bungalow was taken off the hook. They further stated to reporters that Bill Wallace arrived before noon and was in the room for fifteen minutes before the phone was hung up. It rang immediately, with Wallace screaming into the receiver that Belushi was dead. The hotel called the paramedics and sent someone to the room to help, but it was too late. John was officially pronounced dead at 12:45.

Curiously, police records state that Wallace didn't arrive until 12:30. These discrepancies lead many to believe the LAPD is hiding something. It would seem so—their first statement to the press was that John Belushi died of natural causes.

Because of the furor raised over Coroner Noguchi's personal revelations in the deaths of William Holden and Natalie Wood, the County Board of Supervisors had legislated a restraint against him. Thus, he spent five full days checking and rechecking before officially announcing the cause of this celebrity's death, a delay that caused a whirlpool of gossip and speculation that had included everything from choking on food to a heart attack. Death occurred between 10:15 and 12:45 as a result of a drug overdose. Belushi had been "speedballing," intravenously administering a combination of heroin and cocaine, the depressant and the stimulant combining to take the body on a rollercoaster ride—the maximum drug jolt. Both drugs were found in the bungalow. However, if we are to believe Smith's claim that she last injected Belushi at 3:30, then it is highly unlikely this is the shot that killed him. Drug overdoses occur within two hours. If he did die of an overdose and not, as is possible, a heart attack, then he ingested or injected drugs well after that.

Noguchi stated Belushi's weight and poor physical condition had nothing to do with his death. "If he had been in the best of health, the combination of heroin and cocaine would have killed anyone." He noted twenty-four needle marks on Belushi's right arm and more marks on his left, some less than twenty-four hours old. Though Judy Belushi and Dan Aykroyd protested, Noguchi said it appeared that Belushi had been using heroin for two years and cocaine even longer. His body reflected the drug abuse through congestion in his lungs, liver, and spleen, swelling of the brain, and hardening of the arteries.

"I believe he was being assisted in a flirtation with this new and dangerous substance," Aykroyd said. "Three packs a day, a bottle of Courvoisier, la cocaina, maybe, but Jones was not his Jones . . . People, the man who grasped me, danced with me, met my eye and planned the future was not a junkie. As a prop the hypo made us laugh. It was not a tool in his life. . . . The John I knew could have only been assisted into oblivion during the course of an experiment. He hated needles and could never have inserted a hypo into himself. He wasn't that good a mechanic."

"He didn't like needles. He didn't even like taking a blood test," said Judy Belushi. ". . . L.A. was always bad . . . Two days before [he died] John told Bill [Wallace] to throw her [Smith] out of the room. Somehow she showed up and got in [again]. I wish I knew more . . . I don't know what happened."

Smith summed up what happened, "I kept that sucker alive for five days."

One thousand friends gathered on March 8 for a memorial service in New York at the Cathedral of St. John the Divine. The mourners included Carly Simon, Christopher Reeve, Danny DeVito, Paul Simon, Penny Marshall, Charles Grodin, and a group of Hell's Angels. Dan Aykroyd played a recording of The Ventures' "2,000 Pound Bee." He and John had promised to play it for whoever went first.

"He was a nighthawk," Aykroyd eulogized, "but he was not immoral. What we have here is a good man and a bad boy . . . I was his number-one fan . . . he was the only man I could dance with."

Don Novello, better known as *Saturday Night*'s Father Guido Sarducci, was co-writing *Noble Rot* with Belushi. "It was a joy to have known him and an honor to be his friend," Novello said, "and we all know that God now has his hands full"—and Hollywood had lost another hero.

MARVIN GAYE
The Prince of Passion

"I feel safest and most secure in my parents' home," Marvin Gaye told *Ebony* magazine in 1974. "I never really feel secure anywhere else." When alimony and taxes got him down, he moved into the rambling Victorian house he'd bought for his parents, and tried, as he'd been trying all his life, to please the Reverend Marvin Gay, Sr. (the singer added the "e" to the family name). As it turned out, the King of Sensual Soul should have gone anywhere else. Reverend Gay was no fan, and no protector.

Marvin, the third of five children, first sang solo in the choir of his father's Washington, D.C. church, at the age of three. As he grew older he strummed the guitar and sang hymns after his father's sermons.

"Marvin was a very troubled child," recalled a boyhood friend. "He suffered from acute depression and reached out to everybody, looking for love." As a teenager, he took his singing to the streets, hanging out on corners with other guys from the neighborhood. They harmonized, doo-wopped, and diddly-bopped to the new music of the mid-fifties. Allen Freed, who coined the phrase "rock and roll," was bringing the latest brand—a distinctly black sound—to kids everywhere. Marvin's street corner serenades made him popular with the kids, but not with his father, who insisted that his son either find a job or join the service. Seventeen-year-old Marvin picked the Air Force.

His military days were "a horror," but the stringent rules came as nothing new to him. "My father was a strict disciplinarian. I probably have recurrent fears of the beatings I took as a child," he once said. The Air Force didn't whip the harmony out of him; by the time he got his honorable discharge, he knew just what he wanted to do with his life . . . he wanted to sing.

The Moonglows were one of the many close-harmony groups of the late fifties. For almost two years, as first tenor of the moderately successful group, Marvin traveled the rhythm-and-blues circuit. It was his first professional experience and a good one, but "not too satisfying . . ." he told an interviewer. "I got a lot of ego."

Marvin Gaye—the sensitive, satin-voiced "King of Sensual Soul."

Marvin left the group to pursue a solo career. During a gig in a Detroit nightclub in 1962, he met Berry Gordy, founder of the fledgling Motown Records. Intrigued by Gaye's smooth voice and even smoother style, he signed Marvin to his Tamla record label. Gaye had notions of becoming a jazz singer, but Gordy convinced him that his destiny lay in soul. However, Gaye began his career at Motown not as a singer but as a session drummer, playing on several early hits by Smokey Robinson and the Miracles. In October he finally got a chance to record his first single, aptly titled, "Stubborn Kind of Fellow," a big hit in the R & B charts. The twenty-three-year-old Gaye scored a big hit with the Gordy family that same year when he married Anna, Berry's sister, seventeen years his senior. His next recordings, "Hitch Hike" and "Pride and Joy," were both major hits, the latter going all the way to #1.

Gaye delivered a steady string of successes through the early and mid-sixties: "Can I Get a Witness," "Wonderful One," "How Sweet It Is to Be Loved by You"; two-teamed with fellow Motown artist Mary Wells, "Once Upon a Time," "What's the Matter with You, Baby?" and "What Good Am I Without You?" teamed with Kim Weston. He crossed the R & B charts to the national pop charts, and his list of hits continued to grow with "I'll Be Dog-gone"; a duet with his old friend Smokey Robinson, "Ain't That Peculiar"; and another million-seller with Kim Weston, "It Takes Two," but Gaye's most successful partnership was yet to come.

Nineteen-year-old Tammi Terrell had already made a name for herself sing-ing with "The Godfather of Soul," James Brown, when Motown signed her in 1965. She made a minor solo debut with "I Can't Believe You Love Me," and "Come On and See Me," but her first smash hit came with Gaye in 1967. The song was "Ain't No Mountain High Enough." They looked and sounded gor-geous together. "It was a perfect duo," said self-styled rhythm guitarist Wah Wah Watson, who came to Motown in 1968. "There was so much love there between two artists, not two individuals, artists, and it showed in their music."

Many of their duets are regarded as classics: "Your Precious Love," "If I Could Build My Whole World Around You," "Ain't Nothing Like the Real Thing, Baby," "You're All I Need to Get By." During those years, Gaye re-corded what many consider to be his greatest solo hit, "I Heard It Through the Grapevine" (1968). He also showed his skills as a composer, co-authoring "Dancing in the Streets."

Tammi and Marvin, in their hectic schedule of personal appearances to-gether, became very close, but the womanizing Gaye insisted they were never lovers. His touring schedule kept him away from his wife and year-old son, Marvin III, but he rarely spent the night alone. "I can wrap most women around my little finger," he once told interviewers. "That's not bragging, that's truth. . . . Women love me because they know I love them. They come to me like I was a magnet. I'm The Magnetic Man, The Prince of Passion, The Doctor of Love. That sounds arrogant, but what the hell."

Then tragedy struck. During the year-long tour, Tammi began to suffer from violent head pains. Marvin and the crew were worried but she kept on performing until one night, on a Virginia college campus in late 1967, as the duo crooned "Precious Love" to a capacity crowd, Tammi collapsed in Mar-vin's arms. Diagnosis revealed a malignant brain tumor. After several opera-tions she was fit enough to record off and on with Gaye, but in March of 1970, just weeks before Marvin's thirty-first birthday, the twenty-four-year-old beauty was dead. The loss marked a turning point in Gaye's career. He began to have "internal problems" at Motown and he and Anna separated.

"Marvin is probably the most difficult artist I have ever had to work with," said a Motown employee. "He's unpredictable and erratic. He may be where he says he will be at what time and he may not." The singer also refused to

Marvin Gaye, twenty-eight, and Tammi Terrell, twenty-one, in 1967, just months before the diagnosis of the brain tumor that would end her life in three years.

appear on television, claiming the lights bothered him. The employee added that he did see Gaye as "a deeply religious, sincere person."

The Magnetic Man wasn't unappreciative of Motown's patience with him. "They have put up with my nonsense for years. I would have kicked me out a long time ago," he said. Devastated by Tammi's death, he withdrew from touring and public life to reflect on the changes in his life. He struggled to put it into perspective with the social changes happening around him—the trauma of the civil rights turmoil, Vietnam, poverty, pollution. The result of this soul searching was the highly acclaimed 1971 album that Gaye wrote and produced himself, "What's Going On." The album produced two other hit singles, "Mercy, Mercy Me" and "Inner City Blues." Gaye described it as "a very broad social statement." His peers considered it a profound and eloquent concept album.

"I loved that album," said the brilliant Stevie Wonder in 1982. "I still do . . . Marvin's album showed me how musicians could contribute to greater understanding . . . how it could be an influence on people. I had already been thinking about [trying to communicate these ideas], but that album opened the door for me. It was like a blueprint. We all owe Marvin a debt."

"Tammi's death had a great deal to do with 'What's Going On,'" Marvin confided. "My state of being was very profoundly affected because I loved her . . . then there was the war and my brothers' involvement in it, the whole holocaust. I felt it was time to come out as an artist. God was talking to me and guiding me. It was a very spiritual period." With the album's triumph, Gaye's role as Motown's sex symbol changed to one of philosopher and social commentator.

The 6 feet 1 inch, 190 pound Gaye also felt passionately about football, even training with his favorite team, the Detroit Lions, in the early seventies for what he claimed was a serious tryout as a running back. A few of the Lions sang background vocals on "What's Going On." "When I'm playing, I feel safe and in my element. It's really an art; there's always something you can use to save yourself, some kind of play for any situation."

In 1973 "Let's Get It On" assured Gaye's star status. "I'm one of the fortunate ones," he told a reporter. "I'm very creative. I try not to have a swelled head, but I can't help it . . . I get torn up inside by things, things that shouldn't affect me the way they do. Being sensitive gets in the way sometimes. It's uncomfortable. I don't like walking around like an open wound."

By 1974 Marvin's wounds had healed. Still separated from Anna, he was living with Janis Hunter, who was seventeen years younger than he. Later that year she presented him with a daughter, Nona Aisha. Much to the joy of his millions of fans, Marvin started giving concerts again.

"To know that women love me, to know they care, is gratifying. Dudes love me, too. I can feel it. I sing to everybody . . . but the first ten rows," he said with a smile, "are always women." Ladies clawed at his hands and fought for the towels that he'd used to wipe his sweat. Eight-year-old Marvin III handed him the towels on stage and got $50 a week for the job. It was true; women adored hip, smooth-talking Marvin, with his heavy-lidded bedroom eyes. "He was God's gift to women," marveled Wah Wah Watson, who had just completed the guitar work on Gaye's "Distant Lover" about that time. "I've seen women totally freak out and rush the stage, crying and throwing roses."

He was acutely aware of who his fans were and therefore never allowed himself to be photographed with white women. "The least little thing [that could link me romantically with a white woman] can make them [black women] feel that I am being taken away or defecting or something. I'm sensitive to the needs and desires of black women and I'm very conscious of my public position. Besides, I'm an angry black man, whatever that connotes."

He was living at a house he'd bought for his parents in Washington. He adored his mother, Alberta, and spoke of her almost reverently. Mother and son were so close that Marvin, Sr., was frequently jealous.

"Marvin always felt his father didn't appreciate his accomplishments," said Curtis Shaw, Gaye's long-time friend and former attorney. "He said to me on many occasions, 'I wish I had my father's love.' He thought of his father as a prophet."

In 1976 Marvin's divorce from Anna came through, and he married Janis, who gave birth to a son, Frankie, but the end of the decade brought unrelenting bad luck. Anna sued for back support, Janis filed for divorce, and Marvin declared bankruptcy one step ahead of the IRS, which demanded nearly $2 million in back taxes. He admitted that he menaced Janis with a knife during an argument over child custody and then arranged for Frankie to be kidnapped to Hawaii. There, amid the tropical breezes, Marvin became so depressed over the ruins of his life, he tried to kill himself by snorting more than a gram of pure cocaine in less than an hour. He survived and mulled over his life with many regrets. "I used it all—the bad stuff and the good in music," he told friends. "I did some awful things. I became chauvinistic and dived to the depths of degradation. I did music that encouraged the sexual revolution. I never raised myself to the heights of spirituality."

Then he sent himself into a self-imposed exile in Europe. After twenty-eight albums he broke with Motown because of irreconcilable differences and signed with CBS Records. He toured Europe, got off cocaine, and sipped champagne with Princess Margaret. About that time Janis, who had long since been reunited with her son, dropped the kidnapping charges, and the IRS set up a repayment schedule that Gaye could live with. With his burden eased, he returned to the studio and recorded a new album, "Midnight Love," with a smoldering hit single, "Sexual Healing," that reclaimed Gaye's title as King of Sensual Soul. In 1982 he went back to California, not because of his reestablished success but because Alberta Gay was out there in the hospital with severe kidney problems. He remained at her side until she recovered. On the other hand, his relationship with his father had deteriorated to such a state that Marvin told a friend, "I've lost my dad even though he's alive."

At least the world still loved him. "Sexual Healing" won Gaye two Grammy Awards in 1983, and his appearance on Motown's Anniversary Special on TV and a "Midnight Love" tour confirmed that Marvin Gaye's career was on the upswing, despite all his financial woes. He owed $300,000 to Anna and "considerable sums" to Janis, the IRS, and the State of California. As was his pattern during times of trouble, he went where he felt most secure. In January of 1984, he moved into his parents' house in an upper-middle-class black neighborhood in the Crenshaw district of Los Angeles. As a houseguest Marvin had no etiquette. "He'd take drugs and make telephone calls all night and then maybe sleep from 8 a.m. till noon," an anonymous friend told *People* magazine. "His mother would often bring him up breakfast around 1:00 and lovingly watch him eat. . . . Pushers, women, all kinds of people would come to the door all through the night, and Marvin would let them in. God, he'd let the world in, he was so magnanimous. Sometimes his father would search such people. He didn't like them walking around the house. There were so many entrances and exits, so many rooms. His father probably just got fed up." At one point after a quarrel, Gay, Sr., had the police remove his son from the house, but after a short stay at his sister's he returned.

"After all," Marvin confided to a friend, "I have just one father. I want to make peace with him."

"Marvin knew something was going to happen to him," said Deborah Derrick, his current, twenty-two-year-old girlfriend. "He was paranoid about his life. He felt that everybody was against him. He told me somebody was going to shoot him. . . . The last few months of his life, he didn't even go out of the house," except to an occasional party, "or to court." Gaye was also being sued by Carole Pinon Cummings, an ex-girlfriend who claimed that he had beaten

Gaye proudly holds his "comeback" Grammy for "Sexual Healing" at the 1983 awards show.

her several times. Deborah told reporters that she had persuaded Gaye to return to Europe to kick his coke habit and he had agreed, but other friends described him as depressed and suicidal. Some suggest he rode his father to force him to take action.

"He turned into something like a beastlike person," Marvin, Sr., described his son under the influence of drugs. The distrusting singer, in fear of being poisoned or shot, had purchased several guns which he kept in the house for protection.

Saturday night, March 31, the seventy-one-year-old Reverend Gay was tearing up the house in search of a letter from his insurance company. He became angry that he couldn't find it and on Sunday, when it still had not turned up, the retired minister became angry again. From downstairs he began yelling at his wife, who was in her son's bedroom, to help him find it. The couple got into a screaming match. "Don't yell," his son shouted from bed, "come up here."

"I don't have to come up there," the father answered and so it went, back and forth. Eventually, Marvin, Sr., did come up to his son's room and again began yelling at Alberta to find the letter.

"You can't talk to my mother that way," Marvin shouted. "Get out of here. Get out of my room." Gaye was standing now, and when his father refused to leave, he pushed him toward the door, but the elder Gay fell to the floor. "Get out!" Marvin repeated, pushing his father into the hall.

"Stop it! Please, both of you, stop!" wailed Alberta.

"OK, Ma . . . it's over." Mother and son returned to the bedroom and continued their conversation. Suddenly, Gay, Sr., reappeared at the door, brandishing a handgun, one of the pistols his son had purchased. Without a word, he fired one round, catching Marvin full in the chest. The singer slipped to the floor in a sitting position, his head back against the bed. His father stepped forward and fired another shot at point-blank range, turned, and walked out. Quietly, he walked downstairs, out the front door to the porch where police found him, sitting motionless, the .38-caliber pistol lying nearby.

When asked if he loved his son, Gay, Sr., paused for a moment. "Let's say," he finally answered, "that I didn't dislike him. . . . But please," he added plaintively from the jail cell where he was being held for murder, "I want you to believe what I'm saying. I fear God. I respect God. I'm sorry and I regret what happened to this moment. I want you to believe what I'm saying . . . I thought it was loaded with blanks or BBs. I didn't know any bullets was in the gun . . ." explained Gay, who claimed that his son had brutally beaten him. "I was just trying to keep him back off me . . . I didn't mean to do it."

"Life can be a drag if you live too long," Marvin Gaye had mused in a 1973 interview, ". . . but I do think I'm going to break all the rules and outlive everybody. That would be the ultimate dirty trick to play on the world. If anybody could be immortal, it's me." The man who gave him life also took it away from him, but through his legacy of music he has achieved his wish for immortality.

In his twenty-six years at Forest Lawn Memorial Park, the final resting place of many celebrities high in the Hollywood Hills, one employee said he had never seen so many mourners as the 10,000 of Marvin Gaye, lined up to see the Prince of Soul one last time. More crowds remained in a vigil in front of his home. During the private services, Gaye's lifelong friends Smokey Robinson and Stevie Wonder delivered eulogies. Watson reunited the Midnight Love Tour band for a final farewell to "one of the greatest singers of all time . . . a people's person," Watson said. "You didn't have to have a college degree to relate to what he was singing about. He was able to share what he was feeling without intimidating anyone . . . a true artist."

BIBLIOGRAPHY

Anger, Kenneth. *Hollywood Babylon.* New York: Delta, 1975.

Batmar, Richard. "D. W. Griffith, The Lean Years." *Historical Society Quarterly,* vol. XLIV, #3, September 1965.

Bodeen, DeWitt. *From Hollywood.* New York: Barnes, 1976.

Bruce, Lenny. *How To Talk Dirty and Influence People.* Chicago: Playboy Press, 1963.

Bugliosi, Vincent. *Helter Skelter.* New York: Norton, 1975.

Chaplin, Charles. *My Autobiography.* New York: Simon and Schuster, 1964.

Cini, Zelda, and Crane, Bob, with Brown, Peter H. *Hollywood—Land and Legend.* Westport, Connecticut: Arlington House, 1980.

Cremer, Robert. *Bela Lugosi—The Man Behind the Cape.* Chicago: Regnery, 1976.

Dalton, David. *James Dean, The Mutant King.* San Francisco: Straight Arrow Books, 1974.

Dandridge, Dorothy, and Conrad, Earl. *Everything and Nothing.* New York: Abelard-Schuman, 1970.

Dardis, Tom. *Sometime in the Sun.* New York: Scribner, 1976.

Douglas, Carlyle C. "Marvin Gaye Is Back." *Ebony,* November 1974.

Eames, John Douglas. *The MGM Story.* New York: Crown Publishers, Inc., 1979.

Fitzgerald, F. Scott. *Flappers and Philosophers.* New York: Scribner, 1920.

———. *The Crack Up.* New York: Laughlin, 1945.

Fox-Sheinwold, Patricia. *Too Young to Die.* New York: Weathervane Books, 1979.

Frank, Gerald. *Judy.* New York: Harper and Row, 1975.

Friedman, Myra. *Buried Alive.* New York: Morrow, 1973.

Goldman, Albert, and Schiller, Lawrence. *Ladies and Gentlemen, Lenny Bruce.* New York: Random House, 1974.

Griffith, Richard, and Mayer, Arthur. *The Movies.* New York: Simon and Schuster, 1957.

Grossberger, Lewis. "John Belushi—More Than a Pretty Face." *Rolling Stone,* issue 361, Jan. 21, 1982.

Harrison, Joel. *Bloody Wednesday.* Canoga Park, California: Major Books, 1978.

Henaghan, Jim. "The Tragedy of Robert Walker." *Redbook,* November 1951.

Hordern, Nicholas. "The Death of Thelma Todd." *Los Angeles Magazine,* October 1976.

Huxley, Laura Archera. *This Timeless Moment.* New York: Farrar, 1968.

Kasindorf, Jeanie, "Freddie Prinze's Last Laugh." *New West,* 1977.

Katz, Ephraim. *The Film Encyclopedia.* New York: G. P. Putnam, 1979.

Lamparski, Richard. *Lamparski's Hidden Hollywood.* New York: Simon and Schuster, 1981.

Latham, Aaron. *Crazy Sundays, F. Scott Fitzgerald in Hollywood.* New York: Viking Press, 1971.

Levin, Eric, with reporters Carl Arrington, Mary A. Fischer, and Eleanor Hoover. "Marvin Gaye: A Turbulent Life and a Violent Death." *People* magazine, April 16, 1984.

Marx, Samuel. *Mayer and Thalberg, The Make Believe Saints.* New York: Random House, 1975.

Mayfield, Sara. *Exiles from Paradise, Zelda and Scott Fitzgerald.* New York: Delacorte Press, 1971.

Morella, Joe, and Epstein, Edward Z. *The "IT" Girl.* New York: Delacorte Press, 1976.

Noguchi, Thomas T., M.D., with Dimona, Joseph. *Coroner.* New York: Simon and Schuster, 1983.

Polanski, Roman. *Roman by Polanski.* New York: William Morrow and Co., Inc., 1984.

Pruetzel, Maria. *The Freddie Prinze Story.* Kalamazoo, Michigan: Masters Press, 1978.

Robinson, L. "The Death of Sam Cooke." *Ebony,* February 1965.

Stump, Al. "Ten Great Unsolved Hollywood Murders." *Los Angeles Magazine,* September 1979.

Sonnenschein, Allan, and Dana, Jayne. "John Belushi's Last 5 Days." *Penthouse,* December 1982.

Sennett, Mack, and Shipp, Cameron. *King of Comedy.* New York: Doubleday, 1954.

Shulman, Irving. *Harlow, an Intimate Biography.* New York: Geis Association of New York, 1964.

Slatzer, Robert. *The Life and Curious Death of Marilyn Monroe.* Los Angeles: Pinnacle House, 1975.

Spoto, Donald. *The Dark Side of Genius: The Life of Alfred Hitchcock.* Boston: Little, Brown and Co., 1983.

Swanson, Gloria. *Swanson on Swanson.* New York: Random House, 1980.

Swindell, Larry. *Spencer Tracy.* New York: World Publishing Company, 1969.

Thompson, Thomas. "Natalie Wood: Hollywood's Number One Survivor." *Look,* April 2, 1979.

Truitt, Evelyn Mack. *Who Was Who on the Screen.* sec. ed., New York: R. R. Bowker, 1977.

Wagenknecht, Edward, and Slide, Anthony. *The Films of D. W. Griffith.* New York: Crown Publishers, Inc., 1975.

Walley, David. *Nothing in Moderation: a Biography of Ernie Kovacs.* New York: Drake, 1975.

Watson, Tex, and Chaplain, Ray. *Will You Die for Me?* Old Tappan, New Jersey: Revell, 1978.

Young, Charles M. "John Belushi." *Rolling Stone,* issue 271, August 10, 1978.

The Globe

The Los Angeles Herald Examiner

The Los Angeles Times

The National Enquirer

The Star

Jackie Cooper summons his courage . . .

ABOUT THE AUTHOR

Laurie Jacobson is a native of St. Louis, Mo., and received her education at Emerson College in Boston and the American Academy of Dramatic Arts in New York City. In 1974 she moved to Hollywood to pursue an acting career. For five years she worked with Harvey Lembeck in his celebrated comedy improvisation workshop, subsequently performing solo and with groups in clubs and theatres, on television and in film. She continues to act and to direct as well as to write—most recently doing all three for cable TV.